Nutshell Series

of

WEST PUBLISHING COMPANY

P.O. Box 64526

St. Paul, Minnesota 55164–0526

Accounting—Law and, 1984, 377 pages, by E. McGruder Faris, Late Professor of Law, Stetson University.

Administrative Law and Process, 2nd Ed., 1981, 445 pages, by Ernest Gellhorn, Former Dean and Professor of Law, Case Western Reserve University, and Barry B. Boyer, Professor of Law, SUNY, Buffalo.

Admiralty, 2nd Ed., 1988, 379 pages, by Frank L. Maraist, Professor of Law, Louisiana State University.

Agency-Partnership, 1977, 364 pages, by Roscoe T. Steffen, Late Professor of Law, University of Chicago.

American Indian Law, 2nd Ed., 1988, about 319 pages, by William C. Canby, Jr., Adjunct Professor of Law, Arizona State University.

Antitrust Law and Economics, 3rd Ed., 1986, 472 pages, by Ernest Gellhorn, Former Dean and Professor of Law, Case Western Reserve University.

Appellate Advocacy, 1984, 325 pages, by Alan D. Hornstein, Professor of Law, University of Maryland.

Art Law, 1984, 335 pages, by Leonard D. DuBoff, Professor of Law, Lewis and Clark College, Northwestern School of Law.

Banking and Financial Institutions, 2nd Ed., 1988, about 455 pages, by William A. Lovett, Professor of Law, Tulane University.

Church-State Relations—Law of, 1981, 305 pages, by Leonard F. Manning, Late Professor of Law, Fordham University.

Civil Procedure, 2nd Ed., 1986, 306 pages, by Mary Kay Kane, Professor of Law, University of California, Hastings College of the Law.

Civil Rights, 1978, 279 pages, by Norman Vieira, Professor of Law, Southern Illinois University.

Commercial Paper, 3rd Ed., 1982, 404 pages, by Charles M. Weber, Former Professor of Business Law, The Wharton School of Finance and Commerce, University of Pennsylvania and Richard E. Speidel, Professor of Law, Northwestern University.

Community Property, 2nd Ed., 1988, 432 pages, by Robert L. Mennell, Former Professor of Law, Hamline University, and Thomas M. Boykoff.

Comparative Legal Traditions, 1982, 402 pages, by Mary Ann Glendon, Professor of Law, Harvard University, Michael Wallace Gordon, Professor of Law, University of Florida, and Christopher Osakwe, Professor of Law, Tulane University.

Conflicts, 1982, 470 pages, by David D. Siegel, Professor of Law, St. John's University.

Constitutional Analysis, 1979, 388 pages, by Jerre S. Williams, Professor of Law Emeritus, University of Texas.

Constitutional Federalism, 2nd Ed., 1987, 411 pages, by David E. Engdahl, Professor of Law, University of Puget Sound.

Constitutional Law, 1986, 389 pages, by Jerome A. Barron, Professor of Law, George Washington University, and C. Thomas Dienes, Professor of Law, George Washington University.

Consumer Law, 2nd Ed., 1981, 418 pages, by David G. Epstein, Dean and Professor of Law, Emory University, and Steve H. Nickles, Professor of Law, University of Minnesota.

Contract Remedies, 1981, 323 pages, by Jane M. Friedman, Professor of Law, Wayne State University.

Contracts, 2nd Ed., 1984, 425 pages, by Gordon D. Schaber, Dean and Professor of Law, McGeorge School of Law, and Claude D. Rohwer, Professor of Law, McGeorge School of Law.

Corporations—Law of, 2nd Ed., 1987, 515 pages, by Robert W. Hamilton, Professor of Law, University of Texas.

Corrections and Prisoners' Rights—Law of, 2nd Ed., 1983, 386 pages, by Sheldon Krantz, Professor of Law, University of San Diego.

Criminal Law, 2nd Ed., 1987, 321 pages, by Arnold H. Loewy, Professor of Law, University of North Carolina.

Criminal Procedure—Constitutional Limitations, 4th Ed., 1988, 461 pages, by Jerold H. Israel, Professor of Law, University of Michigan, and Wayne R. LaFave, Professor of Law, University of Illinois.

Debtor-Creditor Law, 3rd Ed., 1986, 383 pages, by David G. Epstein, Dean and Professor of Law, Emory University.

Employment Discrimination—Federal Law of, 2nd Ed., 1981, 402 pages, by Mack A. Player, Professor of Law, Florida State University.

Energy Law, 1981, 338 pages, by Joseph P. Tomain, Professor of Law, University of Cincinnatti.

Environmental Law, 2nd Ed., 1988, about 348 pages by Roger W. Findley, Professor of Law, University of Illinois, and Daniel A. Farber, Professor of Law, University of Minnesota.

Estate and Gift Taxation, Federal, 3rd Ed., 1983, 509 pages, by John K. McNulty, Professor of Law, University of California, Berkeley.

Estate Planning—Introduction to, 3rd Ed., 1983, 370 pages, by Robert J. Lynn, Professor of Law, Ohio State University.

Evidence, Federal Rules of, 2nd Ed., 1987, 473 pages, by Michael H. Graham, Professor of Law, University of Miami.

Evidence, State and Federal Rules, 2nd Ed., 1981, 514 pages, by Paul F. Rothstein, Professor of Law, Georgetown University.

Family Law, 2nd Ed., 1986, 444 pages, by Harry D. Krause, Professor of Law, University of Illinois.

Federal Jurisdiction, 2nd Ed., 1981, 258 pages, by David P. Currie, Professor of Law, University of Chicago.

Future Interests, 1981, 361 pages, by Lawrence W. Waggoner, Professor of Law, University of Michigan.

Government Contracts, 1979, 423 pages, by W. Noel Keyes, Professor of Law Emeritus, Pepperdine University.

Historical Introduction to Anglo-American Law, 2nd Ed., 1973, 280 pages, by Frederick G. Kempin, Jr., Professor of Business Law, Wharton School of Finance and Commerce, University of Pennsylvania.

Immigration Law and Procedure, 1984, 345 pages, by David Weissbrodt, Professor of Law, University of Minnesota.

Injunctions, 1974, 264 pages, by John F. Dobbyn, Professor of Law, Villanova University.

Insurance Law, 1981, 281 pages, by John F. Dobbyn, Professor of Law, Villanova University.

Intellectual Property—Patents, Trademarks and Copyright, 1983, 428 pages, by Arthur R. Miller, Professor of Law, Harvard University, and Michael H. Davis, Professor of Law, Cleveland State University, Cleveland-Marshall College of Law.

International Business Transactions, 3rd Ed., 1988, about 484 pages, by Ralph H. Folsom, Professor of Law, University of San Diego, Michael Wallace Gordon, Professor of Law, University of Florida, and John A. Spanogle, Jr., Professor of Law, State University of New York, Buffalo.

International Human Rights, 1988, about 275 pages, by Thomas Buergenthal, Professor of Law, Emory University.

International Law (Public), 1985, 262 pages, by Thomas Buergenthal, Professor of Law, Emory University, and Harold G. Maier, Professor of Law, Vanderbilt University.

Introduction to the Study and Practice of Law, 1983, 418 pages, by Kenney F. Hegland, Professor of Law, University of Arizona.

Judicial Process, 1980, 292 pages, by William L. Reynolds, Professor of Law, University of Maryland.

Jurisdiction, 4th Ed., 1980, 232 pages, by Albert A. Ehrenzweig, Late Professor of Law, University of California, Berkeley, David W. Louisell, Late Professor of Law, University of

California, Berkeley, and Geoffrey C. Hazard, Jr., Professor of Law, Yale Law School.

Juvenile Courts, 3rd Ed., 1984, 291 pages, by Sanford J. Fox, Professor of Law, Boston College.

Labor Arbitration Law and Practice, 1979, 358 pages, by Dennis R. Nolan, Professor of Law, University of South Carolina.

Labor Law, 2nd Ed., 1986, 397 pages, by Douglas L. Leslie, Professor of Law, University of Virginia.

Land Use, 2nd Ed., 1985, 356 pages, by Robert R. Wright, Professor of Law, University of Arkansas, Little Rock, and Susan Webber Wright, Professor of Law, University of Arkansas, Little Rock.

Landlord and Tenant Law, 2nd Ed., 1986, 311 pages, by David S. Hill, Professor of Law, University of Colorado.

Law Study and Law Examinations—Introduction to, 1971, 389 pages, by Stanley V. Kinyon, Late Professor of Law, University of Minnesota.

Legal Interviewing and Counseling, 2nd Ed., 1987, 487 pages, by Thomas L. Shaffer, Professor of Law, University of Notre Dame, and James R. Elkins, Professor of Law, West Virginia University.

Legal Research, 4th Ed., 1985, 452 pages, by Morris L. Cohen, Professor of Law and Law Librarian, Yale University.

Legal Writing, 1982, 294 pages, by Lynn B. Squires and Marjorie Dick Rombauer, Professor of Law, University of Washington.

Legislative Law and Process, 2nd Ed., 1986, 346 pages, by Jack Davies, Professor of Law, William Mitchell College of Law.

Local Government Law, 2nd Ed., 1983, 404 pages, by David J. McCarthy, Jr., Professor of Law, Georgetown University.

Mass Communications Law, 3rd Ed., 1988, 538 pages, by Harvey L. Zuckman, Professor of Law, Catholic University, Martin J. Gaynes, Lecturer in Law, Temple University, T. Barton Carter, Professor of Public Communications, Boston University, and Juliet Lushbough Dee, Professor of Communications, University of Delaware.

NUTSHELL SERIES

Medical Malpractice—The Law of, 2nd Ed., 1986, 342 pages, by Joseph H. King, Professor of Law, University of Tennessee.

Military Law, 1980, 378 pages, by Charles A. Shanor, Professor of Law, Emory University, and Timothy P. Terrell, Professor of Law, Emory University.

Oil and Gas Law, 2nd Ed., 1988, about 402 pages, by John S. Lowe, Professor of Law, Southern Methodist University.

Personal Property, 1983, 322 pages, by Barlow Burke, Jr., Professor of Law, American University.

Post-Conviction Remedies, 1978, 360 pages, by Robert Popper, Dean and Professor of Law, University of Missouri, Kansas City.

Presidential Power, 1977, 328 pages, by Arthur Selwyn Miller, Professor of Law Emeritus, George Washington University.

Products Liability, 3rd Ed., 1988, 307 pages, by Jerry J. Phillips, Professor of Law, University of Tennessee.

Professional Responsibility, 1980, 399 pages, by Robert H. Aronson, Professor of Law, University of Washington, and Donald T. Weckstein, Professor of Law, University of San Diego.

Real Estate Finance, 2nd Ed., 1985, 262 pages, by Jon W. Bruce, Professor of Law, Vanderbilt University.

Real Property, 2nd Ed., 1981, 448 pages, by Roger H. Bernhardt, Professor of Law, Golden Gate University.

Regulated Industries, 2nd Ed., 1987, 389 pages, by Ernest Gellhorn, Former Dean and Professor of Law, Case Western Reserve University, and Richard J. Pierce, Professor of Law, Southern Methodist University.

Remedies, 2nd Ed., 1985, 320 pages, by John F. O'Connell, Dean and Professor of Law, Southern California College of Law.

Res Judicata, 1976, 310 pages, by Robert C. Casad, Professor of Law, University of Kansas.

Sales, 2nd Ed., 1981, 370 pages, by John M. Stockton, Professor of Business Law, Wharton School of Finance and Commerce, University of Pennsylvania.

Schools, Students and Teachers—Law of, 1984, 409 pages, by Kern Alexander, President, Western Kentucky University and M. David Alexander, Professor, Virginia Tech University.

Sea—Law of, 1984, 264 pages, by Louis B. Sohn, Professor of Law, University of Georgia, and Kristen Gustafson.

Secured Transactions, 3rd Ed., 1988, about 390 pages, by Henry J. Bailey, Professor of Law Emeritus, Willamette University, and Richard B. Hagedorn, Professor of Law, Willamette University.

Securities Regulation, 3rd Ed., 1988, 316 pages, by David L. Ratner, Dean and Professor of Law, University of San Francisco.

Sex Discrimination, 1982, 399 pages, by Claire Sherman Thomas, Lecturer, University of Washington, Women's Studies Department.

State Constitutional Law, 1988, about 300 pages, by Thomas C. Marks, Jr., Professor of Law, Stetson University, and John F. Cooper, Professor of Law, Stetson University.

Taxation and Finance, State and Local, 1986, 309 pages, by M. David Gelfand, Professor of Law, Tulane University, and Peter W. Salsich, Professor of Law, St. Louis University.

Taxation of Individuals, Federal Income, 4th Ed., 1988, about 500 pages, by John K. McNulty, Professor of Law, University of California, Berkeley.

Torts—Injuries to Persons and Property, 1977, 434 pages, by Edward J. Kionka, Professor of Law, Southern Illinois University.

Torts—Injuries to Family, Social and Trade Relations, 1979, 358 pages, by Wex S. Malone, Professor of Law Emeritus, Louisiana State University.

Trial Advocacy, 1979, 402 pages, by Paul B. Bergman, Adjunct Professor of Law, University of California, Los Angeles.

Trial and Practice Skills, 1978, 346 pages, by Kenney F. Hegland, Professor of Law, University of Arizona.

Trial, The First—Where Do I Sit? What Do I Say?, 1982, 396 pages, by Steven H. Goldberg, Professor of Law, University of Minnesota.

Unfair Trade Practices, 2nd Ed., 1988, about 430 pages, by Charles R. McManis, Professor of Law, Washington University.

Uniform Commercial Code, 2nd Ed., 1984, 516 pages, by Bradford Stone, Professor of Law, Stetson University.

Uniform Probate Code, 2nd Ed., 1987, 454 pages, by Lawrence H. Averill, Jr., Dean and Professor of Law, University of Arkansas, Little Rock.

Water Law, 1984, 439 pages, by David H. Getches, Professor of Law, University of Colorado.

Welfare Law—Structure and Entitlement, 1979, 455 pages, by Arthur B. LaFrance, Professor of Law, Lewis and Clark College, Northwestern School of Law.

Wills and Trusts, 1979, 392 pages, by Robert L. Mennell, Former Professor of Law, Hamline University.

Workers' Compensation and Employee Protection Laws, 1984, 274 pages, by Jack B. Hood, Former Professor of Law, Cumberland School of Law, Samford University and Benjamin A. Hardy, Former Professor of Law, Cumberland School of Law, Samford University.

Hornbook Series

and

Basic Legal Texts

of

WEST PUBLISHING COMPANY

P.O. Box 64526

St. Paul, Minnesota 55164–0526

Admiralty and Maritime Law, Schoenbaum's Hornbook on, 1987, 692 pages, by Thomas J. Schoenbaum, Professor of Law, University of Georgia.

Agency and Partnership, Reuschlein & Gregory's Hornbook on the Law of, 1979 with 1981 Pocket Part, 625 pages, by Harold Gill Reuschlein, Professor of Law Emeritus, Villanova University, and William A. Gregory, Professor of Law, Georgia State University.

Antitrust, Sullivan's Hornbook on the Law of, 1977, 886 pages, by Lawrence A. Sullivan, Professor of Law, University of California, Berkeley.

Civil Procedure, Friedenthal, Kane and Miller's Hornbook on, 1985, 876 pages, by Jack H. Friedental, Dean and Professor of Law, George Washington University, Mary Kay Kane, Professor of Law, University of California, Hastings College of the Law, and Arthur R. Miller, Professor of Law, Harvard University.

Common Law Pleading, Koffler and Reppy's Hornbook on, 1969, 663 pages, by Joseph H. Koffler, Professor of Law, New York Law School, and Alison Reppy, Late Dean and Professor of Law, New York Law School.

Conflict of Laws, Scoles and Hay's Hornbook on, 1982, with 1986 Pocket Part, 1085 pages, by Eugene F. Scoles, Professor of Law, University of Illinois, and Peter Hay, Dean and Professor of Law, University of Illinois.

Constitutional Law, Nowak, Rotunda and Young's Hornbook on, 3rd Ed., 1986, with 1988 Pocket Part, 1191 pages, by John E. Nowak, Professor of Law, University of Illinois, Ronald D. Rotunda, Professor of Law, University of Illinois, and J. Nelson Young, Late Professor of Law, University of North Carolina.

Contracts, Calamari and Perillo's Hornbook on, 3rd Ed., 1987, 1049 pages, by John D. Calamari, Professor of Law, Fordham University, and Joseph M. Perillo, Professor of Law, Fordham University.

Contracts, Corbin's One Volume Student Ed., 1952, 1224 pages, by Arthur L. Corbin, Late Professor of Law, Yale University.

Corporations, Henn and Alexander's Hornbook on, 3rd Ed., 1983, with 1986 Pocket Part, 1371 pages, by Harry G. Henn, Professor of Law Emeritus, Cornell University, and John R. Alexander.

Criminal Law, LaFave and Scott's Hornbook on, 2nd Ed., 1986, 918 pages, by Wayne R. LaFave, Professor of Law, University of Illinois, and Austin Scott, Jr., Late Professor of Law, University of Colorado.

Criminal Procedure, LaFave and Israel's Hornbook on, 1985 with 1986 pocket part, 1142 pages, by Wayne R. LaFave, Professor of Law, University of Illinois, and Jerold H. Israel, Professor of Law University of Michigan.

Damages, McCormick's Hornbook on, 1935, 811 pages, by Charles T. McCormick, Late Dean and Professor of Law, University of Texas.

Domestic Relations, Clark's Hornbook on, 2nd Ed., 1988, 1050 pages, by Homer H. Clark, Jr., Professor of Law, University of Colorado.

Economics and Federal Antitrust Law, Hovenkamp's Hornbook on, 1985, 414 pages, by Herbert Hovenkamp, Professor of Law, University of Iowa.

Employment Discrimination Law, Player's Hornbook on, 708 pages, 1988, by Mack A. Player, Professor of Law, Florida State University.

Environmental Law, Rodgers' Hornbook on, 1977 with 1984 Pocket Part, 956 pages, by William H. Rodgers, Jr., Professor of Law, University of Washington.

Evidence, Lilly's Introduction to, 2nd Ed., 1987, 585 pages, by Graham C. Lilly, Professor of Law, University of Virginia.

Evidence, McCormick's Hornbook on, 3rd Ed., 1984 with 1987 Pocket Part, 1156 pages, General Editor, Edward W. Cleary, Professor of Law Emeritus, Arizona State University.

Federal Courts, Wright's Hornbook on, 4th Ed., 1983, 870 pages, by Charles Alan Wright, Professor of Law, University of Texas.

Federal Income Taxation, Rose and Chommie's Hornbook on, 3rd Ed., 1988, 923 pages, by Michael D. Rose, Professor of Law, Ohio State University, and John C. Chommie, Late Professor of Law, University of Miami.

Federal Income Taxation of Individuals, Posin's Hornbook on, 1983 with 1987 Pocket Part, 491 pages, by Daniel Q. Posin, Jr., Professor of Law, Catholic University.

Future Interest, Simes' Hornbook on, 2nd Ed., 1966, 355 pages, by Lewis M. Simes, Late Professor of Law, University of Michigan.

Insurance, Keeton and Widiss on, 1988, about 1050 pages, by Robert E. Keeton, Professor of Law Emeritus, Harvard University, and Alan I. Widiss, Professor of Law, University of Iowa.

Labor Law, Gorman's Basic Text on, 1976, 914 pages, by Robert A. Gorman, Professor of Law, University of Pennsylvania.

Law Problems, Ballentine's, 5th Ed., 1975, 767 pages, General Editor, William E. Burby, Late Professor of Law, University of Southern California.

Legal Ethics, Wolfram's Hornbook on, 1986, 1120 pages, by Charles W. Wolfram, Professor of Law, Cornell University.

Legal Writing Style, Weihofen's, 2nd Ed., 1980, 332 pages, by Henry Weihofen, Professor of Law Emeritus, University of New Mexico.

Local Government Law, Reynolds' Hornbook on, 1982 with 1987 Pocket Part, 860 pages, by Osborne M. Reynolds, Professor of Law, University of Oklahoma.

New York Estate Administration, Turano and Radigan's Hornbook on, 1986, 676 pages, by Margaret V. Turano, Professor of Law, St. John's University, and Raymond Radigan.

New York Practice, Siegel's Hornbook on, 1978 with 1987 Pocket Part, 1011 pages, by David D. Siegel, Professor of Law, St. John's University.

Oil and Gas Law, Hemingway's Hornbook on, 2nd Ed., 1983, with 1986 Pocket Part, 543 pages, by Richard W. Hemingway, Professor of Law, University of Oklahoma.

Property, Boyer's Survey of, 3rd Ed., 1981, 766 pages, by Ralph E. Boyer, Professor of Law Emeritus, University of Miami.

Property, Law of, Cunningham, Whitman and Stoebuck's Hornbook on, 1984 with 1987 Pocket Part, 916 pages, by Roger A. Cunningham, Professor of Law, University of Michigan, Dale A. Whitman, Professor of Law, University of Missouri, Columbia, and William B. Stoebuck, Professor of Law, University of Washington.

Real Estate Finance Law, Nelson and Whitman's Hornbook on, 2nd Ed., 1985, 941 pages, by Grant S. Nelson, Professor of Law, University of Missouri, Columbia, and Dale A. Whitman, Professor of Law, University of Missouri, Columbia.

Real Property, Moynihan's Introduction to, 2nd Ed., 1988, 239 pages, by Cornelius J. Moynihan, Late Professor of Law, Suffolk University.

Remedies, Dobbs' Hornbook on, 1973, 1067 pages, by Dan B. Dobbs, Professor of Law, University of Arizona.

Secured Transactions under the U.C.C., Henson's Hornbook on, 2nd Ed., 1979 with 1979 Pocket Part, 504 pages, by Ray D. Henson, Professor of Law, University of California, Hastings College of the Law.

Securities Regulation, Hazen's Hornbook on the Law of, 1985 with 1988 Pocket Part, 739 pages, by Thomas Lee Hazen, Professor of Law, University of North Carolina.

Sports Law, Schubert, Smith and Trentadue's, 1986, 395 pages, by George W. Schubert, Dean of University College, University of North Dakota, Rodney K. Smith, Professor of Law, Delaware Law School, Widener University, and Jesse C. Trentadue, Former Professor of Law, University of North Dakota.

Torts, Prosser and Keeton's Hornbook on, 5th Ed., 1984 with 1988 Pocket Part, 1286 pages, by William L. Prosser, Late Dean and Professor of Law, University of California, Berkeley, Page Keeton, Professor of Law Emeritus, University of Texas, Dan B. Dobbs, Professor of Law, University of Arizona, Robert E. Keeton, Professor of Law Emeritus, Harvard University, and David G. Owen, Professor of Law, University of South Carolina.

Trial Advocacy, Jeans' Handbook on, Soft cover, 1975, 473 pages, by James W. Jeans, Professor of Law, University of Missouri, Kansas City.

Trusts, Bogert's Hornbook on, 6th Ed., 1987, 794 pages, by George T. Bogert.

Uniform Commercial Code, White and Summers' Hornbook on, 3rd Ed., 1988, about 1200 pages, by James J. White, Professor of Law, University of Michigan, and Robert S. Summers, Professor of Law, Cornell University.

Urban Planning and Land Development Control Law, Hagman and Juergensmeyer's Hornbook on, 2nd Ed., 1986, 680 pages, by Donald G. Hagman, Late Professor of Law, University of California, Los Angeles, and Julian C. Juergensmeyer, Professor of Law, University of Florida.

Wills, Atkinson's Hornbook on, 2nd Ed., 1953, 975 pages, by Thomas E. Atkinson, Late Professor of Law, New York University.

Wills, Trusts and Estates Including Taxation and Future Interests, McGovern, Rein and Kurtz' Hornbook on, 1988, about 924 pages by William M. McGovern, Professor of Law, University of California, Los Angeles, Jan Ellen Rein, Professor of Law, Gonzaga University, and Sheldon F. Kurtz, Professor of Law, University of Iowa.

Advisory Board

TORTS

IN A NUTSHELL

INJURIES TO FAMILY, SOCIAL AND TRADE RELATIONS

By

WEX S. MALONE

Boyd Professor of Law Emeritus
Louisiana State University Law Center

ST. PAUL, MINN.
WEST PUBLISHING CO.
1979

Library of Congress Cataloging in Publication Data

Malone, Wex S
    Torts in a nutshell.
    (Nutshell series)

    Includes index.
    1. Torts—United States. I. Title.
KF1250.Z9M28   346'.73'03   79–12748
ISBN 0–8299–2044–7

Malone Torts in Nutshell
5th Reprint—1989

Devotedly to Helen

*

XVII

PREFACE

The concluding portion of the law of torts, devoted to relational interests, is a hybrid area where common law doctrine tends to lose its identity as it merges with statutory and constitutional material in the estuary of public law. It is here that there are spawned from torts such separate topics as trade regulation, labor law, civil rights, family law and the like. The writer who attempts in a compressed text to follow the thread of the common law into this mélange soon finds that he is hard pressed to avoid straying beyond the boundaries of torts proper and into pastures where he should not graze. The effort to isolate the common law component for separate treatment ends up as a half-told story. Such is unavoidably the case here. Other and later Nutshells will be required to complete the full composite picture.

The isolation of relational interests from rights in person and property is a new venture. It is the brainchild of Professor Leon Green, one of the most distinguished law scholars of our time, who has succeeded in reclassifying a mass of apparently diverse torts according to a single characteristic shared by all. The common denominator lies in the fact that they are all harms that are inflicted upon some vital interest of human beings in group living. The advantages to be gained from this novel classification are substantial. The resulting arrangement makes possible the discovery of striking likenesses within old diversities, and this invites thinking about torts in a new dimension. But here I am already writing my first chapter. The table of contents indicates the stretch of the material to be covered.

The writer of even a little book may find himself under big obligations. And I owe so much to so many: There is Martha Salvant, David Robertson, John Wade and Alston Johnson; and there are others—all busy law teachers who have spared the time and patience to read and comment on parts of my text. I owe much to the competence and patience of Mrs. Lena Roshto who typed the manuscript—often over and over as I changed my mind. Finally, I am truly grateful to the Law Center of Louisiana State University which has extended so much assistance to a retired law teacher.

Wex S. Malone

Baton Rouge, La.
May, 1979.

EXPLANATORY NOTES

I have attempted to follow the format of Professor Edward Kionka's Nutshell on Torts—Injuries to Persons and Property, to which I hope this will prove to be a worthy companion. The following notes may be helpful in using this book.

Cases. For obvious reasons cases have been cited sparingly. In general the cases cited are either landmark cases or cases that throw some light on unsettled or disputed areas.

Only the name, court of decision, and date are cited in the text. The full citation may be found in the Table of Cases. If only the name of the state is given, it is the highest court of that state.

Restatement of Torts. Frequent references to the Restatement of Torts are given, but I have not cited every relevant section. Ordinarily it is cited where some portion of its comments provides further illumination of the point under discussion or where it represents only one of several acceptable points of view. In all instances, citations are to the Restatement Second (which is now completed and in final form).

For simplicity and to save space, the Restatement Second of Torts is cited throughout as "R. § —."

*

OUTLINE

PART I. INTRODUCTION

PART II. THE FAMILY RELATIONSHIP

OUTLINE

PART III. THE SOCIAL RELATIONSHIP

OUTLINE

OUTLINE

PART IV. THE TRADE RELATIONSHIP

OUTLINE

*

TABLE OF CASES

References are to Pages

TABLE OF CASES

TABLE OF CASES

H

I

J

K

L

TABLE OF CASES

M

N

P

R

S

TABLE OF CASES

*

TORTS
IN A NUTSHELL:
INJURIES TO FAMILY,
SOCIAL AND TRADE
RELATIONS

PART I

INTRODUCTION

CHAPTER 1

THE NATURE OF A RELATIONSHIP

§ 1—1   **Relationships Defined and Distinguished
from Rights in Person or Property**

Most subjects in the law curriculum suggest by
their titles what is to be expected in the way of
content. Names such as Criminal Law, Contract,
Property and Evidence bring to even the uniniti-

ated at least some vague idea as to what he may encounter. But the title, Relational Interests, is likely to fail completely to identify the subject matter that lies ahead; it may even be actually misleading. Further, the confusion deepens when the reader glances at the table of contents and discovers a baffling array of torts as disassociated as defamation, interference with contract, wrongful death, alienation of affection, et cetera. It is difficult to imagine any connective link that could bind such diverse subjects into an orderly study.

Despite this initial impression, the subject of relational interests actually hangs together very neatly. The common denominator to be found in each instance lies in the unique character of the harm that was suffered by the victim. As we shall see, it is this singular nature of the *interest* invaded by the defendant that affords a nexus for all the different torts that follow.

If, following the language of the Restatement of Torts § 1, we hereafter use the term *interest* to indicate the object of any human desire for which legal protection may be sought, we find that under the traditional common law approach only two species of interest have managed until recently to achieve undisguised recognition in the courts as legal rights. These two were the interests in *persons* and in *property*.

Accordingly, if a human being was injured in a legal sense, the harm he sustained was treated as though it necessarily involved either his body (or personality), or something that he owned, such as an object or a piece of land.   Such was the classic limitation on the nature of rights that was once generally recognized and accepted.   The artificiality of this archaic twofold classification is patent, and a scheme of law whose protective scope was limited to so narrow a range of human needs must prove eventually to fall woefully short of the mark.   In truth, the most important and vital claims to legal protection are far more complex than demands arising from harms to one's body or belongings.   They are claims that originate in our social environment: Man is a creature who is dependent upon numerous human groupings which minister both to his physical welfare and to his needs for recognition and response.   Each group serves a separate purpose.   He is brought into the world as a helpless member of a compact family unit.   The ministrations of parents and other relatives make his survival possible.   Moreover, it is through their efforts that he is disciplined and humanized.   Soon thereafter he is assimilated into an additional grouping as he acquires friends and acquaintances.   It is at this point of acquired social consciousness that he begins his struggle for respect and response.   The pattern enlarges as he later faces the need for self-support.   He is thrust into trade, professional, or employment relationships upon which his material welfare depends. Finally, it is to be observed that the human environment in which he lives is a politically structured one in which he may govern and be governed. The civil rights all men expect to enjoy as citizens in a politically organized society are of tremendous importance in their lives. See Kionka, Torts in a Nutshell—Injuries to Person and Property (1977) § 8–22.

The above suggests that there are at least four basic groups—family, social, trade (or other economic), and political. These groups serve as the groundwork for relationships in which each of us has a vital interest. If a member of a group to which we belong is killed, molested, or otherwise harmed; if the physical environment within which the relationship must operate is worsened in some way; if our own standing within the group is impaired, or we are deprived of an opportunity to enjoy group benefits—in all such instances we may be grievously harmed and will be aroused to prosecute our claim at law against the offender whose misconduct has thus injured us.

It is obvious that none of these interests flowing from relationships could be adequately comprehended within the narrow twofold classification of rights in person or in property. As a matter of fact, law has attempted to accommodate this wider range of needs all along; but unfortunately it has done so from ambush. Courts have been obliged to distort the commonly accepted meanings of property or person.   Judges, for instance, have observed that the head of the family has property in the consortium of his wife or in the services of his children.   In this way, benefits flowing from membership in the family relation have been awkwardly translated into incidents of ownership.   "A man's name is his own property." Through this furtive phase the social relationship manages to acquire a measure of legal protection by becoming a *thing*.   The same result is achieved (but with equal awkwardness) whenever a court regards a man's reputation as a part of his personality.   Presto!   The social interest has become a right in the *person*.   Again, the property label is found readily attached to virtually every benefit that can flow from the trade, the professional, or the employment relationships.   Lawyers are familiar with such expressions as "good will", "the right to the free use of one's hands", "literary property" and ownership of "trade marks".   All these and many other common benefits arising from participation in the economic group have come to be thought of as *things* that are owned, and are protected accordingly by the law.

Unfortunately this confinement of relational interests within the shackles of two archaic notions —*person* and *property*—is something more than mere awkwardness of language.   It seriously impairs discernment.   For instance, it is obvious that the questions of policy that arise from a stolen watch are not remotely similar to those that must be considered in the case of a stolen wife, and one only stumbles over words when he pretends that the two are in some way analogous because each of them can be referred to as a misappropriation of *property*. Clear thinking demands more elbow room in the way of language than this. The needed flexibility can be provided only through a guileless recognition of a third class of rights—rights in human relationships.

§ 1—2   Harms to Relations

Structure of a Relationship. Now that we have brought into focus a scheme of relationships from which innumerable benefits are derived, we next become aware that these are susceptible of being hurt through various kinds of misconduct by others. The types of behavior that cause harms to relational interests can be understood best if we consider briefly the rudimentary structure of a relationship itself. Three parties are necessarily involved in a relation: There is the plaintiff, the defendant, and some other person (or persons) who bears an identifiable relationship to plaintiff. This other "terminal" to the relationship may be a single individual, as in a claim by a parent for wrongful death or for loss of service of an injured child. On the other hand, there may be involved an indeterminate number of "other" persons, such as all possible patrons or customers whose patronage may be lost to a tradesman by reason of the defendant's unfair practices. Similarly, the other "terminal" in a social relationship may be represented by the wide range of friends or acquaintances whose respect for the plaintiff is lost when the latter is slandered by the defendant.

Physical Harms. In all instances this basic tripartite structure is the same. The defendant, a stranger to the relationship between the plaintiff and others, destroys the relation or impairs its value to the plaintiff. The misconduct may take the form of an infliction of a physical harm upon the other party or parties to the relationship, as, for example, an intentional or accidental injury to the plaintiff's child, or the obstruction of the access of a customer or customers to the plaintiff's business establishment. It can be noted that in both these instances the child or customer may maintain its own claim for a bodily harm or indignity. But the injury to the plaintiff, although arising from the same piece of physical misconduct, is separate and must be distinguished. The physical person of the complaining parent or tradesman remains untouched, but the benefits of the family or trade relationship which he formerly enjoyed have been seriously hurt, and it is solely for this loss that he institutes his claim against the same wrongdoer for the same misconduct.

Appropriational Harms. A second type of harm to relations has been aptly termed "appropriational" by Leon Green (and at this point it should be noted that Professor Green's ingenuity is largely responsible for the evolution of the "relational interest" as a concept that can be isolated and used as an everyday analytical tool). Green, Relational Interests (1934) 29 Ill.L.Rev. 460, 1041 (1935), 30 Ill.L.Rev. 1, 314. Green, turning to the appropriational harm, observes that this harm centers on the idea of *deprivation*. The relationship or some of its important benefits are directly taken away from the plaintiff. Usually the defendant seeks to divert the relationship to his own purposes; but this need not necessarily be the case. The salient characteristic of the appropriational harm lies in the fact that either it is directed toward the relationship itself (as is generally the situation), or at least the defendant has acted deliberately with full awareness that the plaintiff will be deprived of the benefit of the relation as a result of his conduct.

The appropriational harm may assume various forms. Usually the defendant behaves so as to induce the other party or parties to abandon the relationship with the plaintiff or to withhold some of its benefits from him, such as in the case of seduction of the plaintiff's wife. The persuasion may be, and frequently *is*, accomplished through a false representation; or it may take the form of economic coercion or some other unscrupulous practice. Finally, an appropriational harm may be the result solely of some piece of physical conduct, as for example, where a defendant erects an obstruction on his own property designed to interfere with the public's view of the plaintiff's advertising sign. By so doing he has appropriated the tradesman's access to his potential customers.

Defamatory Harms. A third type of harm is defamation. This closely resembles the appropriational harms mentioned above. The effect of defamation is to persuade other parties to the relationship to exclude the plaintiff or to withhold some relational benefit from him. Again, defamation, like the typical appropriational wrong, involves falsity of statement. A unique feature of defamation lies in the fact that the untruthful statement in question must refer to the plaintiff or to his behavior or his merchandise in some disadvantageous way. In short, it must be a lie *about* the plaintiff. The treatment of defamation as a separate and distinct wrong is justifiable for the reason that this particular tort has shaped up in history as a tangled skein of legal anomalies. In its structure it is a freak. Furthermore, its obscurities have been recently heightened through innovations by the Supreme Court on the constitutional theme of free speech. A separate consideration of the defamatory harm is therefore unavoidable.

§ 1—3   Summary and Classification

In summary, the study of relational interests boils down to a systematic consideration of four types of relationships:

    (1) Family.

    (2) Social.

    (3) Trade or professional.

    (4) Political.

From each of the above relationships flow various substantial benefits to its participants. These benefits are susceptible of being wholly denied or at least impaired in value through harmful conduct on the part of the defendant, a stranger to the relation. The harms inflicted may be one of three types:

    (1) Physical harms.

    (2) Appropriational harms.

    (3) Defamatory harms.

The essential problem in a relational interest dispute is to determine the extent to which law affords protection of the interest. It may be useful to regard the inquiry here as comprising two stages:

    (1) Is the relationship in question protected at all against the type of harm chargeable to the defendant?

    (2) If so, we may turn to the particular benefit that was lost, and inquire whether

[*10*]

that benefit is included within the range of protection afforded by law against the harm in issue.

This last inquiry usually takes the form of a question regarding the *damages* recoverable. For example, in a wrongful death claim by a spouse, a commonly announced rule is that only *pecuniary* damages are recoverable. This is tantamount to an observation that in the family relationship, the purely emotional benefits derived by one spouse from the presence of the other are not protected against misconduct that results in death.

PART II

THE FAMILY RELATIONSHIP

The compact family unit is the most readily recognized and fully appreciated of all the relationships. The marked dependence of its members upon each other for virtually all their rudimentary needs has impelled courts from the beginning to give serious attention to the family's demand for protection against harm from the outside. But law's earliest move in recognition of the family's claims was cast through history into an awkward mold by reason of the dominant role enjoyed by the family head. The husband-parent was accepted at law without question as the sole representative of the family unit, and all family interests were embodied in him and were recognized as merged within *his* exclusive range of rights. Much of the uneven treatment of the claims of the different members of the family to be noted hereafter can be attributed to this phenomenon.

More recently the interest of the family members in the intimacy, privacy and freedom of family life has come into sharp recognition as a constitutional right which is entitled to a substantial measure of protection against intrusion and regulation on the part of government. This newly

[*12*]

aroused interest on the part of the federal judiciary which is stirring within the womb of constitutional law is exerting and will continue to exert an increasingly liberal influence in damage suits against private persons who interfere with the family interests in one way or another.

Most notable of the harms affecting the family are physical injuries inflicted upon one member of the family by an outsider, with a resulting loss or impairment of benefits for the other members. For reasons noted hereafter, a sharp distinction must be drawn in legal contemplation between those injuries that result in death, on the one hand, and nonfatal (although disabling) injuries, on the other. In history the two harms have developed separately—one as a statutory innovation, the other largely as a creature of judge-made law. For this reason they must be treated separately.

CHAPTER 2

PHYSICAL HARMS—WRONGFUL DEATH

§ 2—1 Wrongful Death at Common Law

Classical Denial of Death Claim. For reasons that are far from satisfactory, courts up until recently have held uniformly that a fatal injury (even though inflicted under such circumstances that the victim could have recovered therefor if he had lived) is not a harm to any surviving member of the deceased's family that can be recognized by law. In brief, there has been no common law right to recover for the death of a human being. This rule was first announced without explanation by Lord Ellenborough as late as 1808 in Baker v. Bolton (K.B.1808), and this single Nisi Prius decision was the only English pronouncement on the matter for sixty-five years. In the meanwhile Parliament enacted a comprehensive remedy for wrongful death by statute, commonly known as Lord Campbell's Act (1846). One result of this legislation was to frustrate common law growth thereafter. When thirty years later a demand for the enforcement of a common law right was again asserted in litigation, the English court found itself faced with the vexatious prospect of recognizing a claim for death at common law directly in the face of an already-developed statutory scheme of recovery. The most feasible escape from this dilemma was to affirm Lord El-lenborough's rule denying the existence of a cause of action for wrongful death at common law, and that position still prevails in England.

In this country, the courts ultimately arrived at the same conclusion in 1848. The prestigious Supreme Judicial Court of Massachusetts approved Lord Ellenborough's position and denied a common law cause of action for wrongful death. Cary v. Berkshire R. R. (Mass.1848). This was the first American holding to that effect. It came at a time when there were already isolated holdings to the contrary in several of the states. The Massachusetts decision, however, set the pattern that was to prevail thereafter, and this holding was followed by a flood of denials of any common law right for death throughout the nation. But the reasons advanced for the denial were specious: (1) The long abandoned medieval idea (if indeed it ever existed) that upon death the civil action becomes merged in the felony; (2) some supposed aversion by common law courts to the placing of a crude monetary value on human life. But however unconvincing both propositions may be, the courts, until very recently, have persistently adhered to to the initial denial of a suit for death at common law. As a result, such rights as the surviving family members may enjoy have been entirely creatures of local statute, and for this reason it must be carefully noted that the treatment accorded death claims has differed in numerous respects from state to state.

Modern Tendencies. Recently, however, a tendency by the courts to reverse their field on the asserted absence of a common law right is becoming clearly noticeable. The first indications came in Illinois. In 1958 the supreme court of that state afforded warning that in an appropriate case a showing of "substantial injustice" under the existing Illinois statutory death provisions might prompt it thereafter to recognize a remedy at common law yielding a fuller relief (Hall v. Gillins). But up until now this has served only as an impending threat. The first definitive recognition of a non-statutory claim for wrongful death was announced in 1970 by the United States Supreme Court in Moragne v. U. S. Marine Lines (U.S.1970). In an extended opinion, the court unequivocally repudiated the traditional Baker v. Bolton position which it had adopted nearly 90 years earlier. The effect of the new position was to make Federal maritime remedies available for a death that had occurred within the territorial waters of Florida, and which was therefore outside the protection of the Death on the High Seas Act. The newly recognized common law remedy served to fill the vacuum. The implications of this important decision will be considered hereafter.

The first action by a state court repudiating
Baker v. Bolton came in 1974. The Massachusetts
Court of Errors and Appeals (which a century
earlier had become the first American tribunal to
espouse the Baker v. Bolton rule) recanted and
openly recognized a common law claim for death.
Gaudette v. Webb (Mass.1971). The only immediate effect of this decision was to enable the court
to treat the prevailing Massachusetts statutory
limitation on the time for bringing a death suit
as merely remedial, and hence properly subject
to being tolled.

**Reconciliation of Common Law and Statutory
Claims.** It is noteworthy that neither the
Moragne nor the *Gaudette* decision obliged the
court to resolve any conflict between the new common law remedy and any existing statutory provision that otherwise would have controlled the
claim. In fact, the Massachusetts court in *Gaudette* volunteered the observation that it intended
to treat the state's statutory limitations as controlling. On the other hand, the position of the
federal courts as it took shape in the maritime
cases that followed *Moragne* gave rise for a time to
considerable confusion. In 1974, the Supreme
Court in a 5–4 decision in Sea-Land Service v.
Gaudet (U.S.1974) held that through resort to the
common law remedy there could be an award for
death within the territorial waters of Florida despite the fact that the decedent had already sued

and recovered for permanent disability during his lifetime. This was a position that had been previously rejected in a line of decisions under the Jones Act going back a half century. By circumventing the statute the court managed to circumvent limitations that adhered to it. In the same case the court allowed the widow damages for the loss of her husband's society and domestic services, contrary both to the express language of the Death on the High Seas Act and to earlier holdings under the Jones Act. Nevertheless it should be noted that in *Gaudet* the Court did not apply its own version of a common law remedy in a situation which fell under the DOHSA. The death occurred in state waters—an area outside the coverage of that measure. Finally, in Mobil Oil Corp. v. Higginbotham (U.S.1978) the Court, dealing with a death which occurred on the high seas, refused to follow the *Gaudet* analogy. It denied an award of damages for loss of society and domestic services where such an award would be in derogation of the express language of Congress in DOHSA.

§ 2—2 Source and Theory of Wrongful Death Claim

The fact that the prevailing suit for wrongful death rests upon statutory foundations necessarily limits drastically the treatment that is possible in a compressed text such as this. There are death statutes in all the states, and these are likely to differ with respect to the persons who may be

[*18*]

entitled to recover, with respect to the elements of loss that can be recognized, the permissible amount of damage allowable, the distribution of the sum recovered, and numerous other matters. At the same time, most of the American statutes are basically modeled after the English Lord Campbell's Act, and a tendency toward uniformity of interpretation in most areas is sufficiently pervasive to make a general discussion useful so long as it is borne cautiously in mind that in each instance the specific controlling statutes and local interpretations must be consulted.

In that great majority of the states whose statutes are modeled after Lord Campbell's Act of 1846 an entirely new cause of action is brought into being upon the death of a victim of a fatal accident. The claim is for the sole benefit of the surviving family members designated in the statutes, and the damages to be recovered are measured in terms of losses these persons sustained by reason of the death. An approach embracing these characteristics will be referred to hereafter as a "pure" wrongful death theory (or statute). This unique death claim is to be distinguished from any suit that also may be maintained on behalf of the deceased for the damages he sustained during his lifetime. In this connection it must be noted that any claim the victim himself may have had, abated at his death under common law. For that reason, special legislation was also necessary if the representative were to be empowered to recover for the deceased's own losses. These measures, which prevail in almost all jurisdictions, are known as survival statutes. Under proper interpretation, they are entirely distinct from wrongful death measures. The chief differences between the two may be noted:

(1) As to the time of accrual of the cause of action: The victim's own right to recover, which is survived, arises immediately upon his injury; while the claim for wrongful death comes into being only when the death occurs, not before.

(2) With respect to the nature of the losses sustained: The victim's claim asserted under a survival statute covers his pain and suffering from the time of accident up until his death. It also includes his lost earnings, which are usually limited arbitrarily to the same period, together with medical and hospital expenses and other costs that accrued prior to his decease. In contrast with the survival suit, the wrongful death claim serves solely to recompense the statutory survivors for the losses that *they* suffer by reason of the victim's death. The victim's own losses are ignored.

(3) As to the proper parties to maintain suit: The survivorship claim is of course

brought by the personal representative for the benefit of the estate. In "pure" death actions, the designated beneficiaries are the real parties in interest, and in some jurisdictions they can maintain suit in their own names. However, solely in order to avoid multiplicity of parties and suits, the death acts of many, if not most states, designate the personal representative as the nominal party, and here he acts in a purely representative capacity. Thus he may serve as claimant in two distinct controversies. These may, or may not be, consolidated for trial.

If the complete separation of the survival and wrongful death claims, which is clear in theory, were consistently adhered to in the language of the statutes and in their interpretation by the courts, the present topic could be adequately disposed of through a few consistent observations. Complications arise, however, from the fact that the legislatures in some states have deliberately or inadvertently departed from the neat scheme of two separate claims suggested above. In a few states (e. g., Connecticut, Iowa, New Hampshire and Tennessee) the prevailing measure appears to be an enlarged survival statute which treats damages sustained by reason of the death as though they are compensation that survives for a harm inflicted upon the deceased himself, or even as reparation for a harm sustained by his estate. In still other states, until recently at least, the death statute has been regarded as penal in character, and the damages awarded are supposed to reflect the extent of the wrongdoing by the defendant. Unfortunately, none of these latter approaches leads to a rational consideration of the individual needs of those surviving members of the family who alone can benefit from the damages awarded.

§ 2—3   Tort Liability—the "Wrong" in Wrongful Death

Torts vs. Contract. The great majority of the American statutes either literally track or at least approximate the language of Lord Campbell's Act, which imposes liability against any person whose "wrongful act, neglect or default" causes the death of another. This phrase, in general, has been held to embrace any conduct that would be regarded as actionable in tort if death had not ensued. Included are intentional misconduct, negligence, and even such no-fault liability as engaging in ultrahazardous activity. Death resulting from a breach of contract has been variously treated. Certainly if the breach also amounts to a disregard of a tort duty toward the person of the deceased, recovery under a wrongful death statute should be allowed even if the action could be maintained as one *ex contractu.* Furthermore it is true, at least in England, that where the one seeking recovery for death was a person to whom a contract duty was directly owed by the defendant, the fact that one of the elements of damage sustained by reason of a breach of that contract duty was the death of a spouse or child should not serve to defeat the cause of action. But where the breach relates to a contract with the deceased and the breach does not also amount to tortious misconduct, a wrongful death claim cannot usually be maintained, even though a "wrongful default" (in the language of Lord Campbell's Act) may have literally occurred. Occasionally a death statute may expressly include (as in Florida) or exclude (as in New Hampshire) a breach of contract.

Products Liability. No-fault liability based upon the sale of a "defective" product has received uneven treatment under the various death statutes. Certainly most earlier cases held that breach of an implied warranty resulting in death was not actionable under them. However, in view of the fact that the newly-emerged entity of Products Liability can be regarded appropriately as a specie of no-fault liability in tort even when it is denominated as a breach of implied warranty, it appears that a death action based on products liability should be maintainable, and the decisions are already moving clearly in that direction.

Prenatal Injury. Recovery for wrongful death is universally allowed for a prenatal injury provided that the deceased infant was born alive and died only thereafter as a result of harm inflicted prior to birth. But there is a sharp difference among the courts concerning the prenatal injury that destroys a yet unborn fetus. Reasons assigned for denying recovery where the child is not born alive include the difficulty of proof of loss of pecuniary services, the non-existence of any "person" whose death can be regarded as an injury, and finally the frequent difficulty encountered in establishing a satisfactory causal relation between the alleged wrongful conduct and the destruction of the fetus. None of the arguments are entirely beyond question, and many courts now allow recovery for the stillbirth of a fetus provided that it was viable at the time of the prenatal injury.

In at least one instance the court recognized a claim for wrongful death caused by the preconception negligence of a manufacturer of birth control pills which damaged the chromosomes of the mother and resulted in the death of the child. Jorgenson v. Meade Johnson Laboratories, Inc. (10th Cir. 1973).

Effect of Tortfeasor's Death. At common law, tort liability for injury to the person was extinguished by the death of the wrongdoer as well as that of the victim. Although this basic shortcoming has been remedied in virtually all jurisdictions through statutes surviving liability, yet difficulties have remained when the tort urged against the wrongdoer's representative is the statutory claim for wrongful death. Strict construction arguments frequently prevailed, notably in the earlier decisions, and resulted in a refusal to recognize the survival of the statutory wrongful death claim, which could not readily be classified as an injury to either "person" or "property" as contemplated by the survival measures. This exclusion, however, has almost entirely disappeared in the opinions or it has yielded to amendments of the survival statutes.

It is noteworthy that a unique problem exists when it appears that the tortfeasor's death preceded that of the victim. It will be recalled that the cause of action for wrongful death does not come into being until the victim dies. If at that moment the wrongdoer is already dead, it becomes apparent that no cause of action for death ever existed during the lifetime of the wrongdoer. Hence, there was nothing upon which a survival statute could operate. But this difficulty, too, has now been generally obviated through specific accommodations in the more modern survival measures.

§ 2—4 The Beneficiaries

A pure wrongful death statute dedicated to the protection of the interests of bereaved family members or "beneficiaries" can operate only where there are such members in existence at the time of death. They may be (and usually are) designated expressly in terms of the family relationship they bore to the deceased.

Spouse. In most jurisdictions the surviving spouse (either husband or wife) is named specifically as a beneficiary, or the spouse may be understood as included within a broader reference such as "next of kin". Although the claimant must be a lawful spouse, the putative husband or wife who "married" in good faith may be included. The few decisions in point indicate that the claimant need not have been married to deceased at the time of the accident, provided that she was his wife when he died.

Children. Similarly, children almost universally qualify as beneficiaries either through express designation or through inclusion as "heirs" or "next of kin". The term *child* almost always includes both adopted and posthumous children. Nor does the illegitimacy of a child serve to deny it wrongful death benefits. Its interests are protected in the event of the death of either the mother or the putative father under the equal protection clause of the 14th Amendment. Levy v. Louisiana (U.S. 1968); Weber v. Aetna Cas. and Surety Corp. (U.S.1972). Moreover, a few statutes provide expressly for the inclusion of the illegitimate child.

Parents. In some jurisdictions the parents are accorded recognition along with the spouse or child. In other states the parents can recover only if the deceased child was unmarried, and, in some instances, only if it was a minor, or if they can establish dependency. We have already seen that the illegitimate child is entitled to the same protection as the legitimate one. Similarly, the mother of a deceased illegitimate is entitled to death benefits just as though the child had been born in wedlock. Glona v. American Guar. & Liab. Ins. Co. (U.S.1968).

Other Relatives. Although the spouse and children are universally covered under one method of classification or another, and the claims of at least some parents are generally recognized, yet brothers and sisters, grandchildren and other more remote relatives have received uneven and often frugal treatment under the various statutes. Sometimes each eligible family relationship will be specified by name; but frequently the statute will provide broadly that the proceeds of recovery shall be distributed to the "heirs", "next of kin", or "as the personal estate of the deceased". These latter terms qualifying the distributees as a group do not appear to contemplate that any detailed inquiry be made into the individual needs of each survivor.

Preferred Classes. In the statutes of a substantial number of states all relatives who are designated either expressly by name or as members of a class are afforded protection without reference to the existence of closer relatives. But it must also be noted that under other statutes the success or failure of the claims of such relatives as those suggested above may depend upon whether the law makers have established exclusive classes of beneficiaries whose claims are entitled to priority over those of other more remote relatives. The presence of a surviving spouse or children, or both, will frequently preclude recognition of any other claimants irrespective of their needs or dependency. Such statutory preferences give rise to special problems whenever the exclusive beneficiary dies without having instituted suit, or even when his death occurs while his claim is still pending. Several results are possible. Conceivably his demise could serve to promote the claims of other beneficiaries who were previously excluded, or it could serve to defeat the cause of action entirely (thus conferring a windfall on the defendant), or, finally, the deceased beneficiary's claim could survive to his own estate. This latter solution is perhaps the one most frequently achieved. The problem, however, is troublesome, for the reason that the claim of the deceased beneficiary is a statutory creature which is neither a right in property or in person. Hence its survival can be made possible only through some special accommodation in either the death or the survival statute.

A remindful word of caution is especially appropriate whenever the claims of beneficiaries are being considered. The preceding observations only indicate the range of general approaches that may be adopted in one statute or another. It is of the greatest importance that each specific measure be examined to determine who in fact are the properly designated beneficiaries.

§ 2—5 Pecuniary Loss

Earnings and Support Contributions Compared. The most commonly recognized item of loss for the survivors is the deprivation of the pecuniary support and maintenance they enjoyed during the lifetime of the deceased. Although his contributions to their needs must usually be extracted from what he earned, the survivors are generally not entitled to an award based on his full earnings. They should recover only that portion that would have been devoted to their own benefit. This allotment could be determined either by subtracting the deceased's estimated personal expenses from his full earnings, or by seeking to fix the actual contributions he made to the maintenance of the survivors over some representative period preceding his death. This latter approach may be preferred in those cases where specific contributions can be fixed, or where personal or business expenses of the deceased are of such a nature that they cannot be isolated from full earnings with any satisfaction.

Life Expectancy of Deceased and Beneficiary. But whichever approach is used, the resulting fig-

[29]

ure must be subjected to further speculation in order to arrive at an estimate of the beneficiaries' loss of support when projected into the future. At this point, the normal life-expectancy of the deceased at the time of his premature death becomes a matter of prime importance, for his future earnings must necessarily be encompassed within this span. Similarly, the life expectancy of each beneficiary marks the outside limit of the period during which he could have enjoyed pecuniary benefits, and if it is determined that his expectancy is shorter than that of the victim, the damages he can recover must be further limited accordingly. Although mortality tables are admissible to assist in determining the expectancy of both the deceased victim and his survivors, the expectancy to be estimated is that of the individual, and general statistics are by no means controlling. Hence, all conditions of his personal health, his longevity inheritance and his history, as well as the safety and health features of his domestic and occupational environment are relevant in reaching an individualized estimate. This applies, of course, to both decedent and survivors.

Factors in Estimating Future Income. In computing the future earnings of the deceased, it is noteworthy that his full life expectancy and the duration of his ability to earn money are not necessarily coextensive. Considering the fact that the survivor's loss of support is represented only by

[*30*]

what he would have received from the earnings of the deceased, the length of time that the latter could have expected to be employed—his worklife —may sometimes be more realistic than his full expected life span.   If he was a wage earner, there should be considered both the physical and emotional strains demanded by the work and also the retirement practices that prevail in employments of the same general character.   Reference must also be made to any special aptitudes or frailties of the deceased that would have affected his continued employment together with his capacity to adapt himself to a change of work in later years. Furthermore, even after a deceased might have been expected to cease work entirely, he may frequently have in prospect the benefit of a pension or social security for the remainder of his life. Such payments are generally treated as equivalent to earnings, and their loss should be compensable to the extent that they would have been shared with survivors.

By reason of the fact that any estimate of earning capacity of the deceased must be projected into the future, there enter into the changing picture numerous factors that are unique to him as an individual: What were the chances for his future advancement or for a shift later into a more lucrative occupation?   This may be a matter of prime importance for youthful employees who were killed before they had an opportunity to achieve their full employment stature. Particularly difficult are situations in which the deceased may have contemplated a radical change in his occupation, as where he was temporarily unemployed at the time of his death, or where he was a student whose prospect for employment lay only in the vague future. But even in the face of such complicating uncertainties as these, benefits should not arbitrarily be denied, for it is the deceased's earning capacity, not his present earnings, that must serve as the proper guide for estimating the loss to his survivors. Conversely, uncertainties of a similar character will be encountered when we face the prospect that a future decline in the deceased's earning power must be expected by reason of advancing age or because of a likelihood that his particular skills and abilities may be less needed in the future. In any conjecture on matters such as the above, the deceased's special skills, his adaptability, his work habits, and his moral temperament are all matters of great importance. Also entitled to consideration are general conditions in the working world: What is the economic outlook for the particular occupation in which the deceased would normally have been engaged? What changes are to be expected in the prevailing wage for his type of work as this may be affected by inflation, collective bargaining, or otherwise?

Deceased's Accumulated Business Assets. Up to this point we have tacitly assumed that all gains to be anticipated during the life expectancy of the deceased would be realized through his own physical effort, skill, talent, or other personal attribute. His accumulated wealth, whether in the form of land, securities or the proprietorship of a business, is not itself to be identified as *earnings* that could serve as a basis for an award to the survivors. Presumably previously acquired assets and the income to be derived from them will continue to be available to his survivors even after his death. Nevertheless, where it can be shown that the returns from deceased's established business were almost wholly the product of his own personal effort, skill and management, and where the role played by invested capital was relatively insignificant, the profits that flowed from such a business may be regarded largely as earnings of the deceased. Even where this is not so, and where the capital investment was substantial there will generally remain a portion of the gains that can fairly be attributed to the personal efforts of the deceased, and that portion should be estimated separately and serve as the basis for an award in the death action. At times the amount contributed through the deceased's own effort may be fixed by estimating what his income would be if he were employed in the same type of business by another person. This, however, may be unfair, as, for example, where it appears that the business could not subsist without the unique services of the deceased, despite the fact that a substantial amount of capital was also required. Even where the income of the deceased was derived wholly from the investment of his capital, his superior skill in management may have played a dominant role in increasing his wealth, and the loss of income that would likely result at his death from an attempt to shift the management to some institutional agency can fairly be assessed as lost earnings of the deceased.

Nature of Survivor's Claim—Dependency. It has been previously noted that the personal character and habits of the deceased are important considerations when an attempt is made to estimate his prospective earning capacity. These are equally important in determining the extent of the loss that was suffered by the survivors. Was the deceased generous and responsible in providing for his family? Was he a good domestic manager? Or, on the other hand, was his manner of living profligate or intemperate? The moral character of the deceased, however, is pertinent in a death suit only to the extent that it may cast light on his ability or inclination to contribute to the pecuniary welfare of the survivors. Isolated instances of sexual or other misbehavior which merely discredit the deceased are generally not admissible.

The economic situation and also the character and personal habits of each surviving claimant may likewise be of importance. But the significance of these factors necessarily depends upon the basic character of the survivor's claim as recognized under the terms of the death statute in question. The interest most readily protected is that of someone who can establish that he was dependent upon the deceased and who has lost his source of support. But the importance of establishing that the claimant was in fact a dependent varies substantially from statute to statute. Under a few of the Acts each survivor must prove that he was dependent upon the deceased, and the amount of support he has lost marks the outside limit of his entitlement (e. g., Va. prior to 1974). In other jurisdictions a nondependent survivor may claim protection under the statute, but, in contrast with the dependent, he can recover only an arbitrarily limited amount (e. g., W.Va.; N.H.). In still other states, all claimants must qualify as dependents, yet the amount of recovery is not limited to their loss of support. Again the dependency of a claimant may be important under a few statutes because it accords him a preference over other survivors in the distribution of damages.

Whenever dependency-in-fact must be established for any of the above purposes the question arises as to what is sufficient dependency? The mere past occasional receipt of benefits from the deceased is not enough. But on the other hand it is seldom required that dire necessitous want be shown; nor is it necessary to establish a legal obligation to support the survivor. In fixing dependency the term, moral obligation, is not infrequently used. The existence of a sustained relationship between the deceased and claimant, the closeness of their family affinity, their relative financial situations and prospects and their respective health and ages are all important for this purpose. Evidence of continued substantial payments to a survivor in the past is persuasive of his dependency.

The overwhelming majority of the death statutes, as interpreted, extend protection far beyond such paltry compensation as would serve merely to prevent utter destitution of the dependent. And this wider liberality prevails even in states where only "pecuniary" damage is recognized. A typical statutory reference to the damages recoverable is "such damage as the jury deems fair and just with reference to the loss sustained by (the survivor)." Loss of the prospect of future gifts or the provision of a generous standard of living far beyond bare necessities can serve as a basis of an award. Thus the claim of a child is not arbitrarily limited to what he could have expected during minority. In addition, there may be evidence of the affectionate relationship between the parties, and of the deserving character or meritorious behavior of the survivor, together with a showing of previous incidents of great generosity. Conversely, evidence indicating an estrangement, or chronic misbehavior by a survivor or his known general unworthiness may appear as detraction from his entitlement.

Loss of Inheritance. The trier, in addition to recognizing prospective gifts, may look ahead and consider what might be the survivor's expectation of inheritance if the victim had lived and acquired an estate throughout his natural life span. The amount in prospect here is scarcely more speculative than in the case of an expectation of a bounty by way of gift. The same considerations seen above that bear on the respective ages of the parties, the affinity between them and the extent of accumulations to be anticipated are all important for this purpose. Assets already in existence at the time of the premature death are obviously excluded except as they may show promise of serving as a basis for future accumulations which might pass by way of inheritance.

Services Within the Family. Even in those states whose statutes restrict the damages recoverable to "pecuniary loss" the courts have almost universally recognized and afforded compensation for the survivors' loss of those household services and familial benefits that are commonplace in most American families. This position prevails in suits for the benefit of the deceased's wife, hus-

band, parent or child; and the elements of loss
that are recognized comprehend the performance
of household chores of all kinds, including work
on the home premises, cooking and other domestic
services, the nursing and caring for ill or indis-
posed members of the family, the provision of religious, moral and other education for the children, et cetera.

§ 2—6 Non Pecuniary Losses

Society and Companionship—Loss of Child. Exchanges of services within the family normally in-
volve ministrations of a more tender and pains-
taking character than those household services
that could be procured in the ordinary labor market. Certainly this does not detract in any way
from their pecuniary value. The question, rather,
is whether loss of this extra quality attributable
to sentimental attachment and feelings of responsibility within the family can itself be assigned a
monetary value in enhancement of damages? At
this point we are on the threshold of the problem
of pecuniary versus nonpecuniary loss. At one
time many courts in states with limitations to pecuniary loss hesitated to include acts of kindness
or affection which were not strictly services meas-
urable in the market place. The narrow position
that formerly prevailed with respect to children,
for instance, was to recognize only the loss of the
child's prospective earnings during his minority

minus the cost of his support. But all this has been undergoing significant change during the past two decades. The decided modern tendency is to afford a measure of protection for the loss of society, companionship, comfort and affection between the family members. The means of achieving this transition have been several: In some jurisdictions there is a forthright recognition that loss of guidance, companionship and protection are proper matters to be submitted to the jury, and in an increasing number of states (presently in excess of twelve) the statutes expressly include such losses. The approach of the Michigan Supreme Court in Wycko v. Gnodtke (Mich.1960) is of particular interest: the "child labor" test (mentioned above) was repudiated. The court observed instead that "human companionship has a definite, substantial and ascertainable pecuniary value." It then proceeded to announce what has since been referred to as the "loss of investment" theory. Under this approach damages could be measured by "the expense of birth, of food, of clothing, of medicine, of instruction, of nurture and shelter incurred by the parent on behalf of the deceased child." Again, other courts, purporting to adhere to the pecuniary value-of-services rule, have endeavored to liberalize the limited recovery it allows by recognizing the prospective loss of the deceased child's earnings even after the attainment of its majority. There is also a manifest tendency by courts to uphold generous jury estimates of the extent of the "pecuniary" loss sustained by reason of the death of the child.

Mental Anguish. Even when sustaining an award for loss of society and companionship a court is likely to insist that this type of positive loss is not to be confused with mental anguish or grief, which is an emotional response to the death and hence cannot be regarded as an element of damage (Sea-Land Services v. Gaudet, supra). Although this is probably the majority position, a few statutes (e. g., Ark., Fla., Va.) provide expressly for emotional losses of all kinds, and occasionally such damages are awarded even in the absence of specific statutory authorization (e. g., La., W.Va.).

§ 2—7 Damages Measured by Loss to Estate

We observed earlier that the statutes in a few states specify that damages are to be measured in terms of loss to the deceased's estate rather than the loss sustained by designated survivors. These hybrid measures are neither survival statutes, nor are they pure wrongful death acts properly geared to protect the relational interests of the surviving members of deceased's family. For present purposes it is sufficient to note that the loss-to-estate death statutes differ from survival statutes in that they serve to create a new cause of action that arises only upon the occurrence of

death. Under these measures the wrongful conduct that caused the death is regarded as an independent injury to the estate of the deceased rather
than to designated survivors, and damages are
measured in terms of the lost accumulations that
would have accrued if the victim had survived to
his full expectancy: What amount would he have
saved and passed on to his estate if he had not
met a premature end at the hands of the defendant? There is a notable lack of consistency with
reference to the measurement of damages under
the various loss-to-estate type statutes. Following
the most widely adopted approach the damages to
the estate are measured by the loss of the deceased's estimated net earnings (commuted to present
value). The only amount deducted is the estimate
of what deceased would have spent for his own
living expenses if he had survived. This most
nearly resembles the loss-to-survivors approach,
since the greater part of the earnings of the deceased not used to cover his own expense would
likely be devoted to his family or would pass to
them by way of gift or devise. In a few jurisdictions (e. g., Ky. and Ga.) the personal representative recovers the full anticipated earnings of deceased undiminished by his own living costs. This,
of course, goes beyond the deserts of the survivors and might be justified (if at all) as a recompense for emotional losses otherwise unrecog-
nized. At the other extreme are those statutes

that limit the loss to what the deceased would have saved and ultimately would have passed to his estate as accumulations. Here it can be noted that although none of the approaches above properly recognizes the needs or deserts of the individual survivors, yet the loss-of-accumulations method of measurement actually works *against* the interest of the dependents, because the pressure of a heavy family responsibility could only serve to lessen whatever amount might otherwise be available to augment the estate.

Courts in all jurisdictions with loss-to-estate type statutes encounter peculiar difficulties with reference to reimbursement for loss of services performed within the family by its members. The wife and mother who will expectably devote her entire life to domestic duties is not likely to accumulate an estate of any consequence, although her continued existence is a matter of tremendous importance to the rest of the family. Similarly, the infant whose life was taken would probably have contributed little beyond the performance of trivial household chores. Even if ultimately he had been placed out as a wage earner, his wages would belong to his father during his entire minority and hence these could not serve as an enhancement of the child's own estate. The difficulties throughout this area are obvious. Nevertheless courts have managed in most instances to so maneuver their loss-to-estate statutes as to permit substantial recovery for family services lost. Not infrequently there is resort to such vague terms as "the value of the life lost", or it may be observed that there should be recognition of "the destruction of (the wife's) capacity to carry on her life's activities as wife and homemaker in the way she would have done had she lived." Chase v. Fitzgerald (Conn.1946).

§ 2—8 Statutory Limitations on Amount of Damages

As recently as 1935 the death statutes in seventeen states imposed an arbitrary maximum limit on the total amount recoverable, varying from five to ten thousand dollars. These limitations were probably imposed out of fear that awards for death might prove excessive unless some restraining hand were laid upon the sympathetic impulses of jurymen. This apprehension may have proved groundless, or possibly it was allayed through the comforting presence of liability insurance. But, whatever the cause, the overall limits on recovery have virtually disappeared. Kansas still recognizes a ceiling of fifty thousand dollars; a similar ceiling exists in New Hampshire, but in that state it applies only in instances where there is no surviving spouse or a dependent child or parent. In Wisconsin there is imposed a limitation of five thousand dollars but which operates only with respect to non pecuniary losses. Somewhat similarly, damages of this character are limited by the West Virginia statute to ten thousand dollars, but significantly an additional award for as much as a hundred thousand dollars is authorized for pecuniary losses sustained by dependent survivors.

§ 2—9   Survival and Wrongful Death Contrasted

The Basic Conflict. An injured person's own cause of action in tort, which at common law would have ended abruptly at his death, is now preserved and vested in his personal representative by means of a survival statute, one of which obtains in every jurisdiction. The existence of such a measure side by side with a wrongful death provision has proved to be a source of concern arising from fear that a duplication of damages could result. Indeed such a fear is not without foundation: Whenever an injured victim while still alive can demonstrate that the impairment of his bodily condition is sufficiently serious to shorten his life expectancy he will become entitled to damages sufficient to replace the lost earnings that otherwise would have been in prospect for him. It is not to be expected that this right would be expunged in the event that death does indeed foreshorten his life before the award has been made. In theory, this element of loss should persist and remain available to his personal representative under a survival statute. If, however, to this survived claim for lost future earnings there were superadded a separate award for his dependants' loss of support under a death statute, the prospect of a duplication of damages would face the defendant. This dilemma has been dealt with in a bewildering variety of ways. In a few states a binding election must be made between a survival claim and an action for wrongful death (e. g., Ky. and Wyo.). Occasionally the survival suit is arbitrarily restricted to those claims of the deceased that were unrelated to his death (e. g., W.Va.). In other states the law makers have deliberately omitted a separate death statute, and lost future earnings in full are provided under the survival measure (e. g., Conn.). There are numerous other varieties in approach. The one that is most satisfactory and which has been most widely adopted is that of affording recognition of both the survival claim and the wrongful death claims but with damages for loss of earnings under the survival suit limited exclusively to those earnings that were lost between the time of accident and the moment of death. All pecuniary loss accruing thereafter must be recovered solely under the death statute. It is noteworthy, however, that funeral expenses, which do not accrue, of course, during the lifetime of the deceased, are frequently made recoverable by express provision in the survival statute.

Defenses. The basic contrast in theory between a statutory survival of the victim's own claim, on the one hand, and the claim created by statute for the benefit of certain surviving family members upon the event of wrongful death, on the other, is brought into focus when certain defenses basic to the defendant's protection are considered:

Prior Adjudication or Settlement. If during his lifetime the tort victim institutes suit which is ultimately reduced to judgment, this judgment is *res judicata* with respect to any attempt by his representative following his death to assert the same claim pursuant to a survival statute. In such case the issues are identical and there are involved the same parties or their successors. This holds true irrespective of whether the judgment in the victim's own proceeding was favorable or unfavorable to him. Similarly, if a settlement is effected by the deceased during his lifetime, this precludes any successful claim thereafter through survivorship.

Parity of reasoning would suggest on the other hand that the family's separate claim for wrongful death should not be adversely affected by any judgment either for or against the deceased during his lifetime. Neither should the death claim be precluded by a final judgment either way in a survival suit instituted by the deceased's representative. In either event there is lacking any identity of parties or their successors; the measurement of damages involved in the two actions is entirely different; and there is no way in which the rights of the family members could be asserted or protected in the deceased's own action, since such rights do not even come into being during his lifetime. The identities essential to *res judicata* simply do not exist. But, however this may be, the overwhelming majority of the courts hold that a judgment either for or against the deceased, or a voluntary settlement of his claim during his lifetime, precludes the maintenance of a wrongful death suit thereafter. However frail this position may be in theory, it has much to commend it from the practical point of view: The likelihood of an overlapping of damage would be substantial in situations where the deceased had instituted suit during his lifetime and had recovered substantial damages while facing an obvious prospect of death or permanent disability. Particularly would a defendant be disinclined to make a generous settlement with a seriously injured person if he were confronted with the prospect of a wrongful death claim in the event that the victim should die thereafter. The rationale most frequently advanced in support of the majority position is the observation that the continuance of a right of recovery in the victim up until the moment of his death is to be regarded as an express or implied condition precedent to the accrual of the cause of action for wrongful death under the

statute. It is noteworthy that in a few jurisdictions the opposite position has been adopted.
Moreover some evidence of a possible turn of the
tide is afforded by the action of the majority of
the Supreme Court in the recent *Gaudet* decision
(supra), which accords a right to maintain the
newly-recognized common law death claim in admiralty despite a settlement by the injured seaman
prior to his death. In that case, however, the
court insisted that recovery under the death suit
be limited to loss of domestic services and society,
thus minimizing to some extent the risk of overlapping damages.

From the standpoint of both theory and practice a recovery on a wrongful death claim should
be allowed despite the rendition of a final judgment in a prior survival suit instituted by the
personal representative following the death of the
victim. Under such circumstances it is obvious
that the deceased *did* have an outstanding claim
at the time of his death, thus obviating the theo-
retical criticism suggested above. Moreover,
from the practical point of view there is little, if
any, reason to apprehend a duplication of damages
so long as the recovery for lost earnings under
the survival claim is limited to such losses as
were sustained prior to the victim's death. Nevertheless, the decisions are not in accord, and in
a substantial number of jurisdictions *res judicata*
is made applicable in cases both where the sur-

vival claim was the subject of the first judgment
and also where the judgment in the death claim
was first. Furthermore, the outcome of the earlier proceeding—whether favorable or unfavorable—appears to be immaterial on the *res judicata*
matter.

*Contributory Negligence, Assumption of Risk
or Consent of Deceased.* If the deceased was guilty of negligence that contributed to the fatal accident, this will obviously be available as a defense to any survival claim brought by his representative. (Similarly, in a jurisdiction where
comparative negligence prevails the damages recoverable by the representative will be subject
to a reduction.) The result is generally the same
in a wrongful death proceeding, although the supporting reasons are not entirely clear. Contributory negligence as a doctrine rests on the premise
that a person should not be rewarded for a harm
that he partly brought upon himself through his
own wrongdoing. But where, as in the wrongful
death claim, the wronged persons are the innocent
family members, a denial of their claims for injury to their relational interests cannot be so
plausibly justified. In treating the victim's contributory negligence as a bar the courts point
out that the right to recover for a wrongful death
depends upon the enforceability of the victim's
own claim. The same reasoning is advanced in
support of the universally accepted position that

the victim's assumption of risk or his consent are
defenses to any claim asserted by way of either
survival or wrongful death.

Contributory Negligence of Beneficiary. The
effect of contributory negligence on the part of
one or more of the beneficiaries is even more
perplexing, and the variations of treatment are
numerous. First, assuming that the deceased victim was free of negligence, his representative's
right to recover in a survival suit is undisputed in
spite of any contributing carelessness on the part
of one or even all those family members who
would benefit from the judgment in the survival
suit. The same generally holds true for the contributorily negligent distributee under a wrongful
death statute of the type in which the death is
regarded solely as a wrong to the estate.

At the opposite extreme is the situation where
the claim asserted is under a true wrongful death
statute brought on behalf of beneficiaries. If the
sole beneficiary (or *all* beneficiaries) are found
negligent, recovery is almost universally denied.
Even here, however, there are exceptions. In a
very few states it is observed somewhat inaptly
that the right to institute suit is vested in the personal representative acting for the blameless deceased. Hence the conduct of the individual beneficiaries could be regarded as immaterial (e. g.,
N.J., N.Y., Pa.). Whenever less than all beneficiaries are contributorily negligent, recovery is

[50]

generally denied under the majority rule only with respect to the share of the careless person or persons, and the claims of the innocent beneficiaries are unaffected. A few courts go so far as to allow recovery for *all* beneficiaries so long as at least *one* of them was free of negligence (e. g., Mo., Or.).

Family Immunities. Until fairly recent years both the husband and wife were clothed with immunity from personal tort liability to each other. Similarly, the parent was not subject to any personal tort claim brought on behalf of its minor child. The spousal immunity clearly appears destined for extinction; it has already been abrogated entirely in about half the states. Furthermore, at least a dozen of the remaining jurisdictions have refused to recognize the immunity where the marriage has been terminated. This includes, of course, a suit for the wrongful death of one spouse. There still remain, however, an appreciable number of jurisdictions that refuse to permit an action against the surviving spouse for the death of the other. The arguments opposed to interspousal immunity are especially convincing when applied to a death claim. In such situations the time honored argument of identity of husband and wife is no longer plausible where death has already severed the matrimonial bonds.

The parental immunity, together with its obverse—the child's immunity from personal liabil-

ity to the parent—is also disappearing, but at a
somewhat slower pace. In fifteen jurisdictions it
has been wholly abolished; but elsewhere the immunity persists as a general proposition.   Here
again, the decisions on the rights of the unemancipated minor to maintain a wrongful death suit
against the parent are not entirely harmonious.
However, the growth of authority in favor of the
child's death claim is clearly in evidence.   It is
significant that the Restatement of Torts Second,
although reluctant to regard the parental immunity as wholly abolished, nevertheless adopts the
position that it no longer obtains for the wrongful death of the parent or child, or for the wrongful death of the other parent (R. § 895h(2)(f),
(g)).

Limitation of Actions.   Statutory periods of
limitation for the institution of tort suits come
into operation the moment that the cause of action arises.   It follows that when the personal representative institutes a survival claim based on
the deceased's own right, he must proceed within
the statutory period which began running at the
time the initial injury was sustained.   If the deceased's claim was barred at the time of his death,
the survival action will be defeated; and even if
the claim was enforceable at the moment of death,
the period continues to run and the survival suit
remains subject to the same limit as though the
victim had not died.   In a few states an additional
short period is wisely allowed the representative

if the claim was enforceable at the time of death (e. g., N.H., S.D., Wis.). Through parity of reasoning it follows in general that the period of limitation for a wrongful death claim does not start running until the death occurs, since the cause of action does not come into being until then. The time limits within which the death suit must be instituted are usually designated by the authorizing statute itself, and the period varies from one to three years from time of death (with two years the period most frequently specified). Occasionally the period runs from "the accrual of the cause of action", which is generally regarded as the time of death.

It must be noted that the period of limitation imposed by legislature in the death act is a condition upon which the very existence of the right of action for death itself depends. Hence, saving provisions applicable to general statutes of limitations have not been available to a claimant under the death statute. If, however, there is no period designated within the death statute and resort must be had to general statutory limitations on actions, the usual savings provisions apply to the death claim as well as to other suits. The same result is to be expected in any jurisdiction whose courts should choose to endow the wrongful death claim with a common law pedigree (Gaudette v. Webb, supra, § 2–1).

When it appears that at the time of his death the deceased's cause of action was already barred

by the applicable statute of limitations, a wrongful death claim asserted thereafter may be defeated even though it was instituted within the period
authorized by the death statute itself. This is for
the reason that the very existence of the death
claim may depend upon the fact that the deceased
was vested with an enforceable claim at the time
of his death. The answer here may rest upon
the precise language of the statute. Consider, for
example, the New York Death Act, which author-
izes a death claim only in cases in which the defendant would have "been liable to an action" if
deceased had remained alive. With this compare
the West Virginia Act which allows a wrongful
death claim whenever "the act, neglect or default is such as would (if death had not ensued)
have entitled the party injured to maintain an
action to recover damages .   .   .". This latter
phrase can be fairly interpreted to require only
that the injury was one for which recovery would
have been warranted initially. Nevertheless even
in states whose statutes are so phrased the decisions are far from harmonious. The courts of Illinois, North Carolina, Ohio, and West Virginia,
among others, adopt the interpretation suggested
above, while still other states (e. g., Fla. and Va.)
deny the death action whenever the deceased's
claim was barred at the time of death. The entire difficulty is easily remedied by an express
provision in the statute, and this is frequently the
case.

CHAPTER 3

PHYSICAL HARMS—NON FATAL INJURIES

§ 3—1 Source and Nature of Family Members Rights

Common Law Origin. A physical injury (especially a disabling one) inflicted on one member of
a family will usually entail tragic hardships for
other family members also, and the provision of
financial repair for these consequential losses is
as much a matter for serious concern as is the
compensation of the victim himself. When the
injury is not fatal the common law courts provided from the beginning a remedy for the husband
or father of the injured wife or child, and this
without need for legislative intervention (in contrast with the fatal accident picture (Chapter 2,
supra)). Notice, however, that in accord with
legal tradition relief was confined strictly to the
male parent or husband, and this limitation persisted until very recently. The reason, already
suggested in the preceding chapter, lay in the his-
torically dominant role of the male head of the
family. In legal contemplation he *was* the family
—the owner of both his wife and children, who
were his mere chattels subject to his command.

Husband. The husband had a right to his wife's services which was analogous to and probably derived from the master's action for loss of the service of his servant, and his claim for an injury to his wife was maintainable in *trespass per servitium amisit*. But in the husband's suit the *servitium* was broader than that of the ordinary master. It came to embrace three elements—services, society and sex—which are now universally known under the aggregate term *consortium* (or, more popularly, the S's). The tidal wave of Emancipation of Women statutes that arose during the Nineteenth Century (discussed hereafter) gave rise to a vexatious problem concerning the continued validity of this claim of the husband. In several jurisdictions the courts came to the conclusion that the husband's right to his wife's consortium was one which was justifiable only by the fact that in past history he alone served as sole spokesman for the family, and that the family's rights were wholly absorbed in his legal personality. Hence it would appear to follow that when the wife's legal rights emerged through the emancipation acts and terminated this exclusive role of the husband, all his former rights to her consortium were extinguished. At one time this position prevailed in a substantial minority of the jurisdictions. Today, however, it persists in only a handful of states (i. e., N.C., Conn., R.I., Va. and Kan.), and in several of these the result is dictated by special language in the emancipation statutes. The great majority of the courts have continued even after emancipation to uphold the husband's right to damages for loss of the domestic services and the company, affection and sex benefits of his injured wife. The wife's earnings outside the home, however, have become her own property, and for these she alone can recover. Occasionally an emancipation provision goes further and expressly confers upon the wife herself the right to recover for the impairment of her domestic services as well as the loss of her outside earnings (Va. and Kan.). Under such circumstances it is obvious that the husband cannot recover for these same losses. Whether he still retains an enforceable claim for impairment of his more intangible interest in her society and marital affection even under such statutes is open to question.

Parent. From the standpoint of history the character of the parents' entitlement in the child has conspicuously been that of service, as contrasted with the husband's right to his wife's consortium—an indiscriminate blend of services, society and sex. Hence the claimant's right to the custody of the minor has been traditionally regarded as an essential prerequisite to recovery for a disabling injury to the child. Although the male parent will normally be the exclusive custodian and hence the sole possessor of the right to services, yet his death or abandonment of the family can serve to promote the mother, or even an outsider, to the role of custodian entitled to maintain suit for loss of the child's services. It may also be noted that the mother of an illegitimate child may be the custodian and hence is in a position to sue and recover. The character of the parent's claim as one in services has persisted and its restricted character has been emphasized occasionally in recent decisions. See Borer v. American Air Lines, Inc. (Cal.1977). Thus even today there must be some appreciable impairment of the present or prospective ability of the child to render service to the custodial parent, and the victim must be an unemancipated minor.

Wife. As long as the wife was wholly denied personality at law she obviously could enforce no claim on her own behalf against anyone who injured her husband and impaired her interest in his society and services. Legal standing to maintain law suits was finally conferred on her during the latter half of the nineteenth century through the universal adoption of Married Women's Property acts. One might expect that thereafter courts would recognize and enforce on her behalf a claim to the consortium of her wrongfully injured husband similar to the right that he had traditionally enjoyed with respect to her. Such, however, was not to be the case for more than half a century. The reasons advanced in support of a continued denial were not convincing. The recognition of a woman's legal status, observed the courts, did not have the effect of conferring on her any new substantive right to her husband's consortium. The lack of precedent, and the portent of double recovery if she, as well as he, were premitted to sue for a single injury, were some of the stock arguments marshalled against any recognition of her claim.

The turn of the tide came in 1950 with a landmark decision of the Court of Appeals for the District of Columbia, Hitaffer v. Argonne Co., and at present it can be stated that the courts of last resort in a majority of the states recognize that the husband and wife enjoy equal rights in the consortium of each other and that each can proceed against any third person who tortiously injures the other. This recognition of the wife's claim may well become universal. Rodriguez v. Bethlehem Steel (Cal.1974). It has been confirmed by statute in several states. The cogency of the new position is intensified by the argument that a denial of the wife's right could be in derogation of the equal protection provisions of the United States Constitution. This same argument, however, could lead to the conclusion that the consortium claim of the husband as well as that of the wife, should now be denied.

In recognizing the wife's claim to her husband's consortium the courts must face the prospect that a duplication or at least an overlap of damages could follow. Already in court is the disabled husband with a claim for his lost earnings—earnings which otherwise would have been used in part for the benefit of his wife. Obviously the wife should not be allowed to recover this same item under the guise of lost support or services. A somewhat similar risk of confusion might be apprehended even with reference to nonpecuniary losses. Both partners may suffer impairment of their previous enjoyment of companionship and sexual pleasures with each other in the event that either of them is injured. Although the individuality of the interest of each spouse should be fully recognized, yet permitting the parties to proceed by way of separate suits can be expected to lead to confusion and to possible overpayment (or underpayment) despite all efforts to prevent it. Such prospects have prompted courts in some jurisdictions to wholly deny recognition of the consortium claim of either spouse unless the suit is joined with the personal injury claim of the other.

Minor Child. The recent acceptance and enforcement of the wife's right to recover for a negligent injury to her husband has not as yet led courts to recognize an analogous right on the part of the child with reference to the loss of the parent's companionship, training and similar relation benefits. The same arguments of lack of precedent, danger of double recovery and remoteness of damage which ultimately came to be rejected when urged against the wife's claim have met with success when the child has attempted to assert its rights. Borer v. American Air Lines (Cal.1977). R. § 707A. Many writers have insisted that any distinction between the rights of spouse and child is unsupportable, and even opinions denying the child's claim are frequently apologetic in tone. Indeed, very recently an intermediate court of appeal in Michigan has recognized the right of a child to maintain a claim for the loss of the society and companionship of its mother who sustained accidental injuries, setting off an anxiety reaction which caused the mother to have indiscriminate sexual relations. Berger v. Weber (Mich.App.1978).

§ 3—2 Relational Harm and Physical Injury Compared

Relational Claim Distinct. The spouse's or parent's loss of consoritum or services is a distinct harm which is not to be confused with the invaded right to bodily security of the injured husband, wife or minor child. The family member claiming a relational injury (the relational claimant) must be prepared to establish that his own harm is of a character protected by law. Worry or concern for the welfare of the injured person, for example, is not enough. If one member of the family is insulted, defamed or disfigured, this itself cannot

serve as a source of liability to another member
(§ 6–12). But if a wife becomes ill or mentally
unbalanced as a result of defendant's words or
conduct, so that her husband is obliged to provide her cure or is denied her company, he can
recover for the physical harm thus inflicted upon his own relational interest. To the extent that
an item of damage can be recovered directly under the suit for bodily harm any relational injury
claim for the identical loss must yield. Hence
neither husband nor wife can recover for the other's loss of outside earnings, and a parent cannot
recover (under the guise of loss of services) for
an impairment of the child's prospect of such
earnings as may accrue after it has attained majority.

The separateness of the two actions is manifested by the fact that a settlement or a favorable
or an adverse judgment in one action is not binding upon either party to the other. The two suits
may be tried separately or together unaffected by
any inconsistency of verdicts.

Liability for Physical Harm Required. Although the claim for harm to the family relation
and the claim of the physically injured victim
are entirely separate with reference to proper
claimant and to proper damages, nevertheless
both have their origin in the same conduct of the
defendant. The latter must be subject to liability
in tort to the family member whose person was

injured. All the usual essentials to a recovery for bodily injury must be shown by the relational claimant, and if the victim assented or assumed the risk of injury, or if he is not a person to whom a duty was owed, there can be no recovery by any family member.

Noteworthy here is a group of decisions in which the parent has been allowed recovery for loss of the services of a child to whom the defendant has unlawfully supplied habit forming drugs. He may also recover medical expenses reasonably incurred in treatment of the child (R. § 705). The right of recovery here is not lost because the child voluntarily purchased and used the drugs. The same liability does not attach to the sale of an alcoholic beverage to a child. In many states, however, there are statutes forbidding the sale of intoxicants to minors. Many such measures provide for civil liability to the parent.

Fault of Victim or Claimant. What has been said above applies equally with respect to the contributory negligence of the victim. Here, as in the wrongful death situations (§ 2–9, supra), the victim's negligence is a defense to all relational claims. This is true despite the criticism of many writers who have maintained that the blameless parent or spouse should not be denied a recovery solely because of the contributing fault of the injured person. This, it is argued, resurrects the discredited notion of imputed contributory negligence, or at least treats the relational harm as though it were in some way a derivative of the victim's own right instead of an independent claim.

Again, as in the wrongful death claim (§ 2–9, supra), the relational claimant's own negligence that contributed to the harm or his consent to the victim's exposure will preclude his recovery.

§ 3—3   Damages

Spouse's Loss of Services and Consortium.   The husband and wife are each entitled to recover the value of the lost domestic services of the other. Household chores of all kinds, both past and prospective, which the spouse was capable of performing are included, even though there is no showing that they were in fact regularly rendered. Although the market cost of replacement of such services can always serve as a minimum, yet the jury can properly place such value on family ministrations as will take into consideration the devotion and tender care bestowed by one who is a member of the family.   Outside earnings of either spouse, as we have seen, remain the sole property of the earner, except possibly where he or she is employed directly by the other spouse.

The spouse's loss is by no means limited to bare household services.   The most significant aspect of marriage is the interest of each partner in the consortium of the other.   This, we have seen, embraces the society, companionship, solace, access to sexual relations and opportunities for parenthood which obtain in varying degrees in every marriage. Loss of sentimental aspects of consortium is treated in terms of a deprivation—an affirmative loss taken from the complainant spouse and which must in some way be translated by the jury into dollars. It is frequently observed in instructing the jury that this deprivation must be distinguished from the grief, sorrow or anguish experienced by the spouse upon being faced with such a loss. The factors that are pertinent in fixing the amount of an award for loss of the consortium of an injured spouse are basically the same as those that must be considered in claims for the deliberate alienation of a spouse's affection, and hence the matter can be deferred for treatment under that topic (§ 4–2, infra).

Parent's Loss of Child's Services. We observed previously (§ 3–1) that the only formal element of damage recoverable by the parent is replacement of loss of the child's services. Even today an instruction to the jury that it can award damages for loss of the child's companionship is likely to result in a reversal. But despite this formal adherence to the service requirement, the conception has lost some of its earlier importance, and its hold on the law may have loosened. It is not generally required that the child be one who has rendered any actual service or even that it is likely to do so. Thus the custodian's bare right to the service is frequently enough to ground his claim against the third party wrongdoer. Once an impairment of this right is established, a generous award of damage is frequently tolerated, as in the wrongful death cases. In many jurisdictions today the parent can recover medical expenses actually incurred without even an attempt to establish a right to services, and the formal services requirement has been completely abolished by statute in three states (Idaho, Iowa, Washington). It has recently been abandoned by judicial decision in at least one jurisdiction. Shockley v. Prier (Wis.1975). On the other hand, the Supreme Court of California has recently emphasized that the parents' right is strictly limited to loss of the economic value of the child's services and that loss of affection cannot properly be included. Baxter v. Superior Court (Cal.1977).

CHAPTER 4

APPROPRIATIONAL HARMS

§ 4—1 Nature of the Harm

Up to this point we have considered a relatively narrow group of situations in which one member of the family has been killed or seriously injured under circumstances that would entitle him (or his representative) to recover for the physical harm sustained. Only when liability to the physically harmed person could be made to appear did there arise a second cause of action in favor of some other member of the family entitling the latter to recover for the loss of relational benefits he previously enjoyed with respect to the killed or injured victim.

We come now to a more complex picture where no recognizable tort has been committed against the person whose service or consortium has been lost. Instead, the harm is one that is directed, not to a person, but toward the relationship itself. The complaining member of the family alleges that the defendant has knowingly deprived him of family benefits he previously enjoyed. In such situations the defendant's conduct can be regarded as intentional in the sense that he either was motivated by a desire to take away some family benefit or at least he proceeded deliberately while aware that such a deprivation would follow. His conduct can be meaningfully characterized as *appropriational*. (*Deprivational* carries much the same meaning). Usually, but not always, he was seeking to capture the benefits of the relationship for himself. The means employed to attain such an objective may vary. There is frequently a persuasive effort brought to bear by the defendant on some member of the family, as we shall discover in such torts as seduction, alienation of affections and criminal conversation. This may at times be accompanied by fraud, defamation or coercion. But often the inducement is actionable even though it amounts to no more than sheer unperjured persuasion. Again, the conduct complained of may take the form of a denial of access, as when one member of a family is physically prevented from visiting another member, or where the defendant confiscates, destroys or damages a corpse of a deceased relative, or refuses to surrender it to family members for religious rites or burial. The particular form that the conduct assumes is not decisive of its appropriational character. What is important is that in some way it is directed toward the relationship as indicated above. Seldom are such harms committed through sheer negligence. Appropriational harms have certain characteristics in common, which justifies the use of the term. It should not be regarded as a classification that necessarily entails tort liability on anybody's part, any more than does the expression "physical harm."

§ 4—2   Interference Between Husband and Wife

Spouse's Rights to Consortium—Equality of the Sexes.   A cause of action for deprivation of the consortium benefits of marriage was originally vested exclusively in the husband, who was the sole representative of the family.   However, the nationwide enactment of Married Women's Property acts during the 19th century had the immediate effect of according recognition to a corresponding right in the wife with respect to the consortium of her husband.   This prompt extension to the wife of full protection against appropriational harms stands in sharp contrast with the tardy recognition of any claim on her own behalf for a physical injury inflicted upon her husband. This latter claim, as we know, was ignored entirely by the courts until the last twenty years.

The claim of each spouse with respect to consortium embraces the exclusive right to sexual relations with the other, the right to the presence of the other and even the right to the other's affections.   Hence there are three distinct appropriational torts to be considered—Criminal Conversation, Enticement, and Alienation of Affections. Considering that the purpose of all three actions is to protect the marriage institution, it is essential that the complainant establish the existence of a man and wife relationship. Those who are merely affianced have no such rights. However, even a common law marriage or a union that is voidable because of the underage of one partner serves to afford a sufficient basis for a loss-of-consortium claim.

Criminal Conversation. The insistance of each spouse that he or she alone is entitled to have sexual relations with the other is protected against outside intermeddling through the suit for criminal conversation. Although such claims are fairly infrequent today, yet the cause of action can readily be established merely by making a satisfactory showing that the defendant, a third party, voluntarily had intercourse with the spouse of the offended plaintiff. The violation of the exclusive marital right is of itself sufficient to justify an award of damages. The validity of the claim is unaffected by the fact that the partners to the marriage themselves seldom, if ever, had sexual relations with each other. Neither need it be shown that the defendant was the procurer, so long as he or she submitted, even reluctantly, to the prohibited intercourse. Indeed, criminal conversation is the only appropriational tort against the family in which even total ignorance by the defendant of the fact that his partner in the act is married does not prevent liability. Although the violation of the claimant's exclusive right to intercourse is sufficient without more to ground the action, yet a showing that the affections of the miscreant spouse were alienated from the plaintiff or that the spouse was enticed to absent him or herself from the plaintiff's home will serve to aggravate the offense and thus enhance the amount of recovery.

Enticement. The husband's right to damages for the enticement of his wife from home was a claim protected originally by the ancient writ of Ravishment. This, in turn, gave way to an action of trespass for depriving a master of his servant— a class of menials which included his wife. The essential interest invaded here was the husband's right to the presence of his wife to assure performance of the services demanded of her. If it could be shown that she was enticed or counseled by defendant to leave the shelter of his roof or that, having run away, she was harbored by the defendant, the requirements of an enticement were met. At one time it made no difference whether the defendant acted out of selfishness and malice or, on the other hand, was prompted by the most praiseworthy of motives. Nor need he have diminished in any way her affection for her spouse.

The tort of enticement still persists as a distinct cause of action. It is now available to both spouses, protecting the access of each to the physical presence of the other. In practice, however, it is usually regarded as concomitant to each spouse's broader claim to the affection of the other—an interest that finds its protection in the more recently recognized action for alienation of affections. The two interests are frequently lumped together under the term consortium, to which may be added, when appropriate, a count for criminal conversation. But each tort retains its own identity as guardian of a distinct marital interest. The affections may be alienated although no physical separation of the spouses has occurred and there has been no sexual intercourse with the defendant.

Alienation of Affections. Alienation of affections did not emerge as a distinct tort until its recognition in New York in 1866. Its spread thereafter was rapid, and today it is recognized in virtually every jurisdiction, except as provided otherwise by statute.

Intention. With alienation of affections, as with most other appropriational harms, it must appear that the defendant directed his (or her) conduct toward the relationship itself. This means that he must have been fully aware that the object of his attention was a married person and that he deliberately took steps calculated to diminish the marital affection formerly existing between this person and the complaining spouse. It need not appear that defendant was motivated solely by a desire to impair the affection or that he acted through ill will. But certainly negligence alone cannot ground a claim for alienation of affections, and even awareness by the defendant that his behavior might serve to deprive one spouse of the other's affections does not give rise to the tort.   Sometimes, as where the defendant is cast in the role of a lover, his (or her) objective is to attract to himself (or herself) the alienated affection.   But perhaps more often the defendant is a parent whose intermeddling in the marriage of its child is prompted only by a desire to extricate the child from what the parent may regard as an undesirable match.   The worthiness of the impulse that prompted such conduct is a matter to be dealt with later under the subject, privilege.   It does not affect the element of intention.

Conduct.   The alienation must be carried into effect through affirmative conduct of some kind. Merely serving as the passive (although willing) recipient of a married person's affection is not enough to give rise to liability.   On the other hand, the defendant need not have actually initiated the process.   The line here is difficult to draw.   Few single items of behavior standing alone can be very meaningful.   The apparent innocence of the defendant's motive in following a given course frequently lends color to his conduct. If, for instance, the plaintiff's spouse is an established customer or business associate of the defendant, his active participation with such spouse in private conferences or his invitation that she join him at lunch may fall short of being alienatory conduct even though the defendant is aware that by so doing he is attracting her affection. On the other hand, declarations of love or intimate bodily contacts usually tell their own story. It has been observed that this is no way to conduct a business.

Causation.   Even conduct clearly designed to alienate the affections is not actionable unless it does have that effect. It need not have been the sole motivating cause of the loss; but when such conduct appears in combination with other independent operating factors such as a deeply grounded hostility between the spouses or profound misbehavior by one of the partners, the inducement extended by the defendant must have played a role that was something more than trivial. It must be shown to have served as a substantial factor in impairing the marriage.

Effect of Prior Estrangement or Separation of Spouses.   The observation that alienatory conduct may be actionable even though it was not the sole cause of the loss of affection, is a proposition that can be readily couched in terms of duty. We can appropriately observe that the rules of law that operate to condemn the defendant's behavior are rules designed to protect even those marriages that were already strained and tenuous. To put the matter another way, it can be said that the chance of patching up a marital rift is a chance that is protected against outside intermeddling. Evidence showing that the marriage was unhappy even before the defendant appeared on the scene or that there was previous misbehavior by either party does not defeat recovery per se, but such may be considered in fixing the amount of damages. What was the value of the chance that the marriage might otherwise have regained a more even keel? Even the fact that a separation had taken place at the time of the defendant's intervention does not preclude a claim for alienation of affections. Of course the earlier behavior of either spouse in voluntarily separating or otherwise manifesting an indifferent attitude might serve to defeat the action totally, by indicating consent.

Privilege as a Defense. A claim for alienation of affections, like other intentional torts, may be defeated by a showing that the defendant acted pursuant to some privilege: That is to say, he was impelled to act by an interest in the health, safety or morals of the spouse whose affections were alienated. Such a privilege is asserted most frequently by the defendant who is the parent of one partner to the marriage. Such parent who interferes is aided by a strong presumption that he (or she) was properly motivated, and the burden is upon the aggrieved spouse to show the impropriety of the parent's interference. In order to

justify the recognition of a privilege the motive
of the defendant must be to serve some substantial interest of the alienated spouse. The parent's
mere pique at the plaintiff spouse or distaste for
the latter's habits, behavior, or religion will not
suffice unless the health, safety or moral welfare
of the child reasonably appears to be endangered.
The privilege is a qualified one, which means that
it can be defeated if it is abused by the defendant.
This may happen when there are no reasonable
grounds for the parent's belief that an impending
threat of harm exists, or where the means adopted
are fraudulant, coercive, or where the parents
otherwise exceed the bounds of acceptable behavior.

The privilege may be extended beyond the parents to other near relatives and occasionally even
to strangers. But, apart from the parents, the
intermeddler must persuade the court that his
relationship to the alienated spouse or the circumstances under which he acted were such as to
warrant the recognition of a privilege. The privileged actor may be one who has counseled the
spouse in his role of physician, attorney or religious advisor. But even in the absence of such
a professional relationship the defendant may be
privileged as a confidante to reply to an inquiry
or to furnish advice that has been requested by
the alienated spouse. Once the occasion has been
recognized as a privileged one, it will afford pro-

tection to the defendant unless the complaining spouse can persuade the trier that the privilege was abused as indicated above.

§ 4—3 Interference Between Parent and Child

Abduction of Child. The interest of the parent in the physical presence and company of the minor child is afforded protection against one who abducts the child or entices it to leave or remain away from home. Traditionally the parent's right here has been beset by limitations similar to those attendant on the parent's right to recover for a physical injury to the child. Thus the claim is grounded on the right to services, and it can be maintained only by that parent who is entitled to the child's custody. Hence so long as the marriage of the parents remains intact, only the father can recover. Indeed the mother might even become subject to liability to her husband if she should leave home, taking the child with her against his wishes. The male parent's exclusive right to bring the action, however, may be giving ground in face of the increased recognition of equality of rights between the spouses. Even today there need be no actual service rendered, and a "constructive" loss is all that is required.

The abduction may be accomplished by force, in which case the child's own right to bodily freedom may be impaired. But the conduct may not be tortious toward the child, as where the latter is simply enticed or persuaded to leave home or to remain away from home. The child's own consent does not adversely affect the parent's claim. As in the case of husband and wife, the enticement must be knowingly directed against the parent-child relationship, and the defendant must be aware that the parent has not consented or must at least be cognizant of such facts as would charge him with bad faith. As in the case of other appropriational harms to the family, negligence is not enough.

Damages include compensation for the parent's mental distress and anxiety, to which may be added damages for any alienation of affections brought about as a result of the loss of companionship. But in the absence of an enticement or other recognized tort affecting the parent-child relation, alienation of the child's affection for its parent, standing alone, is not actionable.

Seduction of a Daughter. The recognized right of the father to maintain a claim for the seduction of his daughter is similar to the claim for enticement of a minor child from home. The female may be forcibly ravished or her consent may be procured by fraud, in which event she may recover in her own right. But, as with enticement, the consent of the child to intercourse does not deprive the father of his right. Again, the foundation of the claim is the right to the daughter's service which is impaired when presumably the child is made ill or pregnant. Again, as with enticement, the loss of service is almost wholly fictional. The unfortunate seducee may not leave the family roof and she may escape pregnancy. The true basis of the award is the damage to the parent's sense of honor and respect. Moreover, compensation for the disgrace suffered by the entire family may be included. Nevertheless the token showing of lost service that must be made sometimes proves to be awkward and it serves at least to restrict the right of recovery to the parent who has custody of the child. For this reason the courts in a few states have discarded the service basis entirely, and a similar result is frequently achieved by statute. Occasionally the father of an adult child who resides under the parent's roof and renders service in the household has been allowed recovery. Marriage of the child to defendant or consent of the parent to the defilement serves to defeat the action. There is no authority as yet to support a parental cause of action for the seduction of a male child or for enticing a child to engage in homosexual or pornographic behavior.

Enticement of Parent From Minor Child. In most jurisdictions the minor child's interest in the continued presence of its mother or father is not protected against the defendant who entices the parent to leave the home, although a few courts have allowed the action (Ill., Mich., Minn.). The

prevailing arguments against the child's recovery
are the same as those urged where the child seeks
damages for a disabling injury to its parent (§
3–1, supra).   Such reasons appear even more specious here where the parent is enticed away from
home and is thus wholly lost to the child.   Alienation of the parent's affection for the child, without
more, is clearly not actionable.

§ 4—4   Heart-Balm Statutes

Claims for the appropriational harms discussed
above, in so far as they may relate to amatory
behavior or sexual misconduct of the defendant,
have been sharply criticized on several grounds:
(1) that they are frequently illfounded and afford
opportunities for extortion and blackmail;   (2)
that the sensitive spouse or parent will probably
retreat from the prospect of becoming involved in
a sensational court proceeding, and the claimant is
therefore likely to be a hardened individual motivated by greed;   (3) that imposing tort liability
serves little or no preventive function and may
even tend to add to the animosity between the
spouses;   (4) that the modern generation's reaction to marital irregularities is less adverse than in
earlier times, and that a home readily broken by
an outsider's attention to one of the partners is a
home that was probably destined to break up in
any event.

Arguments such as these have induced the legislatures in a number of states to abolish or at least to modify the common law claims for alienation of affections, criminal conversation and for seduction of a daughter. The suit for alienation of affections is made unenforceable in all this group of states (thirteen); although in one (Pennsylvania), the parents of one spouse are still subject to liability for intermeddling with their child's marriage without privilege. The claim for criminal conversation is outlawed in eleven of the thirteen states. Six of the thirteen still permit the claim for the seduction of a minor daughter, although four of these six prohibit the claim where the daughter is an adult. One jurisdiction, Louisiana, has traditionally denied all claims for intrusion into the family. Louisiana even refuses to recognize actions by family members for non-fatal injuries, as discussed in the previous chapter.

Interference by Conduct Independently Tortious. It should be observed that the appropriational harms discussed above (alienation of affections, etc.) have usually involved only inducement or persuasion by the defendant, and hence would not be regarded as tortious apart from the harm to the family. However, an outsider may impair the family relationship through conduct that is independently actionable, such as defamation, fraud or imprisonment. When the conduct is thus tortious the resulting harm may extend so as to include the impairment of some benefit of the family relationship as an item of damage. In such case the claim should not run afoul of Anti Heart-balm legislation. For instance, alienation of marital affection may serve as an element of loss whenever an actionable defamatory statement concernig one spouse is communicated to the other. It is similar with fraud. In one notable instance, Work v. Campbell (Cal.1912) a wife who believed the defendant's defamatory statements concerning her husband became enraged and she so severely upbraided the poor innocent man that he left her, disappeared, and never returned. She was awarded damages against the husband's defamer, based on the deceit practiced by the defendant. Again, intercourse procured by violence (battery) against a non consenting female child that deprives the parent of her services is actionable by the parent as a physical harm independent of any tortious seduction. Liability is also imposed where the child is forcibly kidnapped, or even where the plaintiff himself is tortiously imprisoned and he claims separation from his family as an element of his damage.

§ 4—5   Engagements to Marry and Family Status as Affected by Deceit and Defamation

A person who is engaged, but not married, lacks the status necessary to recover for alienation of

affections or enticement against the defendant outsider who merely persuades the other party to
withdraw from the engagement. R. § 698. If,
however, the defendant goes further and defames
the plaintiff, he lays himself open to a defamation
suit in which loss of the marriage may be the principal item of damage.

It is notable that a misrepresentation can also
have the effect of bringing about a marriage or a
counterfeit marriage. One who is falsely led to
enter into what is believed to be a valid marriage
and later discovers that the partner already has a
spouse living or that the ceremony is otherwise a
sham, is entitled to recover damages based on the
value of the household or other services performed
or for such other pecuniary benefits as were conferred in reliance on the mistaken status. Courts
here have proceeded under various theories, such
as deceit or implied contract. The indignity suffered by the "wife" who engaged in sexual relations with one who she believed was her husband
may be reparable as damages for a battery. R.
§ 555.

Sometimes the misrepresentation is by a third
party defendant and relates to some matter that
was basic to the marriage, such as the health or
the fertility or the virginity of the proposed mate.
R. § 556. It may even consist in a gross misrepresentation concerning his finances. Here recovery has been allowed against the outsider for such

damage as can be established to the trier's satisfaction.   Strictly speaking, these are harms to the
personality of the deceived spouse, who has had an
undesirable family relation thrust upon him.

§ 4—6 Wrongful Interference with Expectancies

The Nature of the Expectancy.   One marked
benefit of belonging to a family is the frequently
justifiable expectation of each member that he may
receive gifts or bequests from relatives.   Once the
expectancy has attained a tangible existence in
the form of a delivered gift, an executed non-revo-
cable contract, or a devise made final by death, it
enjoys unquestioned legal protection as a property
or contract right.   But up until it has become thus
finalized the expectancy must yield in the face of
the superior right of the donor or testator to
change his mind and revoke the bounty or confer
it upon others.   Furthermore, third persons are
free during this time to persuade him to change his
mind, so long as they adopt means that are neither
dishonest, violent nor unlawful.   But even bare
expectancies of family bounty normally ripen into
completed gifts, devises or inheritances if left
alone, and they are entitled to some measure of
protection against nefarious intermeddling by
third persons who exceed the bounds of decent
persuasion and resort to defamation, fraud, surreptitious destruction or alteration of documents,
or who gain their objective through aggressive

[*84*]

behavior. Even in such instances, however, liability is not easy to establish, because the interest in expectancies is precarious and the countervailing interest in preserving a broad freedom of action for the benefactor is compelling. First, it must appear that the frustrated expectancy was something more than a vague hope for a bounty. If a testator had already executed a will favoring the claimant as beneficiary there may be a fairly solid basis for a recovery by such intended legatee against an intermeddler. Under such circumstances the latter, if he is to defeat the plaintiff's interest, would be obliged to take steps to induce an affirmative change of position by the benefactor in order to prevent the expectancy from reaching its normal fruition. On the other hand, the situation is more difficult for the claimant who can only point to the fact that a relative had assured him that he intended to remember him in a future devise or to designate him as beneficiary in a policy of insurance which was yet to be taken out. In such situations the prospect that the proposed initial step will indeed be taken by the benefactor must be imminent at the time the defendant interferes. Second, the trier must be fairly convinced in any case that the intention favoring the claimant would have continued up until the benefactor's death or until such time that he could no longer exercise a free choice. No case has been found in which a tort claim for intermeddling with a will was enforced while the testator was still alive and sane. Similarly, the trier must be persuaded that the change depriving the claimant of the fruits of his expectancy was brought about solely through the defendant's misconduct or overreaching. If it appears likely that the change of mind would have occurred ultimately even if the defendant had not interfered, recovery will be denied. In most instances of recovery the benefactor died or became incompetent very shortly after acceding to the defendant's unlawful persuasion.

Wrongful Inducement. As indicated above, the defendant's behavior inducing the change must be wrongful. It may be obviously tortious, as where he forges or destroys a will or takes the life of an intestate in order to prevent the execution of a will favoring complainant, or resorts to force to prevent a gift or devise. Or it may take the form of deception or psychological coercion. R. § 553. False statements made by him may serve to defame the complainant, or may be misrepresentations of fact affecting the desirability of ignoring the heir or favoring the defendant. Again, a claim for the restoration of diverted benefits may be grounded on the exertion of extreme emotional pressure in the form of coercion or undue influence on the benefactor. This is true even though, strictly speaking, such measures hardly qualify as common law torts. But no action can lie against one who merely persuades the benefactor to change his mind, even though his arguments may be vigorous and persistent. It is generally stated that mere negligence that prevents the realization of an expectancy is not actionable. Occasionally, however, in recent years a few courts have sustained claims against attorneys whose negligent preparation of testaments has caused the loss of a bequest to some intended beneficiary. Lucas v. Hamm (Cal.1961). See generally R. § 774B.

§ 4—7   Interest in Deceased Relatives

Living family members have a very real and profound interest in the custody and disposition of the remains of a deceased relative. Their claim embraces the right to be present during the crucial period immediately following death and to participate in the ritual of the funeral and interment. It continues thereafter in the preservation of the privacy and dignity of the place of burial. These profound and tender interests in departed family members may be invaded by outsiders in a variety of ways. The body may be intentionally mutilated through an unauthorized autopsy, or the place of burial may be desecrated. Again, the harm may be appropriational, as where an undertaker delays or refuses delivery of the body for the funeral or denies some family member access to view the remains. In all such instances awards of damage and injunction are frequent. The courts have encountered much difficulty, however, in devising some acceptable theory for protection. The harm here is clearly to the family relation. But the persistence of the classic notion that all actionable rights adhere in either person or property has proved particularly troublesome in claims relating to dead bodies. In the earliest cases of body snatching or the performance of unauthorized autopsies recovery was possible only through resort to the fiction that there is a "quasi" property right in a dead body which belongs first to the husband or wife and then to the next of kin. Thus there has emerged an ordered preference of property rights to be administered by the court when forced with often bitter warfare between various relatives seeking preferment for burial privileges. The matter of a public right to perform an autopsy is now regulated largely by statute and conformity with the limitations of such measures governs civil liability.

Misconduct by embalmers, transporters, funeral directors and others entrusted with the body or with the conduct of the ceremony is frequently made actionable under a contract theory. In these cases the courts have generally managed to allow recovery for the emotional loss by either ignoring the usual limitations on the range of damages allowable for breach of contract, or by treating the conduct as willful and wanton or as outrageous and hence actionable in tort under doctrines of emotional distress.

Following the more recent tendency, recovery has been allowed for mere negligence, often even in the absence of any service or custodial contract respecting the body. The variety of situations in which relief has been afforded include delays in telegrams affecting funeral arrangements or transmitting funds to enable some close relative to attend the service; negligence in extricating a body from a wreck; shock resulting from a collision involving a hearse in traffic; loss of ashes; unauthorized disposition of a fetus; improper embalming or preparation; or confusing bodies in custody or shipment *et cetera*. However, the continued insistence that there be a quasi property right has tended to limit recovery to the spouse or next of kin entitled to the disposition of the body, or, where there is a contract, to the contracting party.

The right to recover for the desecration of a monument is vested in him who erected it, but after the death of the erector the right appears to be in the next of kin of the deceased. An action for disturbing the burial place is vested in the surviving family members, even though they may have no proprietary claim to the land where the body was interred, and suits have been sustained even against the title holders of burial lots where they act maliciously or without due notice to the surviving family members. It is difficult to define the temporal duration of the right to proceed for the desecration of a grave. Certainly the right continues so long as the place of interment is recognized as a burial ground. The remoteness of the relationship and the fact that the deceased ancestor was not personally known to the plaintiff will be considered in determining the amount of damage, but does not automatically terminate the right. Acts of desecration of burial places for which damages or injunctive relief have been allowed include the removal of subsurface support, agricultural cultivation of a burial ground, or drilling for minerals, building on the spot, or even the interment of an unwanted person in a family burial plot.

§ 4—8   Parent's Interest in the Delivery of Child

The interest of family members in being present together during the solemn occasion of the funeral rites for a deceased relative has an interesting parallel in the situation where the husband insists on being in close attendance on his wife on the occasion of the delivery of their child. Novel techniques for childbirth include the LaMaze procedure which contemplates the presence of the father in the delivery room at the critical time of the delivery. Since this is frequently prohibited under hospital regulations, even though the physician is willing, there may arise a serious legal dispute. On the few occasions on which injunctive relief has been sought against a reluctant hospital recovery has been denied. The husband's relational interest in being present with his wife at the moment of birth (sometimes erroneously referred to as a "right of privacy") has been regarded as subordinate to the interest of management in an unimpaired right to control the hospital's operations and processes.

§ 4—9   The Interest in Attaining or Avoiding Parenthood

The Attainment of Parenthood. The interest of husband and wife in becoming parents enjoys rather full protection against physical harms to the person. The spouse who sustains an injury that deprives *him* of his procreative power or denies *her* the capacity to conceive and bear a normal healthy child is entitled to recover for such losses as elements of damage in a suit for negligence. Furthermore, if either spouse is injured, the other spouse has an independent right to recover for his or her own individual loss of a prospect of parenthood as an element of consortium (§ 3–1, supra).

The Supreme Court has recently held that a wife's right to an abortion within a trimester of conception [Roe v. Wade (U.S.1972)] prevails over the interest of the non-consenting husband in becoming a parent. Planned Parenthood of Central Missouri v. Danforth (U.S.1976).

The Avoidance of Parenthood. Parenthood is not always to be regarded as a blessed state. Particularly is this true where there has been no marriage. The female's right to an abortion was noted above. Furthermore, the non-consenting unmarried woman who seeks to recover for ravishment will be entitled to damages that will include the pain and expense of childbirth and the cost and embarrassment of raising an illegitimate child. The unmarried mother who has consented to intercourse will encounter more difficulty. It has been frequently observed that a woman cannot recover for her own seduction so long as she was not induced to believe that the seducer was her husband. But even this disability has been removed in a number of states. Again, she may be entitled to damages when she can show that she surrendered her virtue relying on a promise to marry. We have already seen, however (§ 4–4), that the suit for breach of promise has been outlawed by statute in a number of jurisdictions.

The interest of married persons in avoiding parenthood has received considerable attention in recent years through the recognition of a cause of action for negligence of a physician that resulted in an unsuccessful sterilization of either parent, or for the failure of contraceptive drugs or devices or for the furnishing of unsound medical advice that encouraged the conception of an unwanted child.

Courts are far from unanimous in their reactions to such negligence suits, and the decisions favoring or rejecting the claims are about equal. Apparently some courts are not ready to lend encouragement to an effort to frustrate the time-honored family function of bearing and raising children. It is argued that even though contraceptive practices are no longer criminally prohibited it does not follow that an opportunity to resort to them is entitled to affirmative protection in a damage suit. On the other hand, the social policy underlying family delimitation is gaining favor in the public eye. The economic burden of the large family in urban society, the unhappiness and frustration that are frequent wherever a large family group must subsist together in close quarters—all these afford strong arguments favoring a recognition of the claim. In those jurisdictions where the suit is recognized, the courts are still not in accord on the matter of damages. In some jurisdictions, for instance, only the expenses of pregnancy and delivery are compensable. Other courts would allow full play for the jury's discretion, including damages for the wife's pain and suffering in childbirth, the cost of supporting the unwanted child, and the husband's loss of the wife's services during and following her confinement. It has been observed by some courts and writers that the benefits that accrue from having a normal child should be considered as mitigating factors in determining the amount of damage. This may suggest that parents are to be viewed as enjoying a "blessed event" despite their strenuous protests to the contrary in the courtroom.

Up to the present the courts have not recognized a claim on behalf of a brother or sister who would be obliged to share in the economic hardship brought on by reason of the arrival of the unwanted new sibling. The obstacles to a recovery here are serious. We have previously observed in other settings that a child has no right of recovery against an outsider who abducts a parent or otherwise wrongfully deprives a child of parental care and attention (§ 4–3, supra.)

There is a related question concerning a possible damage claim on behalf of the unwanted child itself. We have already observed that the raper or seducer who forces an unwelcome illegitimate child upon the mother must usually answer in damages for the harm she sustained. Should the wrongdoer be required also to repair the harm suffered by the child who is brought into the world as an illegitimate and is thus denied a respected family status and all rights of inheritance? The child's claim has been denied in the few cases in which courts have been obliged to face the problem. One obstacle facing an allowance of recovery relates to causation: following the "but for" test we must inquire as to what would have been the situation if the defendant had abstained from wrongdoing? The inescapable answer here is that without the defendant's misconduct the infant would have remained unborn. This poses a difficult dilemma as to what should be done about the wrong that serves solely to bring a life into being? It should be noted that the same problem for the child can arise in the setting where the parents are married, but, as suggested above, they have sought unsuccessfully to avoid childbirth. True, the child here is not stigmatized, but nevertheless is denied a normal welcome into the family through the defendant's fault. We may conjecture that the child's chance of recovery may be enhanced if the defendant's negligence had caused it to enter the world as a deformed or otherwise physically handicapped person. Recently a New York trial court overruled a motion to dismiss a petition brought on behalf of a child born with polycystic kidneys due to the negligence of defendant physician in advising parents to conceive and bear a child. This was affirmed by the Appellate Division. Park v. Chessin (S.Ct.N.Y.1977).

A husband may be subjected to unwanted parenthood by reason of his wife's submission to artificial insemination without his consent. His right, if any, against the participating physician presents a difficult problem. What familiar theories are available here? There is no seduction or abduction of the wife, nor have her affections been

alienated. Her consent precludes any successful
claim for loss of services through physical harm.
If the insemination process can be regarded as
equivalent in law to intercourse between the wife
and the physician there remains the prospect of
a suit for criminal conversation. Occasionally
courts have granted the husband a divorce against
the wife by treating her submission to insemination as adultery. Again, there might be suggested an analogy here to the claim against the
physician who negligently sterilizes the mother
with the result that the father is burdened with
parenthood. This analogy is weakened by the
fact that the claim for unsuccessful sterilization
does not present a conflict between the individual
interest of the husband as opposed to that of his
wife.

Finally, is it arguable in view of the right
of the wife to submit to an abortion despite her
husband's protest, thus depriving him of parenthood, that she enjoys a similar right in the disposition of her body to force an unwanted parenthood upon him?

PART III

THE SOCIAL RELATIONSHIP

CHAPTER 5

PHYSICAL AND APPROPRIATIONAL HARMS

§ 5—1 Physical Harms

Although the need to acquire and maintain contact with other human beings is basic in our lives, our interest in social relations is but sparingly recognized at law, and such notice as it does receive is usually at a tangent only. Damages for false imprisonment, for instance, may extend to include recompense for the social isolation suffered by the victim. It should be noted, however, that his loss in this respect is only a parasite that depends upon his claim against physical restraint. It follows that although the imprisoned plaintiff himself can recover for being denied the enjoyment of the company of friends, those same friends, who may value his companionship just as high as he values theirs and who sustain a corresponding social loss, have no legal basis for complaint when he is taken from them. It is interesting at this point to recall by way of contrast that if the same falsely imprisoned victim has a *wife,* she—as contrasted with his friends—will be entitled to damages when her husband is abducted (see § 4-2), indicating that the family interest here enjoys a measure of protection that is denied the social relationship.

§ 5—2   Appropriational Harms—Exclusion from Group Membership

In only two areas of controversy does the social relationship emerge as a direct object of legal attention. Of these two, the most prominent by far is the proceeding for defamation, which will be considered in detail later. The remaining area, to which we should turn briefly at this point, is represented by a class of controversies, usually under equity jurisdiction, in which the plaintiff seeks to forestall his exclusion from membership in some non-profit organization, or he attempts to establish an advantaged standing for himself in such an organization. The usual harmful conduct which he charges against officers or other members is the exertion of effort to induce the group to take some sort of action unfavorable to the plaintiff's standing or prospects. In these controversies over membership it is to be noted that the interest in the social relation is seldom presented as an unalloyed human need for the comfort of friendship. Nearly always it is infused with strong overtones of property or religion, or it is entangled with the activities of commerce, politics, labor, or the like. This involvement with more corporeal interests is of some assistance in achieving recognition for the social relation. It helps to commend the latter to a court of chancery, which traditionally has tended to restrict its jurisdiction to matters of property only.

At stake in the membership controversies is the claim of the individual to participate in the group's activities and to share in its prestige. The merits of this claim must be placed in opposition to the claim of an autonomous organization that it be allowed to manage its own affairs as it sees fit. This interest of the defendant in being left alone rests on principles basic to a democratic society, including prominently the right to freedom of assembly. Courts are reminded that any organized grouping of persons, however trivial its purposes, is nevertheless a minuscule unit of government and hence it is entitled to political respect. The reluctance of courts to interfere with the conduct of organized groups is heightened by their appreciation of the markedly diverse and often esoteric character of private group activities and by their awareness of the specialized knowledge and the expertise often required in dealing with the peculiar internal problems of nonprofit institutions, which frequently serve important purposes in society. As Professor Chaffee observed, "the injury to the member may be outweighed by the enormous amount of time and effort required for the decision of the case." To these considerations militating against court interference it should be added that the objectives of some private organizations are tinctured with religion, and groups of this kind enjoy a constitutional sanction of freedom of worship. The group decision to exclude a church member because of his refusal to conform with accepted church doctrine is not a matter in which a court should readily intervene.

Against these and other considerations that would dissuade court interference there is to be opposed the seriousness of the consequences that an expulsion would visit on the plaintiff under the circumstances. The excluded member may be exposed only to some minor inconvenience or sustain an injury to his pride or a loss of pleasant companionship that could be substantially replaced by another group or in a new setting. On the other hand, the continuance of his membership in the defendant organization may be vital to his livelihood or welfare, as in case of expulsion from a powerful professional or labor organization or the denial of an opportunity to attend school. Both the variety and the extent of the harm that can be suffered are almost unlimited.

The many delicate considerations that must be balanced by a court in its effort to resolve membership controversies are beyond any treatment possible here. One dispute recently up for resolution before the Supreme Court of Pennsylvania, Bear v. Mennonite Church (Pa.1975), will serve to illustrate the complexity of the problem. Plaintiff was a member of the Mennonite Church, a very strict and tightly controlled religious group. His criticism of the teaching of the Church and its bishops led to his excommunication and subjected him to an order whereby all church members, including his wife and children, were commanded to "shun" him—a practice that includes a sweeping boycott and obliges all church members to abstain from any contact whatsoever with the unhappy renegade. A demurrer to the plaintiff's petition for an injunction and reinstatement to membership was sustained by the trial court. But this was reversed on appeal, and the case was ordered for hearing on the merits. Observed the opinion, "Even action in accord with one's religious convictions is subject to governmental regulation when it poses some substantial threat to public safety, peace or order." It is noteworthy that the excluded plaintiff was in position to press the seriousness of an injury both to his family and his business relations. The sheer social aspect of the ostracism (which was almost total) was not stressed in support of the conclusion—indeed it was hardly mentioned. Cf. § 7–11, infra.

Apart from the cases involving exclusion from organizations there are but few decisions indicating that protection may be afforded the social relationship against physical or appropriational harms. If physical pressure or economic coercion were exerted by a defendant against one's friends or neighbors, and such exertion were clearly motivated by a desire to injure the plaintiff's social relationship, we can surmise that the court would probably undertake to afford relief. Often cited in this connection is a decision of the Louisiana Supreme Court, Deon v. Kirby Lumber Co. (La. 1927), enjoining a saw mill employer in an isolated area from threats to dismiss all of his workers who visited the plaintiff's store.

CHAPTER 6

DEFAMATION

§ 6—1 The Anomalous Character of Defamation

Defamation is clearly a cause of action dedicated exclusively to the protection of relational interests. The familiar three-party structure of all relational harms, previously discussed, is a prominent characteristic of this tort. That is to say, the plaintiff enjoys a relationship with an indeterminate number of other persons variously described as friends, acquaintances, business associates, customers and the like. The beneficial aspects of this association enjoyed by him are commonly referred to as his "reputation" or "standing" when the relationship is social or professional, while the term "good will" or "patronage" is generally used whenever standing in the trade community is at stake. At any rate, the plaintiff, on the one hand, and the remaining members of the group in question, on the other, constitute the terminals of the relation, and this relationship is susceptible of being impaired by reason of the defendant's calumny. Hence, there can be no defamation apart from an injury to a relationship. Law may afford some redress for the sheer insult and mental upset occasioned by outrageous language charged against a person in private, but unless there is discoverable an injury to a relationship through publication, the remedy for sheer emotional distress must be found outside the law of defamation.

Perhaps the tort of defamation could be treated satisfactorily as merely another division of the broad classification of Appropriational Harms. Like other appropriations, defamatory conduct is directed toward the relationship itself, and it is behavior calculated to impair the victim's standing in the community. It's essential character as a falsehood which seduces others away from the plaintiff is remindful of many of the appropriational torts affecting the family, already observed. Nevertheless, for reasons to be seen hereafter, defamation can more appropriately be treated as a distinct harm.

Defamation is distinguished from other injurious falsehoods in that the harmful language must relate to the plaintiff himself. It must be *about* him, and characterize him in such way that others, upon hearing the remarks, will hold him in lower esteem and perhaps avoid him altogether. It is interesting to note that the person to whom the defamation is addressed and who is induced thereby to shun the plaintiff may, upon discovering the truth, learn to his dismay that the defendant's lie has served to deny him a valued social contact with the plaintiff. However, he and other persons to whom the lie was addressed and who accepted it at its face value have no recognized action for deprivation of the plaintiff's company, although the latter, being the "victim" of the calumny, may recover for the loss of *their* society. At this point a comparison with the family relation is interesting: An intermeddler who falsely informs a wife of her husband's infidelity, thus prompting her to leave him, may be obliged, when the truth is out, to answer in damages to the now sadder-but-wiser wife who misrelied on the statement as well as to the defamed husband himself. Work v. Campbell (Cal.1912).

Similarly, a merchant's interference with the more materialistic trade relationship through resort to some lying practice such as disparagement of a competitor's goods may serve to confer a cause of action upon the competitor and also at the same time it may give rise to a suit for fraud on behalf of the deceived customer who relied on the falsehood to his detriment. But a cause of action rooted in misreliance on another's falsity, which may protect other relations, does not reach to cover any resulting harm to the social relationship standing alone.

§ 6—2 Defamation Before and After Reform

The Traditional Law of Defamation—an Inept Tort. To work one's way through the quagmire of Traditional defamation doctrine is an arduous undertaking. It is a body of law beset by sophistry and fiction which can be appreciated only after one has gained some understanding of its anomalous history. There are, in fact, two torts of defamation—libel and slander—each with its own historical origin. The factual distinction between the two depends solely on whether the objectionable language was delivered orally or in writing. Largely through historical accident many words that are legally innocuous when spoken become actionable as libels when they are written. Similarly, the damages recoverable for a written libel may differ substantially from those that can be awarded for oral slander. But, as we shall see, in many other respects both libel and slander are governed by the same rules, and the distinction between them serves no useful purpose and appears unnecessary and confusing.

It should also be noted that the Traditional law of defamation became stagnant at a comparatively early period. It persisted as a tort of strict liability after other wrongs had shown themselves more resilient to the needs of changing times. Despite sporadic efforts by legislatures to soften its archaic rigors, defamation failed to prove responsive to the growing need for freedom of a modern press. Moreover, many of the strict features of Traditional defamation are hidden behind a deceptive veil of fiction which is confusing to the uninitiated. It is defined as a tort of "malice," yet a defendant who is concededly blameless may never-

theless be held fully liable. Defamation is commonly referred to as a false disparagement, yet
falsity is presumed until the defendant affirmatively establishes truth as a defense. The damages recoverable for a Traditional defamation are
described as payment for an injury to the reputation, yet in most proceedings under the Traditional law of libel the plaintiff need show only that
the words were susceptible of injuring the reputation—not that they actually did so.

**Constitutional Reform of Defamation—a Free
Press.** The Traditional law of defamation with
its shortcomings and artificialities thus became
seriously out of joint with the times. Efforts to
update it had been long anticipated when, in 1964,
the Supreme Court took the matter in hand and
moved into action with the widely discussed decision in New York Times v. Sullivan. In an unprecedented step the Supreme Court insisted on
encompassing the law of defamation within the
confines of the First Amendment. Following this
momentous opinion there emerged a line of decisions—still in course of development—which impose substantial limitations on the right to recover
for defamation—limitations which were dictated
by the apparent need for more freedom of speech
and press. Whether a beneficial loosening of the
fetters on writers and publishers has indeed really
been achieved and, if so, whether the gain has
been at too great a cost to the interest in reputa-

tion are matters on which opinions have differed. Also not beyond dispute is the question as to whether the law of defamation has indeed been reduced to simpler proportions as a result of the new line of attack, or, on the other hand has been subjected to novel expedients which, presently at least, appear difficult both to understand and to administer.

Whatever the answer to these questions, it is clear that the present reformed state of the law of defamation can not be appreciated until after we have gained some understanding of the fundamentals of the law of defamation as that law existed *prior* to the *New York* Times decision of 1964. This earlier body of law, which, it must be noted no longer affords a dependable chart of the present state of affairs, has been and hereafter will be referred to in these pages as the Traditional law of defamation. No special veneration is intended by this adjective, but we are obliged at least to understand first what it is that has become the object of reform before we can deal effectively with the meaning of the reforms themselves.

§ 6—3   Slander (Oral Defamation)

Evolution of Slander. Much of the eccentric character of the tort of slander must be attributed to its historical beginnings. Being an offense whose essential characteristic is falsity, it was regarded at first as a charge against the conscience of the slanderer and for this reason it fell within the exclusive jurisdiction of the church court, which moved into action whenever the words used by the defendant charged an offense cognizable under the canon law. The object was to compel a public confession by the sinner, and the determination of guilt led to penance under pain of excommunication. No damages were awarded in this proceeding. Common law courts avoided any recognition of slander until the middle of the sixteenth century, when, obliged by the pressure of a growing middle class, they began the recognition of a cause of action whenever the words in question charged an offense indictable at common law. The suit was in the form of an action on the case, which meant that damages must be proved. This required showing of a temporal loss is a feature of the action for slander which has continued to characterize it and places it in sharp contrast with the suit for libel, which was of later origin and in which, as we shall see, injury to the plaintiff's reputation is presumed and no proof is necessary. In slander the injury must be pecuniary in character and the victim must be able to point to the specific items of temporal loss on which he relies. R. § 575. Humiliation and loss of general standing in the community is not enough. These elements can be recovered only as parasitic damage once an item of pecuniary loss has been established.

As soon as the doors of the common law were opened to claims for slander, the action became highly popular, and judges began to search for some means whereby the ensuing flood of litigation could be contained. Resort to the doctrine of *mitior sensus* enabled the courts to lay a restraining hand on the number of recoveries for words charging the commission of crime. At one time the alleged charge by the defendant must have been in language that almost literally tracked the technical phrases of an indictment. This has since disappeared and the specific language used by the defendant is no longer decisive. It is now sufficient in most states that the words impute to the plaintiff conduct that constitutes a criminal offense punishable by imprisonment or which is regarded as involving serious moral turpitude at the place where the words were spoken. Indeed, it is no longer necessary even that a specific offense be charged. But nevertheless, the language used by the defendant must be such as to leave the impression that the plaintiff is exposed to a present risk of prosecution. An accusation only of a prior conviction is not enough (R. § 571).

Slander per se. By the seventeenth century a charge of the commission of a crime assumed the character of an exception to the general rule that pecuniary loss must be affirmatively proved in slander. Since such language would place the plaintiff in danger of prosecution, the portent of temporal damage was too obvious to require further proof. The charge of crime came to be known as slanderous *per se*. This change proved to be an enormous advantage for plaintiffs, since the establishment of a specific pecuniary loss is nearly always virtually impossible. There soon came to be recognized two additional classes of words that were similarly treated as slanderous *per se*: (1) words affecting the plaintiff in his business, trade, profession, office or calling, and (2) words imputing a loathsome disease. The recognition of these charges as actionable without proof of specific loss probably arises from the fact that a temporal damage can readily be deduced from the very nature of the words (R. § 570).

Interference With Livelihood. The second class of words referred to above as slanderous *per se*—those that tend to interfere with one's livelihood —have been dealt with cautiously and restrictively by the courts. Since almost any derogatory remarks may have a tendency to impair somewhat one's effectiveness in his trade or calling, it is obvious that the quality disparaged must be one that is peculiarly valuable to the plaintiff's business or profession. Hence a charge of insolvency or of indifference to indebtedness when spoken with reference to a minister or a physician will probably not be treated as slanderous *per se*, while the same charge will be regarded as actionable when applied to a merchant or banker. However, the latter two persons may be referred to as atheists or as heavy drinkers without risk to the speaker, while such charges would give rise to a successful slander suit when applied to the minister. The language used may be very general, such as "shyster", when applied to an attorney, or "quack" when referring to a physician. On the other hand, charge of a single incident of impropriety or incompetence is insufficient to be regarded as slanderous *per se* unless it is of such character or committed under such circumstances as would imply a continuous incompetence or a defect of character. Even words usually thought of as laudatory may become slanderous *per se* when applied to persons in specific callings—as, for example, a reference to a burlesque queen as being *modest* on the stage. The relative importance of any given skill or the absence of any specific training or education when considered with reference to any one of the numerous trades, professions or callings is necessarily a matter on which opinions may differ sharply. We can only observe that in doubtful cases there is still a noticeable tendency on the part of courts to proceed cautiously and to regard the affinity as insufficient to warrant recovery without proof of special damage (R. § 573).

Imputation of Loathsome Disease. The third class of words actionable *per se* are those imput-

[*112*]

ing to the plaintiff a presently existing disease which is loathsome, which is commonly regarded as contagious and is lingering or chronic in character. The most common and almost the only disease falling clearly within the classification is venereal disease of any variety, and quite irrespective of whether it was acquired innocently or through immoral practices. Other diseases whose imputation has been regarded as actionable without proof of special damage are leprosy and the plague. The controlling feature is the public attitude toward the affliction rather than any incurable nature or any actual danger of contamination it may possess. Thus scarlet fever and smallpox, though clearly contagious, are not included; while venereal disease, which generally yields to modern treatment, constitutes the commonest of the per se charges. The few decisions passing upon tuberculosis for present purposes are not harmonious (R. § 572).

Imputation of Unchastity. Originally an oral charge of unchastity of a woman was not actionable *per se* since a shortcoming in sex virtue did not result in pecuniary damage and could not be construed as a charge of serious crime. Hence actual damage, such as loss of a marriage, must be shown. Such was the state of affairs until recently. The charge was made actionable in England through the Slander of Women's Act of 1891, and thereafter most American courts have reached the same result either through a direct holding or through treatment of illicit intercourse as a criminal offense. In a few states the older position has been corrected by statute. There are as yet no decisions supporting the position that either an imputation of unchastity to a male or a charge of homosexuality against either sex is actionable without proof of damage (R. § 574).

Slander Per Quod. If the words used fail to qualify as slanderous *per se*, they may nevertheless serve as the basis for a successful slander claim if the plaintiff can establish pecuniary damage, such as a loss of customers, patients or clients, or a definite decline in business clearly attributable to the defamatory statement. Included also may be the loss of items or opportunities upon which a value can be placed, such as a voyage, or even the respect of persons whose esteem for the victim could be found to be of prospective pecuniary value. In such events the words are commonly referred to as slanderous *per quod* (R. § 575). Cf. § 8–2, infra.

§ 6—4   Libel (Written Defamation)

Evolution of Libel. The separate treatment accorded oral defamation (slander) and written defamation (libel) by the common law must be attributed to historical chance. In administering the early law of slander the common law courts recognized both written and spoken words indis-

[*114*]

criminately. Slander by way of mouth predominated only because of the generally prevailing illiteracy during the middle ages. Nobles and other great men who might be expected to read and write or to have ready access to a scribner tended to avoid the courts and sought their redress for insult at sword's point.

Feuds and disorder among men of influence persisted and was a matter of serious concern to the court, which recognized that here were harbored the germs of insurrection. As early as 1275 the Statute of Edward I *De Scandalum Magnatum* condemned the spreading of "false gossip" concerning the nobility and other persons highly placed in government, and it provided for jail terms. Apparently this measure, administered at first by the common law courts, was seldom used. It was reenacted in 1389 and at that time its enforcement was entrusted to the Council which, in turn, passed the administration to an *ad hoc* committee which ultimately emerged as the Star Chamber. Again, as with slander, redress was not expressly limited to either oral or written calumny. However, since the tribunal's dominant purpose was to maintain internal order it devoted its chief attention to the ever-increasing tide of pamphlets and published poems attacking the government and its principal agents. Fleeting gossip and oral slander was regarded as too trivial and transitory, and it came to be ignored by the Star Chamber.

As time went on, the Star Chamber extended its jurisdiction to non-political private libels, since these, too, proved disruptive of the king's peace. Libel's origin, however, as a criminal bulwark against politically motivated literature has left its imprint in several respects: Since any written criticism of the gracious sovereign or disparagement of his lordly officers must necessarily be looked upon as utterly false, it followed that libelous charges were regarded as actionable by the Star Chamber even in the absence of any proof of falsity—a characteristic which has persisted down through the years.

Similarly, after the action was later expanded to include an award of damages to the defamed victim it was not regarded as necessary to introduce the slightest proof that any loss was in fact sustained. If the language fell appropriately into the libel category, general damage resulting from the utterance was conclusively presumed. How could words be regarded as being sufficiently grave to warrant criminal action by the Star Chamber unless it were assumed at the outset that the person against whom they were directed had been grievously harmed thereby? So ran the argument.

The historical origin of libel as a safeguard against sedition and disruption of the royal government and which was administered by a powerful commission is largely responsible for still another salient characteristic of the tort—the technique for determining when a statement is libelous. This determination was made exclusively by referring to a broad formula which, as will be seen, controls even today. It was asked: do the words tend to expose the plaintiff to *hatred, ridicule* or *contempt*? If so, they are libels. This method of attack through resort to a generality stands in sharp contrast with the approach to slander, in which the words uttered must be such as would cause a provable monetary damage or else they must fall within one of the four exceptions of words actionable *per se.*

The Star Chamber was abolished in 1641, and twenty years thereafter, following the Restoration, the common law courts took over the administration of the Chamber's former functions, including the adjudication of libel. Concern over seditious literature persisted with the Restoration, and this probably impelled the common law judges to ignore any opportunity to merge libel and slander into a single tort. Libel, with the three distinguishing characteristics observed earlier, remained as it was under the Chamber, and in 1670 Chief Baron Hale formally confirmed the separation of written and spoken defamation into the now familiar molds of libel and slander. This bifurcation has persisted and until recently it has prevailed unimpaired in every American jurisdiction except Louisiana. We shall consider later what, if any, effect the new jurisprudence since New York Times v. Sullivan has upon this Traditional law of defamation as it has thus emerged from the chrysalis of history.

§ 6—5   The Libel Formula

Under Traditional libel it is not necessary that a written communication must actually cause harm to another's reputation in order to be actionable. The test is, rather, whether it has a tendency to have such harmful effect. And this, in turn, is ascertained through resort to a broad formula under which libel has been variously defined as a communication that: (1) tends to hold the plaintiff up to hatred, contempt or ridicule, or (2) tends to lower him in the estimation of the community or to deter third persons from associating with him. This second version has been preferred by the Restatement (R. § 559).

The Makeup of the Community. The hatred or contempt need not be universal. The words do not fall short of being libelous merely because there are some persons in the community who would not be induced thereby to hold the plaintiff in lower esteem. Nor is it even necessary that he be so regarded by a clear majority. On the other hand, the fact that some single individual or mere handful of persons may be led to hold the plaintiff in low esteem does not serve to qualify the words as libelous. Perhaps "substantial minority" is about as accurate a designation of the required number of persons as is possible. Furthermore, if the words would injure the plaintiff in the eyes of only a comparatively small group within the community, it must be shown that they were heard by some member of this group.

When used in a definition of libel, such terms as "adverse community reaction" are unavoidably vague and even misleading. Seldom is there to be found a single community sentiment that prevails with respect to any particular person, incident or condition. Instead, in the same community there are radicals and there are reactionaries; there are prudes and there are the morally insensitive. Doubtless, some must be regarded as renegades from society. Each person has his own set of opinions and reactions. In a democratic society courts could ill afford to confine defamatory charges to those matters which would arouse the contempt only of strict conformists or "rightminded" persons. On the other hand some groups may be so clearly outcast from society that their reactions should be ignored by courts in determining what is libelous. Certainly it would not be actionable to charge that the plaintiff, a burglar, became penitent and "squealed" to the police, although such a charge would hardly enhance his popularity with other members of his calling. But apart from such extreme situations, the courts have tended to suppress their own preferences in morals or taste and to accept the public as it is, in all its variety. Hence it might equally be actionable to charge a normal person with being a homosexual and to charge that a true homosexual is engaged in a blatant crusade against homosexuality. Charges concerning attitudes or beliefs on matters of morality, religion, politics or race, or that falsely impute membership in a church, party or racial group have all been regarded as actionable libels if communicated to those who would view with contempt any person so charged. Words whose only tendency would be to arouse disapproval of some conduct falsely charged against the plaintiff or that prompt persons to disagree with some point of view attributed to him are not sufficient to be regarded as libelous. Neither are revelations of some startling unfortunate fact concerning him, such as that he is dead, that he is in debt, or that he has been excluded from a club, unless these would injure him in his trade or calling. In order to be libelous the words must excite a markedly unpleasant reaction with respect to the person. Most commonly such a feeling is derogatory or adverse—often reaching the level of hatred or contempt. But again, the words may be actionable although they do no more than substantially lessen the esteem the victim formerly enjoyed.   Statements that arouse only pity may nevertheless be actionable if, but only if, they also suggest a debasement of some kind, such as an imputation of insanity or a charge that a woman has been sexually abused or that she has been abandoned by her husband.

It may be noted that all the above instances of libel share a common characteristic.   All are falsehoods that have in some way misled the reader or viewer so as to prompt him to alter his feelings toward the victim in an unfavorable way.   When this essential injury to the relationship is lacking it is difficult to conclude that the plaintiff has been libeled, even though he was humiliated or embarrassed.   Merely to induce one person to laugh at another's expense is hardly actionable.   But if the jest reaches the point of being heartless or cruel, as where it creates even a fleeting appearance of hideous deformity or ludicrous behavior, it may reach the level of libel. This may be true of photographic distortions or typographic blunders, even though the misimpression is only momentary.   Nearly always, however in such cases there has been wide publicity, and the conduct could be regarded more properly as an actionable violation of privacy.

Statements of Opinion.   A libelous statement may be couched in the form of an opinion so long as the opinion is reasonably understood as one based upon some derogatory fact or facts that are known to the speaker. A charge, for example, that a person is a "crook" carries the implication that he has engaged in fraudulent or furtive acts. The Traditional common law attitude toward expressions of sheer opinion, when divorced from all implication of fact is not clear. This will be discussed hereafter in connection with a privilege known as Fair Comment. As we shall presently see, all dispute on this matter has now been laid at rest by the Supreme Court as a result of the recent constitutional reform movement. There can be no doubt today that sheer opinion is *not* defamatory.

Non Defamatory Falsehoods. Finally, any words which, if spoken, would be regarded as slanderous per se, will be actionable libels if written. Again, with libel as with slander, false words which cause a monetary loss to the person concerning whom they were uttered will give rise to a cause of action for the specific damage sustained, even though they fail to qualify as libels under the formula. The resulting tort under these circumstances might be designated more appropriately by another name, such as injurious falsehood. Especially prominent here are false statements impugning the title to land or disparaging the quality of goods being offered for sale. These falsehoods are commonly referred to as *slander* of title or trade *libel*, although the means through which the lies are disseminated, whether orally or in writing, is quite immaterial to the cause of action. The matter is treated hereafter (§ 8–2).

§ 6—6   Libel and Slander Distinguished by the Mechanical Means of Communication

As we have seen above, it is obviously to the advantage of a plaintiff whenever he can show that the defamatory matter is to be regarded as libel rather than slander. As the distinction between the two torts took shape it was between those words that were spoken and those that were written. Later, however, libel came to embrace any defamatory communication conveyed through sight, including pictures and cartoons, statuary, and even symbolic pantomine, such as burning the plaintiff in effigy or erecting a fiery cross at his door. For some reason, however, communications through the sign language of the deaf-mute or the use of deprecatory gestures are treated as slander only. Oral statements dictated to a secretary or communicated to a reporter who later writes down the matter as contemplated by the speaker are regarded as libels, and presumably the same would be true with the use of sound tape or a phonograph record even though the communication will ultimately be understood through the sense of hearing only (R. § 568).

Radio and Television Broadcasting. The lack of any rational policy in support of the distinction between libel and slander is reflected in the contradictory treatment accorded defamation by radio and television in both the decisions and the statutes. Words communicated through these media have been regarded indiscriminately as libel or as slander, depending on the chance of jurisdiction. To further complicate the matter, statements read over radio from a prepared script have sometimes been treated as libel, while extemporaneous words have been regarded as slander. If a majority position on any of this is discoverable from an examination of the statutes it would support the treatment of both radio and television as slander only. Group pressure on the legislatures from the broadcast media is evident here. If it is desirable to protect commercial users of the airways from excess liability for defamation, the same result might be better achieved directly rather than by compounding the already confused distinction between libel and slander. The Restatement has adopted the position that in the absence of statute all broadcast material is treated as libel (R. § 568A).

§ 6—7 Publication

In view of the fact that the function of defamation is to protect one's reputation in the social, professional or trade community, it follows that the plaintiff's standing must have sustained a depreciation. This, in turn, contemplates that at least one member of the community, other than the plaintiff himself, has received an adverse impression of him as the result of a publication of some kind initiated by the defendant. The form of the communication—whether through printed or spoken word, through gesture or pantomine—is immaterial in so far as the existence of a publication is concerned (although the means adopted may be of vital importance in determining whether the defamation amounts to libel or slander). Moreover, the number of persons who receive and are affected by the communication is unimportant in determining whether a publication has taken place, although the number of recipients may substantially affect the amount to be recovered. It is enough that there was one recipient, and this is true even though that one person was made aware of the defamatory information sheerly in his capacity as a secretary, a postman, or a telephone or telegraph operator and was wholly indifferent to what he learned. Neither is the result affected by the fact that the recipient was not even acquainted with the defamed person, nor that he disbelieved the statement. All such matters have a bearing only upon the amount of the recovery. For purposes of publication the individual employees of a single corporation are not submerged into the corporate personality. Hence a communication by a clerk to a secretary within the common employment constitutes a publication by both the clerk and by the corporate employer.

However, a publication does not take place unless some third person understands the communication. It is not enough that he hears the sound or witnesses the sight without knowing what it means, as where the speaking or writing is in an unfamiliar tongue. Even if the recipient understands the words but he is totally unaware of some extraneous fact necessary to make the apparently harmless statement defamatory, there is still no published defamation as to such recipient.

Intentional or Negligent Publication. The making of the publication is the one element of Traditional defamation in which some showing of fault on the part of the defendant is necessary. He must be blameworthy at least in letting loose a communication which is ultimately found to be defamatory. The most commonly discovered fault in publishing is that of intention. But even where this is lacking, it may appear that the defendant was negligent, as in allowing a privately written piece to lie on his desk at a place where there was an unreasonable risk that it would be seen by others. Or perhaps he chose to insult the plaintiff at a time when he believed the two were alone, but he neglected to ascertain whether some other persons might be within earshot.

In order to find a publication it is necessary only that the actor's conduct play some appreciable part in bringing the defamatory information to a new recipient. How he did it is not important. If he delivers a newspaper, releases a book from a library, operates a telegraph machine, or a motion picture projector or participates in the mere mechanics of broadcasting at a time when he is aware that intelligence is being communicated, his role as a publisher is complete. The fact that he is carrying out his routine duty as an employee is immaterial. The question as to whether or not his participation in some such routine capacity as above (while he is innocent of wrongdoing) will serve ultimately to render him liable for defamation is another matter (§ 6–10, infra). But if he is to be excused, it is not because his conduct failed to qualify as a publication [R. § 577 (1)].

It may be asked whether in addition to the duty to refrain from any positive act of publication there is an affirmative duty to remove or destroy defamatory material discovered by the possessor on premises under his control once he realizes that failure to do so will attract the material to the attention of others? In the few cases decided up to date the answer has been "yes", provided that he has actual knowledge and that the removal would not be unduly burdensome [R. § 577(2)].

Repetition as Publication. Where there are successive repetitions, each repeater, as well as the originator, is a publisher. Nor does it matter that the person repeating reveals the source of the statement and even disclaims any belief in it.

Again, the repetition does not fall short of a publication because the recipient may already have heard or seen the defamatory material elsewhere or because he doubts its truth, although such matters may serve to reduce damages (R. § 578).

As indicated, the originator himself remains liable for any repetition of the defamatory matter for the purpose of establishing the area within which the defamation took place and thus determining the extent of the general damage suffered. This is true even though the repeater assured the originator that he would keep the matter secret. If, however, recovery is sought for some specific harm occasioned by the repetition, it must be shown that the person repeating was privileged to do so, or that the originator authorized the repetition or at least that he reasonably expected it (R. § 576).

Multiple Publications. It appears to follow from the above observations that each new communication to a different person amounts to a fresh publication, affording a basis for a new and separate cause of action. The implications of this are staggering when it is considered that there may be millions of readers of the same issue of a leading magazine and that tens of millions of persons may witness a single television performance. Let it then be added that a popular motion picture may enjoy a run of several successive years and may ultimately pass into the realm of

[*128*]

television replays and it is obvious that the number of possible defamation suits becomes so incalculable that no private fortune could pay the litigation costs alone.

Modification of the separate publications rule obviously became essential. The problem was particularly acute with venue when it appeared that the plaintiff might move from county to county with successive suits, and also with the statute of limitations where a long delayed distribution of an ancient publication could extend liability almost to infinity. To meet this, many courts devised what has come to be known as the "single publication rule" under which a single communication heard or witnessed at the same time by two or more third persons is to be regarded as a single publication for which only one action for damages may be maintained, and in such suit *all* damages suffered (at least within the same jurisdiction) can be recovered. Similarly, all issues of a single edition of a book or newspaper or all exhibitions flowing from a single broadcasting event by radio or television are embraced within the single publication rule (R. § 577A).

Several features of the single publication rule must be noted. First, it relates only to multiple publications by the same publisher. Thus a delayed sale by a retailer of a defamatory book which has rested on his shelf for several years can give rise to a defamation suit against such retailer, even though an attempted claim against the publisher of the same book would be barred by the statute of limitations if the prescribed period had elapsed since the publisher first released either the specific copy in question or even any copy from the same edition. For the same reasons a recovery against a national broadcasting system does not preclude a separate suit against any participating radio or television station. Similarly, even though a recovery has been allowed against the manufacturer of a defamatory phonograph record, a claim can still be maintained against the performer and even against the operator of the juke box through which the material is heard. Presumably, the usual rules affecting joint tort feasors and principles of indemnity within a particular jurisdiction are controlling in all such cases. Indemnity agreements are frequent among mass media participants.

Second, new releases of defamatory material on successive occasions do not fall within the single publication rule. There arises, then, the question as to what is a "new" publication for this purpose? All copies of a single edition of a newspaper, although distributed at different times and by different agencies, are regarded as a single publication. Probably the same would be true of a single broadcast news program even though it may be repeated at successive hours throughout the country in order to accommodate differences

[*130*]

in time zones. But a defamatory article appearing in the morning edition of a newspaper could not be republished in the evening edition without a separate publication having occurred. The same would be true of a repetition in the evening of material from an earlier morning broadcast over radio or television. Perhaps the closest estimate of the proper distinction between the successive and the single publication is suggested by inquiring whether the two publications were so scheduled as to indicate that the purpose was to reach about the same general group of recipients with each publication. The single publication rule is an obvious artificiality which serves only as a rough compromise between the need to avoid ruinous litigation, on the one hand, and the need to afford the victim of defamation a fair opportunity to have an adequate recovery, on the other.

Multiple Jurisdictions. The imponderables of multiple publication increase manyfold whenever it appears that some or all of the separate publications took place in different states. The resulting conflicts of law problems are too complex to admit of treatment here. Both the Restatement (R. § 577A) and the Uniform Single Publication Act (NCCSL1953) provide in substance that a recovery in one jurisdiction includes all damages sustained in all jurisdictions, and that such a judgment bars all actions in all states founded on the same publication.

§ 6—8   Reference to the Plaintiff

No person can succeed in establishing an actionable defamation unless the words are reasonably understood by a recipient as referring to the claimant. There is no need that the latter's name be used or even that he be accurately described. Nor is it necessary that all recipients, or even a substantial number of them, conclude that the plaintiff was the person referred to. It is sufficient that *some* recipient did so understand and that his understanding was reasonable in the light of facts known to him. Such extraneous facts, when necessary to complete the identity, must be established by the plaintiff, and such evidence is known as the *colloqium.* Resort to a fictitious name does not arbitrarily serve to prevent the recipient from reasonably identifying the plaintiff as the one who was actually intended. The same may be true of a disclaimer in a book or performance. Indeed a person may be defamed without any direct reference to him whatever, as where the statement is made that *C* is illegitimate, and his parents, *A* and *B*, claim that they were thereby defamed as adulterers. Under the Traditional common law position the only matter of importance was the reasonableness of the recipient's impression that the plaintiff was the person intended. A complete absence of intention or even negligence on the part of the defendant was entirely immaterial under the Traditional view (See § 6–10, infra). This, as we shall see later, has now been repudiated.

Defamation of a Member of a Class. When a defendant refers disparagingly to an entire class of persons it may be difficult or impossible to conclude that he should be reasonably understood as referring to any single member of it. But if the group in question is small and the defendant refers to the entire group without qualification, the plaintiff may succeed in establishing that he was one of those referred to merely by showing that he was known to the recipient of the statement as a member of the group in question. Such statements as "This jury has been bribed" can fairly be interpreted as a charge against any one of the jurors. But as the group becomes larger, this is not possible. The observation, "All lawyers are shysters" is not likely to be actionable on behalf of any one lawyer. An intent to refer to a single individual is even more difficult to discover when the defendant has levelled his charge at only a fraction of the group. Such statements as "a few" of the group, or "some" of them, "many" of them, or even "most" of them will not generally be regarded as a sufficient reference. But the chances of recovery are improved as the group referred to becomes smaller, such as a reference to "one of you three". The same is true as the intended proportion of the group becomes impressive. It has been held, for example, that a statement, *"Most* of the sales staff are fairies" (referring to a staff of twenty-five) referred sufficiently to the plaintiff (R. § 564A).

§ 6—9   Libel Per Quod

As previously indicated (§ 6–4), a statement that is innocent on its face may nevertheless be defamatory when taken in connection with special facts known to the recipient. For example, the apparently innocuous statement that Mr. and Mrs. X announce the birth of a child could serve to hold this couple up to ridicule and contempt in the eyes of a recipient who is aware that they are newlyweds. Similarly (§ 6–7), a derogatory statement which ostensibly refers only to some fictional character and hence would appear not to be defamatory of anyone, may still be reasonably interpreted as a reference to the plaintiff when communicated to a person aware of special facts that would make such an identification plausible in his mind. In such cases of incomplete defamation the plaintiff must set forth the specific facts known to the recipient which would render the statement defamatory (termed *inducement* in the pleadings), or that would establish a reference to the plaintiff (termed *colloquium* in the pleadings). But once this hiatus has been satisfactorily filled there would appear no reason why the case should not proceed just as though the defamatory implication or the reference to the plaintiff appeared clearly on the very face of the defendant's statement.

The position described above is the one originally adopted by the overwhelming majority of the courts both in England and in this country, and damages were allowed without proof of special harm whenever the recipient's reaction to the published matter in question was attuned to the broad libel formula of contempt and ridicule toward the plaintiff. For this purpose it was immaterial whether the defamatory implication was gained through the writing standing alone or whether, on the other hand, it required knowledge of outside facts in order to complete the picture. However, during the latter part of the past century this entire matter became confused. A number of American courts adopted a position that whenever the defamatory character of a statement cannot be determined except through resort to extraneous facts the statement must be regarded as merely libelous *per quod*, with the odd result that only special damages established by the plaintiff could be recovered. Libel *per quod* was set up in contrast with libel *per se*. The latter term was used to indicate works that meet the libel formula without any need for outside explanation. This group of courts adopted the same position of libel *per quod* with respect to the reference to the plaintiff, which, under

their view, must be clear on the face of the libelous matter if general damages are to be allowed.
The suggestion has been made that the so-called
libel *per quod* rule is an awkward adaptation to
libel of the familiar distinction between slander
per se and slander *per quod*. We know, however, that this distinction in slander is one that
depends exclusively upon the subject matter of
the spoken defamation, and that the completeness
or incompleteness of the statement on its face is
a matter of no consequence in defining slander
per se (§ 6–3). Perhaps the much debated *per
quod* rule as related to libel can be better accounted for in another way. It might be regarded as
an effort calculated to soften somewhat the rigor
of the Traditional position—to be considered hereafter—that a publisher is subject to liability for
defamation even though he was entirely unaware
of the fact that he was defaming anyone by
publishing the matter in question. It is obvious
that the libel *per quod* limitation would serve to
relieve such an innocent publisher of liability for
general damages whenever the publication appeared to be harmless. If this is the proper explanation, the *per quod* rule is now devoid of any
basis in policy; for, as we shall see, the no-fault
rule has been entirely obviated by the Supreme
Court under constitutional free-speech decisions
within the last few years. Libel *per quod* is not
recognized under the Restatement (R. § 569, comment *b*).

§ 6—10   Traditional View of Defendant's Intention or Negligence

The Traditional attitude that formerly prevailed toward the mental state of the defendant in defamation is accurately summarized in Lord Mansfield's observation, "Whenever a man publishes, he publishes at his peril."   King v. Woodfall (K.B. 1774).   True, as we have seen, the defendant must be regarded as being to blame in some way in connection with the actual making of the publication.   But apart from this, fault or absence of fault was almost universally disregarded whenever the defendant was the originator of the defamation. The extreme to which this attitude might be carried is well illustrated by the English case, Cassidy v. Daily Mirror, Ltd. (K.B.1929).   A character well known in racing circles was accurately reported by defendant newspaper as saying that he was engaged to marry a certain young lady, whom he introduced to the press.   In fact, however, the speaker was already married to the plaintiff, who successfully maintained that the above published statement was reasonably susceptible of an interpretation that she (although unmentioned in the printed report) had been deceiving her friends and acquaintances by falsely holding herself out as the speaker's wife, or that she was living with him in sin.   Under these facts the publisher was subjected to liability for a statement which he regarded as wholly innocent and which did not carry on its face the slightest reference to the defamed plaintiff. Other instances of liability without fault under the former law included references in books or plays to characters believed to be fictional, or newspaper entries intended to refer to one person, but which were reasonably understood by a few readers as referring to the plaintiff, who may have the same name or initials. In this connection it is noteworthy that the statement in question may have been true or privileged when applied to the person intended by the publisher, but it becomes defamatory when related to the plaintiff. In any event the innocent publisher paid for his mistake according to the Traditional view.

The same indifference in Traditional defamation law toward the blameless quality of the defendant's behavior is apparent in another connection—that of his belief in the truth of his statement. Even though the hapless publisher had made every reasonable effort to assure the truthfulness of his statement before venturing to make it, he was nevertheless subject to liability under the universally accepted older view.

Even prior to the wave of constitutional reform (to which we shall turn presently) there was sharp questioning of the wisdom of an unqualified no-fault attitude toward all defamation. Conceding that mass communication media such as publishers of newspapers, periodicals and giant promoters of motion picture, television and radio

should be regarded as engaged in an ultrahazardous activity and hence held strictly accountable,
yet there is force to the argument that courts
should retreat from any prospect of subjecting the
private writer of a letter or the sender of a tele-
gram to an unqualified liability for mistakes that
were not intended and could not be reasonably
avoided. However this may be, no distinction
was drawn under the Traditional view between
the giant and the pygmy so long as the defendant
was an originator of the defamatory matter
charged against him.

Routine Disseminators. We have seen that each
participating step in the vast process of disseminating information is to be counted as a separate
publication (§ 6–7). Such being the case, must
we now face the prospect that the linotype operator, the radio or television mechanic, the newsdealer or book retailer, the librarian, even the bus
passenger who thoughtlessly leaves his magazine
on a seat when leaving—that all these routine
disseminators would be held responsible in defamation under the Traditional view for a single
item or picture whose libelous purport they neither knew nor could know! At this point the
courts drew in their horns and contented themselves with a more moderate basis of liability for
many of those who merely deliver or transmit material published by some third party. Responsibility attaches to such an agency only when it

knows or has reason to know of the defamatory character of the material in question.

Who is such a favored disseminator within the contemplation of the law? The classification certainly does not embrace all those who could avoid in some way being labeled as originators. The gossip for example, should certainly be held strictly accountable, and the newspaper publisher who prints and markets material prepared and submitted by another should be similarly treated. It may be suggested that the disseminator is appropriately characterized as one who is unable to exercise any control over the content of what passes through his hands. Under this approach the newsdealer, bookstore proprietor and librarian, and the telegraph or teletype service operator clearly qualify for preferred treatment. It may be emphasized that distribution by these agencies adds little or nothing to the authenticity of the material they pass along. From another standpoint it can be added that they are seldom so posited economically as to distribute the damage cost of their mistakes along to the public. Apart from one Florida decision, Layne v. Tribune Co. (Fla. 1933), courts have been unwilling to extend the benefit of the disseminator view to the publisher of a newspaper which innocently prints a defamatory Associated Press dispatch.

If the newsdealer, the librarian and other similar disseminators are to enjoy truly effective protection against inadvertant libel, they must be accorded something more than the prospect that they will not be responsible so long as they succeed in remaining free of negligence. Due care usually includes a duty to make an affirmative inquiry, and this is not feasible in the setting under discussion. The news dealer could not carry on his trade without loss if he were obliged to examine each publication he offers for sale in order to ascertain whether there may be some defamatory item concealed between its covers. It is only after the disseminator becomes aware for some special reason that a particular copy is likely to harbor defamation that he comes under a duty to take the trouble to ascertain the innocence of what he is handling. Thus the continued distribution of a serial publication which is widely reputed to carry scandulous material or the persistent sale of the books of a notorious muckraker can expose the indifferent distributor to liability.

Telegraph Companies. The telegraph company which transmits a message under its public duty as a utility enjoys not only the tolerance extended other disseminators, but in addition it is free to accept material defamatory on its face unless its falsity is evident. It may be added that even matter which is obviously both false and defamatory may be transmitted under a special privilege to be discussed hereafter [R. § 612(2)].

Radio and Television. Considered in the light
of the foregoing, the proper treatment of radio
and television broadcasters poses a difficult problem. At times these agencies are in a peculiarly
helpless situation. Defamation through ad libbing
is difficult to anticipate and control, and the same
is true of broadcasts originating in the streets
or other public places. Although there is room
for difference of opinion as to what treatment
should be accorded these enterprises, their close
analogy to the newspaper and the fact that their
own staff originate much of what they transmit
prompted most courts under the Traditional view
to treat broadcasters as originators subject to the
same strict liability as newspapers [R. § 581(1)].
Even before the advent of the constitutional reforms to be considered later, the broadcaster's
dilemma had been afforded relief in whole or in
part through statutes in several jurisdictions.
These measures varied: A few conferred complete immunity for any statements originated by
persons who were not members of the staff, while
others offered relief for only the non-negligent
broadcaster. Furthermore, we have already considered the palliative effect on mass media of the
Libel per Quod rule in some of the states, and we
know that there is a tendency in a number of jurisdictions to regard defamation by radio as merely slander, rather than as libel, with the result
that proof of damage is required unless the words
are slanderous per se.

Inadvertent Libel and Retraction. A retraction does not serve to exonerate a defendant from liability for defamation, even though he had acted with complete innocence. It may, however, be considered in mitigation of punitive and sometimes actual damages. In a great many states special newspaper retraction statutes have been enacted. Some of these go no further than to affirm the common law position, above. Most, however, require that a plaintiff who seeks general damages against a newspaper defendant must first call the libel to the attention of the publisher within a period specified by the statute and demand a published retraction and apology. If this demand is ignored, or if the retraction is not timely or is not allotted space of at least the same prominence as that of the original libel, the plaintiff is entitled to his full general damages. But if the request is complied with, as above, the plaintiff is limited to such specific pecuniary losses as he can establish. Some, but not all, of these retraction statutes are available only to inadvertent defamers.

§ 6—11   Truth

Defamation is a tort that harms the victim's reputational interest by polluting with falsehood the stock of facts and impressions stored in the minds of others and upon which the victim's standing depends. Hence falsifying is the very

backbone of this tort, and it would seem to follow
that the plaintiff should be obliged to establish
the untruthfulness of the alleged defamatory matter as a part of his *prima facie* case. However,
under the Traditional approach the victim of a
defamatory statement enjoys a presumption that
the utterance is wholly false, and this prevails
until the defendant sets up truth as a defense
and satisfies the trier to that effect. As we have
seen, the reason is partly historical. But, in addition, there is also a strong practical justification
in support of the presumption: Any effort to establish at the outset that a proposition is false is
certain to prove extremely difficult. Especially is
this the case whenever the falsehood is in the
form of a generality, such as "A is dishonest."

The establishment of the truth of a defamatory
statement affords an absolute defense, and it is now
settled that this is the case quite irrespective of
any ill will or malice that may have prompted the
utterance. When the plea of truth is successful no
damages of any kind—nominal or otherwise—can
be recovered. At issue is the accuracy of the specific defamatory statement. Hence, if the defendant charged that the plaintiff had committed
an assault upon a designated victim on a particular
occasion, a mere showing that the plaintiff was
a violent man who had been known to engage in
numerous brawls would not be a satisfactory
showing of truth. However, when the defama-

tory charge is a generality, such as, "A is a violent man," the defense of truth may succeed under a showing that A did in fact commit an assault on a particular occasion. If the defamatory statement is in form the repetition of a report or rumor, proof that there was in fact such a report is not enough to exonerate the defendant so long as the substance of the report remains false. A showing by the defendant that the defamatory statement is true only in part does not enable him to avoid liability, although partial truth may serve to mitigate the damages. It may be noted in this connection that evidence of a plaintiff's bad reputation may have the same mitigating effect.

The recognition of truth as a defense despite the malice that may have prompted its utterance has been attacked as affording a refuge for those who may be tempted to resurrect and publish long-forgotten sins or misfortunes, and in some states statutes require that in order to escape liability a publication of defamation must be shown to have been made with a good motive or for justifiable ends as well as being supported by the true facts. The constitutionality of such measures as these is highly doubtful, as will be seen later.

Still before us for consideration later is the question as to whether truth should now be considered merely as a matter to be raised in defense, or whether, on the other hand, in light of current constitutional reform, the duty to establish the falsity of the defamatory statement must now be regarded as a part of the plaintiff's burden in making out a *prima facie* case (R. § 581A).

§ 6—12   Who May be Defamed

The Defamation of a Third Person.   Any living person may maintain a suit for a defamation that is injurious to his own reputation; but he cannot have a cause of action for the defamation of another person, even though he has sustained serious emotional harm because of the injury to the reputation of such person, who may be a close relative, business associate or friend. The pity that the world may feel for the unfortunate plaintiff who is the spouse or child of a thief or murderer is not regarded at law as equivalent to the contempt or ridicule necessary to a defamation. The same considerations lead to the conclusion that there can be no defamation of the dead, however deep may be the humiliation of the surviving members of the deceased's family (R. § 560).

Distinguishable is the situation in which one person himself is defamed by reason of derogatory statements made concerning another. A charge, for example, that one's ancestor was afflicted with an inheritable insanity may well be regarded as defamatory of his descendants.

Defamation of a Corporation.   Similarly, a corporation (which, for the purpose of defamation, is regarded as a person having a professional or business reputation) can be the victim of an actionable defamation whenever prominent officers or employees are charged with misbehavior or unethical practices which reflect upon the prestige of the corporate employer.   Recovery has been denied, however, in the converse situation where a dominant stockholder of a corporation seeks to recover for injurious defamation of the company.

An eleemosynary institution whose support depends on donations or grants of public funds receives the same treatment as a profit-making corporation.   But in the absence of a prospect of some loss of financial support, non-profit groups, such as those organized for political purposes or for the propagation of some ideal, have had little success in recovering for defamation which tends to lower their functions or objectives in the public eye. Finally, for reasons not readily appreciated, municipal corporations have been denied a right to maintain a suit for defamation in the few decisions that have considered the matter.   The Restatement has cautiously suggested a caveat as to these last observations (R. § 561).

Defamation of a Class.   Unorganized groups of individuals who constitute a "class" because of some common national, racial, or religious characteristic have had no success in maintaining a suit for defamation of the entire group. It is only when some single individual can claim injury to his own reputation by reason of a false aspersion concerning the group of which he is a member, intending thereby to reflect upon him as an individual, that a cause of action for defamation comes into being.

§ 6—13   Privileges to Defame Under the Traditional View

Although no showing of fault or blameworthiness on the part of the defendant has been required under the Traditional approach to defamation, it does not follow that under the old scheme there was no effort to strike an acceptable balance between such competing social values as may be involved in a defamation controversy. Any useful purpose served by the making of the defamatory statement is brought into focus for judicial consideration when the defendant undertakes affirmatively to justify his behavior despite the prima facie showing already made by the plaintiff. The defendant may point to the fact that he belongs to a class of persons whose freedom to speak without restraint is so vital to some operation of government that they enjoy complete immunity from defamation claims while so acting. Apart from and beyond this, the defendant may escape liability by a showing that the harmful statement was made on an occasion recognized

[*148*]

by law as being qualifiedly privileged because of its tendency to assist in the protection of some social need. The two types of privilege differ from each other. In the instance of an absolute privilege, recognition by the court of the defendant's immunity concludes the matter in his favor without further ado. On the other hand, if the defendant succeeds only in establishing that the occasion on which he spoke or wrote was qualifiedly privileged, he is still faced with the prospect that the plaintiff may prevail by showing that the defendant was careless with respect to the truth or falsity of what he said or that his conduct was otherwise extravagant. In such event the defendant will be found to have *abused* the privilege and hence will incur liability.

In seeking to consider what fate may befall these two privileges in the light of recent Constitutional reforms, one can safely predict that the absolute immunity enjoyed by those acting in the furtherance of some governmental activity will persist in full force as at present. But the role (if any) that may be assigned to qualified privileges under the new Constitutional order is a matter of considerable uncertainty. This will be discussed later (§ 6–20).

§ 6—14   Absolute Privilege to Defame in the Performance of a Public Function

Nature and Source of an Absolute Privilege. Courts have long recognized that certain per-

sons acting in roles that directly further some governmental operation should be free to speak or
write without the slightest fear of being called to
account in a defamation proceeding. The privileged person may be an official serving either of
the three branches of government, typically judge,
legislator, governor or mayor. Or he may be a
mere private person who at the time in question
was serving as attorney, litigant, witness, or an
advisory assistant in connection with some public
proceeding. The immunity of these persons to a
defamation claim depends, not upon any reasonable, or even honest, belief by them in the truth
of their statements, but rather on the public need
that such statements be freely made even at the
risk of their proving ultimately to be wholly false,
malicious and injurious. Obviously so free a rein
for villifying can be afforded only when some
matter of vital concern, such as conduct of the
essential processes of government, is at stake.

Participants in the Litigation Process.

The Judge.

Upon the occurrence of litigation, all the participants in the process—the judge, the attorneys,
the witnesses and the jury—enjoy an unqualified
immunity to liability for defamation. As to the
judge, it is important only that he was engaged
in the performance of a judicial function. He
may be a trial judge or an appellate justice, a

commissioner, a referee, a master, or even an executive officer in the conduct of an extradition hearing. It is enough that he was purporting to act in a judicial capacity under some slight color of jurisdiction. The arbiter under a collective bargaining agreement is so protected. The immediate source of the claimed authority is immaterial so long as it is ultimately governmental. Also immaterial is the seriousness or the triviality of the controversy involved. For purposes of conferring immunity the judicial function is not limited to acts that demand an exercise of discretion or that are intended to lead to a final determination. It includes, rather, any operation appropriate to the litigation process in its broadest reaches. The judge's immunity can sometimes be invoked even before the institution of proceedings, provided that they were in prospect at the time. Similarly, it can extend beyond the time when final judgment has been pronounced. But, whenever or wherever uttered, the objectionable remark must bear some reasonable relation to the subject of inquiry. This requirement has been variously stated. Certainly technical relevancy is not necessary; but a statement that is wholly foreign to the matter at hand may lie outside the pale of absolute protection.

Other Participants. For similar reasons jurors, the litigants themselves and their attorneys, as well as witnesses, all have the benefit of an unqualified privilege to defame. Complete freedom of access to the courts appears to require no less than a total immunity for all participants. This protection is not limited to statements made during the conduct of the hearing itself. It extends to preliminary communications on pending litigation between the attorney, litigant and witnesses so long as the matter bears some reasonable relation to the conduct of the proceeding. Libelous matter in the pleadings is protected. Statements by a witness on the stand may be accommodated under this broad approach even though the same remarks might be clearly excluded under the rules of evidence. On the other hand, the fact that a subject under discussion between attorney and client is one that might eventually lead to litigation does not serve to justify an absolute privilege, and the same is true of statements made to the press which refer to some pending litigation. They are not for that reason a part of the litigious process.

The question as to what is a judicial or quasi judicial proceeding so as to warrant an absolute immunity for contestants, witnesses, or those seeking the assistance of a public body or officer is not settled. Included within this marginal group are zoning commissioners, licensing officials and bodies regulating professional activities. Persons who seek the assistance of such commissions, or who are opposing a threat of official action, may enjoy only a qualified privilege of the type to be discussed later.

The Legislative Process. The United States Constitution, Article I § 6 provides " . . . for any speech or debate in either house they (members of the Congress) shall not be questioned in any other place." Similar provisions are found in the constitutions of many of the States. Measures of this kind afford an immunity even when the defamatory matter does not relate to any legitimate object of legislative concern, so long as it is made in the course of performing a "Legislative Act". This term embraces the introduction of material at legislative committee meetings, its unhampered discussion, the voting on reports or on legislation, and anything generally done in a session of the house in relation to the business before it. It does not follow, however, that all the activities carried on by legislators are Legislative Acts within the intendment of the Speech and Debate clause. Acts to influence the Executive Branch of government, for example, are frequent, but they are not embraced by the immunity provision. Whether a gratuitous communication to constituents or to the press informing the public concerning the speaker's legislative activity is itself a Legislative Act is a subject on which pronouncements in the Supreme Court opinions are not harmonious.

Although the terms of the Speech and Debate Provision refer only to "members of the Congress," it has been interpreted to afford protection to a congressional aide so long as his conduct would be a protected Legislative Act if performed by the congressional member himself. On the other hand, public circulation of committee reports by the Superintendent of Documents is not a Legislative Act which serves to confer constitutional immunity (although the reporting of public records may be qualifiedly privileged, as will be seen later.) The witness who participates in the conduct of a legislative proceeding enjoys the same absolute immunity as a witness in a judicial proceeding. Communications relative thereto are included.

The immunity discussed above is available to members of the highest legislative body of a State. The treatment accorded members of city councils and other inferior legislative bodies is uneven. In some jurisdictions minor legislative officers enjoy only a qualified or conditional privilege, such as will be discussed later.

The Executive Process. For many years the absolute privilege to defame was denied to all officers of the executive branch of government except the President of the United States, the Governors of States, cabinet officers of the United States and State offices corresponding thereto. This restriction in coverage still applies to State executive officers in most jurisdictions. In 1959, however, the United States Supreme Court extended the absolute privilege to *all* Executive officers of the Federal government irrespective of their standing in the heirarchy of authority. It is required only that the defamatory statement be made in the outer perimeter of the performance of a duty of the office, and that it be one that the officer is authorized to make. This immunity has been held to embrace a release to the press explaining the official's conduct in office.

There are also statements in the Supreme Court opinions to the effect that the executive officer's immunity, fashioned by the courts, is available to *legislative* officials in addition to the legislative immunity provided for them under the Speech and Debate provision, discussed earlier. If such is the case, it would appear that a legislator's report to his constituents or to the press should be absolutely privileged. Here the proper test of immunity would be the relevancy of the statement to the performance of the legislator's duties rather than inquiry as to whether the statement was made on the occasion of performance of a Legislative Act.

Although, as indicated above, absolute immunity is usually denied to those State officers who do not occupy positions of highest authority, it does not follow that these lesser officials are wholly without protection against defamation claims. Their privilege, however, is a qualified one, and of a character to be discussed hereafter (§ 6–17). Similarly, persons complaining to or otherwise seeking the aid of inferior officials, enjoy only a qualified privilege, in contrast with parties litigant and witnesses in judicial or legislative proceedings.

§ 6—15   Other Absolute Privileges

Aside from the need for unrestricted freedom of expression in discharging governmental functions, only a few special needs have been regarded as important enough to justify conferring an absolute privilege to defame which would protect even the conscious liar.

Husband and Wife. Freedom of confidential communications between spouses is encouraged by protecting their statements to each other against any claim for defamation. This protection exists quite apart from any general intrafamily tort immunity. Furthermore it applies only to communications between the spouses. The matter complained of need not relate in any way to the protection of any family interest or the preformance of any familial duty.

Communications Required by Law. Any agency required by law to publish statements of others without discrimination is entitled to an absolute immunity from liability. The Federal Communications Commission, for instance, requires that all radio stations afford equal opportunities to all political candidates. A station broadcasting under these circumstances is denied any power of censorship over what is said. Hence it enjoys a corresponding exemption from liability. This absolute immunity can be profitably compared with the merely qualified privilege of a telegraph agency which is obliged to accept all messages proffered it except those known to be defamatory. Even if it is aware of the nature of the statement it remains immune unless it is also aware of facts affording reason to know that the sender himself is not privileged to communicate the matter in question. Nevertheless, it follows that the privilege of the agency acting thus under its general public duty, as indicated above is not an absolute immunity as we have used the term.

§ 6—16　Qualified Privilege

The following discussion of the qualified privilege to defame must be understood as strictly limited to the Traditional approach to defamation as it existed prior to 1974. In that year, as we shall see (§ 6–20), the Supreme Court subjected the law of defamation to a constitutional requirement that fault be established as a part of the prima facie showing incumbent on the plaintiff.

Prior to this change the element of blameworthiness would not be brought in focus until the defendant had interjected the meritorious charac-

[*157*]

ter of his conduct into issue by affirmatively claiming that the statement in question was made upon an occasion that was at least qualifiedly privileged. It was incumbent on the defendant to establish the circumstances upon which the existence of a privileged occasion would depend.

The effect of judicial recognition of the privilege was to deny recovery to the plaintiff unless he could come forward and show affirmatively that the defendant's conduct constituted an "abuse" of the qualifiedly privileged occasion on which he acted. If the plaintiff succeeded in doing so, his right to a recovery was restored. It follows that our inquiry into qualified privilege is two-fold: First, under the Traditional approach, what constitutes a qualifiedly privileged occasion? Second, what conduct by defendant will amount to an abuse of the occasion?

A qualified privilege is accorded for the purpose of enabling the speaker or writer to protect some interest of his own or of another person whom he is under a legal or moral duty to protect, or to protect the interest of a group of which he is a member. In order to merit protection, the interest must be of sufficient importance in the eyes of the law to justify a conclusion that the injury to the reputation of the defamed plaintiff would be offset by the social advantage to be served by the communication if the statement should turn out to be true. The statement must be motivated by the desire to protect, and it must be made to some person whom the defendant reasonably believes to be in a position to assist in carrying out the purpose for which the privilege was accorded. The fact that he was mistaken in so concluding is immaterial. Similarly, in fact there may be no privileged occasion to be served. But this does not preclude protection of the defendant's conduct if he reasonably believes that such an occasion does exist.

Protection of the Publisher's Interest. Interests of the defendant himself which he may properly seek to preserve by means of a defamatory utterance include the protection of his possession of real or personal property, as where he complains to an appropriate party of a thievery. Somewhat similar is the privilege to slander the title of an adverse contender in a bona fide effort to defend one's own claim to the property (Cf. § 8–3, infra). However, he cannot engage in defamation of the person in an effort to protect his interest as a rival claimant. Nor can he justify a defamation solely as an effort to further his interest in legitimate competition with the plaintiff. He may safeguard the interest of his family through derogatory statements concerning outsiders whose conduct might impair the serenity of the domestic institution. Again, the publisher's own reputation is an appropriate object to be protected by a privilege whenever the defendant is seeking to discountenance statements made against him by the plaintiff. His reply, however, must be limited to matters that detract in some way from the credibility of his attacker or that tend to clear up the charge.

Protection of the Interest of Another Person. The interest sought to be protected through the recognition of a conditional privilege may be an interest of the recipient of the defamatory communication or of a third person. Obviously the defendant cannot assume gratuitously that the interest of some other person will be served if he speaks, and thus gain a privilege to defame. The intended object of his protection must be someone to whom he owes a legal duty, or there must be a clear moral obligation to speak recognized under the usages of decent society. When the defendant relies upon a legal duty, the person intended to enjoy the benefit of the statement may be someone who bears a recognized relationship to the speaker, such as that of principal and agent or trustee and cestui que trust, or the defendant may be acting in a professional capacity, such as attorney or physician. The person being protected by the statement may even be a stranger whose life or property is apparently subjected to immediate peril by violence at the hands of the plaintiff. Under such circumstances the defendant may with impunity communicate with a police officer or even with a private person who appears to be in a position to help. Again, a qualified privilege may be available to one who is hired as an investigator to protect an employer or prospective employer of the defamed plaintiff, or to afford information needed to assist the hearer in determining whether to enter into or remain in a business relation with another.

Similarly, a former employer of the plaintiff may be qualifiedly privileged to counsel a present or prospective employer of the plaintiff on the latter's character and qualifications as they relate to the performance of his duties. Whether a request is necessary in order to justify the statements may depend upon a number of factors, such as the closeness of the relation between the two employers, the apparent urgency of the need for the specific information and the expected seriousness of the injury the plaintiff's reputation would suffer if the statement should turn out to be untrue. At one time there was a serious difference of opinion in the courts concerning the privileged status of credit agencies. It now appears fairly settled, in this country at least, that these agencies perform a useful service in the commercial world, and so long as such an agency confines its disclosures to those persons who have requested specific information, it enjoys a qualified privilege to reveal matters that have been ascertained through reasonable inquiry. However, an open compendium of credit ratings available to subscribers at large can bring the publisher to grief whenever the

[*161*]

statements prove to be untrue. A mutual credit organization operating a cooperative venture, and which restricts its findings to its members, enjoys a qualified privilege which is more secure.

Courts are more wary in extending the protection of a qualified privilege with reference to a remark volunteered by the defendant in the interest of the recipient's purely domestic or social affairs. If the recipient is closely related to the defendant by family ties and the topic is a matter of apparently substantial concern to the hearer, a privilege will frequently be recognized. The same may be true even between persons who are not members of the same family but where the relationship between them is one of great intimacy and the need for the information by the recipient is fairly apparent. But otherwise the law frowns upon the gossip who presumes to speak for what he considers the hearer's "own good". A privilege to speak on such matters is more likely to be upheld where the statement is made solely in response to the direct request or urging of the recipient, thus affording some assurance that the matter is considered, at least by the hearer, as being of sufficient importance to his interests to justify the communication.

Protection of Common or Group Interest. When the making of a statement would reasonably appear to serve both an interest of the speaker and an interest of the recipient its qualifiedly privileged character is apparent. The interests of the parties may be substantially identical. But they need not be; as where a bank officer in speaking to a depositor accuses the plaintiff, a third party, of forging an endorsement on a check drawn by the depositor, or where a person who, himself, is accused of some offense against the recipient of the statement attempts to identify the plaintiff as the true culprit. In so doing he seeks both to exonerate himself and to assist the other by pointing out the wrongdoer.

Frequently the speaker and the recipient or recipients are members of the same group, and the statement is made for the purpose of protecting a common interest of the group membership. They may both be partners, employees of the same employer, stockholders in the same corporation, members of a trade union, or, perhaps, creditors of the same debtor or bankrupt. The person being discussed may himself be a member of the group, or an officer or a candidate for office in the group, or merely a candidate for membership. But members of a group are also free to discuss among themselves the character—or conduct of an outsider whose dealing with the group or whose behavior may substantially affect the common interest in any respect.

Although the most readily recognized group interests center around matters of business, profes-

sion or employment, yet family, religious and social groupings may also be protected by a qualified privilege. Members of the immediate family
enjoy a relatively free hand in advising and counseling with each other. Statements, for example,
reasonably believed by a parent to be true may be
volunteered with the objective of discouraging a
child from entering a marriage that the parent regards as unsuitable. More caution may be required, as we have seen (§ 4–2, supra), where the
object of the statement is to disrupt an existing
marriage. In such case liability may be incurred
by the parent even though it has avoided defamation or has spoken the truth. A conditional privilege may be accorded statements made without
prior request within the family on matters of social, professional, or business relations with outsiders where the object is to protect some family
interest.

Also enjoying protection are exchanges of information between members of a church, an educational or even a social group, such as a fraternity, where the statements are made in good faith
for the protection of the welfare of the group and
are reasonably confined within the membership
itself. It is not necessary that the statement be
made during the course of a formal meeting or
even that it be accompanied by a demand for immediate group action, so long as its purpose is to
further the interest of the group. However, en-

gaging in idle gossip under a claim of protection by reason of group membership is not to be countenanced.

Although the defamatory statement is privileged only when directed to persons within the group, the fact that the means of publication chosen reaches also some disinterested persons outside the membership does not automatically defeat the privilege. Whether, for example, a statement concerning matters of importance to a labor union ceases to be privileged when published in a newspaper of general circulation depends on the reasonableness of resort to that means of publication in view of the number of union members to be reached, the need for haste, the unavailability of a more restricted agency for distribution and the breadth of the exposure involved through use of the means selected.

§ 6—17 Special Situations of Qualified Privilege

Privilege to Discuss Matters of Public Concern —Traditional Approach. Following the same approach in recognition of a group interest discussed in the preceding section, a private citizen may, as a member of the political community, report to proper authorities matters believed to be true concerning the commission of a crime or the misbehavior of a public officer or the conduct of any public affair of the body politic. The qualified privilege is grounded on a hope or expectation by the speaker that curative action of some kind may be undertaken, or at least that the matter will be further investigated. Perhaps a similar communication directed to a group of private citizens who are dedicated to furthering the public purpose for which the statement was made might enjoy a similar privilege. But broad dissemination of facts concerning the political community or behavior in public office, such as matters of public concern that appear in newspapers or statements of a derogatory character broadcast by a candidate for office have been denied protection in the majority of jurisdictions under the Traditional approach to qualified group privilege. This refusal to recognize the political community as a group which is entitled to the same protection as a social fraternity or a church membership has been defended by the argument that the broad area of dissemination (usually through mass media which are not characteristically members of the group) could prove disastrously harmful, and that worthy persons would be discouraged thereby from seeking public office. This refusal of protection has been discountenanced and rejected in a substantial minority of the courts, and it has been the target of much sharp criticism by writers. The importance of this diversity of opinion will become obvious later when we come to discuss the constitutional protection now accorded statements in the press concerning public officials and public figures (§ 6–19).

Fair Comment.　Although derogatory statements of fact on matters of public concern were
denied qualified privilege protection under the Traditional approach, nevertheless, a speaker or writer was accorded a privilege of Fair Comment
which allowed him the freedom to express his
own opinion so long as he avoided any false as-
sertion of fact.　As will be noted hereafter (§ 6–
20), the human interest in freedom to assert an
opinion has since been recognized by the Supreme
Court as a constitutional right, and it is no longer
regarded as a mere privilege confined to a limited
group of topics and subject to abuse, as was formerly the case.　Nevertheless, the now obsolescent
privilege of Fair Comment deserves brief notice
because the courts, in determining the outside
boundaries of its protection, restricted it to matters of Public Concern.　As so used, the privilege
embraced a wide range of matters relating to the
behavior of public officials and the conduct of public business.　This was true even though the same
writing referred to private individuals such as
contractors, seekers after influence, and the like.
Also permissible were discussions of the management of charitable, educational and religious institutions, and criticisms of literature, art, drama,
and similar public cultural offerings.　Why there
should ever have been any limitation on the range
of topics properly subject to pure critical opinion
is not clear.　It has long been argued that the ob-

servation, "I do not like you, Doctor Fell; the reason why I cannot tell . . . " should not be considered in any sense as a defamatory statement even though Doctor Fell were an obscure private person.

A major difficulty encountered in an attempt to administer the Fair Comment privilege is the need to distinguish statements of opinion from statements of fact, since the latter are not protected. Seldom can an expression be regarded as "pure" opinion when examined critically. Usually the opinion amounts to a comment upon some fact or facts, which may be express or implied. In either event, if the speaker is to escape liability on the basis of Fair Comment, the element of fact in his statement must either be true, or independently privileged, or it must be one that is generally known already.

The requirement that the comment must be "fair" does not mean that the opinion must be temperate or reasonable in any way. The term, rather, expresses the requirement that the statement be confined to such matters as are of public concern. One may be tempted to conclude that the obsolescent Fair Comment privilege with its artificialities and tenuous distinctions afforded the speaker or writer on public affairs a dubious protection at best, and perhaps we are well rid of it.

Report of Public Proceedings. The publication at large of a judicial, legislative or administrative proceeding is conditionally privileged. Everything said or done at such proceedings is properly a matter of record in which the public has a legitimate interest. For this reason, wide dissemination, whether by newspaper, radio, or whatever means, is permissible. The privilege does not extend beyond the proceeding itself and those documents which can be regarded as a part of it. In the case of a judicial proceeding the reporter's privilege does not attach in most jurisdictions until some official action has been taken on the pleading or other document in question, although such action need not be a final disposition. Since the privilege rests upon the interest in public access to official activities, it is immaterial whether the publisher does or does not believe in the truth of the content of what was said during the course of the proceeding. The only requirement is that his statement be a report that is both truthful and fair as to what transpired. Errors in naming the parties and mistakes as to what occurred on the reported occasion, even though unintended by the reporter or believed by him to be true, serve to exclude the account from the privilege under the Traditional view. The same is true where the reporter resorts to insinuation or indirection in order to convey a false impression. Similarly, what is a mere allegation in a pleading cannot be reported as a statement of fact, and a witness's testimony must be reported for what it is, nothing more. Misleading headlines or fragmentary or garbled reports are not protected. This does not mean, however, that a report must be literal, so long as it fairly reflects what happened.

Providing Means of Publication for Privileged Originator. If the exercise of a privilege to defame is to be protected effectively, it may be necessary to so extend the privilege as to confer immunity on certain persons or agencies which provide appropriate assistance in disseminating the privileged material. If, for example, a person who has been accused in public of a crime is to enjoy the benefit of a privilege to broadcast in reply that his accuser is a liar, this privilege is worth little unless a newspaper or other appropriate medium can make its facilities available to him without fear of becoming subject itself to a claim for damages. The material so published may be the subject of an absolute or a qualified privilege. The disseminating agency must be one that reaches an appropriate audience or reasonably believes that the publication will not extend unduly beyond the area necessary to afford protection to the person for whose benefit it is acting. If the published material is covered by an absolute privilege, the disseminating agency will avoid liability even though it is aware of its falsity. If the material is only conditionally privileged, the situation of the disseminating agency is not clear. Certainly such agency is without protection when it is aware that the holder of the original privilege knows the statement is false. Even if the agency suspects that the originator was ignorant, it may be under a duty to alert him as to the untruthfulness before undertaking to assist him. Under these circumstances, both privileges would disappear. Similarly, it is essential that the disseminator have some reason to believe that the statement was one that the originator was privileged to make.

On the other hand, where the disseminating agency is a telegraph company or other public utility which is obliged to accept and transmit messages, it must be affirmatively shown that the disseminator had reason to believe that the originator was not acting pursuant to a privilege of any kind. He is under no positive duty to investigate such matters.

§ 6—18 Abuse of Qualified Privilege

In order to determine whether liability should be imposed upon a defendant despite the fact that he acted on a qualifiedly privileged occasion, the court resorts to a balancing process by which it attempts to individualize the situation. In so doing it weighs the interest of the defamed person against the gain that hopefully would accrue to society by tolerating the publication in question in the light of the particular circumstances that attended it. If the balance here is resolved against the defendant, he is regarded as having *abused* the occasion and hence is vulnerable to liability. The basic inquiry is whether the injury he inflicted on the plaintiff's reputation was in fact avoidable or was one that was greater than would reasonably appear necessary to protect the interest in question. Did the end justify the particular means which he was shown to have employed? The abuse of a qualified privilege is not infrequently characterized as "malice"—an equivocal term which unfortunately tends to divert focus away from the essential balancing process and toward some vicious state of mind which is attributed to the defendant. Sometimes it is true that a showing of contempt or ill will toward the victim suggests that the communication was not directed toward serving the interest in question, or that the communication was not an appropriate means for protection. But if the statement made by the defendant was one that did tend to serve its protective purpose and if it inflicted no unnecessary harm, the privilege is not abused by the fact that the defendant also satisfied his resentment by defaming the plaintiff.

Abuse of a qualified privilege may result whenever the circumstances attendant on the publication suggest to the trier that more harm to the plaintiff's standing was inflicted than was reasonably necessary in order to attain the objective that prompted the communication. Abuse may also result whenever the trier concludes that the defamatory matter was not of a character calculated to assist in achieving the objective that prompted the communication. Each of these aspects of abuse—excessive harm, and lack of utility—require brief mention.

Excessive Harm. Excessive harm to plaintiff's reputation is threatened whenever the defamatory statement is communicated to persons who have afforded no reasonable indication to the defendant that they could be of assistance in attaining the objective sought. Such excess of publication, however, must be substantial, and it must be fairly avoidable. A realization by the defendant that persons other than those intended may see or hear the statement is not fatal to the privilege so long as their awareness is reasonably incidental to an effective communication to the appropriate recipient. It may be unavoidable that a defamatory statement be made in the presence of other persons, or that a matter that is of concern to only a limited group be published in a newspaper of general circulation. Even if the method adopted is not absolutely essential to the effectiveness of the communication, it may nevertheless be privileged if it is usual or customary. Thus a defamatory letter may be dictated to a secretary if intended for transmission to an appropriate person.

Even though a publication to an additional person or persons is regarded as excessive, the defendant may be subjected to liability only with respect to that part of the harm fairly attributable to the inappropriate communication, if the excess can be severed and fairly evaluated separately. Otherwise the abuse of privilege exposes the defendant to liability just as though no privilege existed.

Statement's Lack of Utility. If the matter published consists of statements that serve no useful purpose in achieving the objective for which the privilege was given, its publication falls outside the privilege and thus amounts to an abuse. This is true even though it is communicated only to those recipients who would be appropriate persons. Thus, although a citizen may be privileged to report to a police officer his belief that the plaintiff had committed a criminal offense, yet resort to a broadside disparagement of the latter's character unrelated to the incident reported, or the use of highly intemperate language embroidered with extraneous defamatory observations may be regarded as an abuse. If the harm to plaintiff's reputation inflicted by the inclusion of unprivileged material in an otherwise privileged communication can be isolated and assigned a separately estimated price, this may be done. Otherwise the privilege is lost in its entirety and defendant must answer for the total harm.

Defendant's Awareness of Falsity as Abuse of Privilege. Obviously the dissemination of a statement which turns out to be wholly false can serve no useful purpose. Hence the publication of a statement known by the defendant to be untrue is a clear abuse of a qualified privilege. But on the other hand, an honest effort to protect some vital interest of the speaker or others need not be penalized because it later appears that the speaker was unavoidably mistaken as to the facts narrated by him. To frustrate such good faith efforts by imposing liability would severely discourage needed protective measures, and society would be the loser thereby. For this reason a privileged communication is abused only when something more than a bare mistake by the defendant is discoverable. It is noteworthy that under the Traditional view the effect of an innocent mistake made on a qualifiedly privileged occasion must be distinguished from an equally innocent mistake made in the course of a wholly nonprivileged occasion, in which latter event the defendant's complete ignorance of falsity is immaterial. There remains the question as to what mental attitude on the part of the defendant toward truth or falsity must be shown in order to defeat a qualified privilege. A defendant may have an honest belief that he is telling the truth but without any reasonable foundation. Perhaps an affirmative investigation would have correct-

ed the error. Is he under a duty to make such
an investigation—always? Sometimes? Never?
Must it be shown that he was faced with some
suspicious circumstance suggesting that an affirmative investigation would be in order? The
answer is not entirely clear under the Traditional
view. Not infrequently it has been held that so
long as he entertained an honest belief in the
truth of his statements he has not abused his
qualified privilege. Sometimes the defendant's
required mental state with regard to truth has
been described in terms of "honesty" and "absence
of malice". Again it may be said that the privilege is not lost so long as defendant had "probable cause" for his statement. In short, the an-
swers are frequently equivocal, and perhaps they
betray a felt need by the courts to maintain a
flexibility of approach. However, the majority
view prior to the intervention of the Supreme
Court on constitutional grounds was probably
that negligence with respect to truth or falsity
would serve to defeat a qualified privilege, even
if the defendant was honest in his belief. At least
this position was adopted in Section 601 of the
first Restatement of Torts (1938).

The Burden of Establishing Abuse of Privilege.
With respect to the burden of proof resting on
the respective parties, a finding that a privilege
was abused should be distinguished from a finding that no privilege ever existed. It is incumbent

on the defendant to assert and persuade the court that the communication complained of was made on a privileged occasion. Thereafter the burden of showing that the occasion was abused by excessive publication, or otherwise, rests upon the plaintiff, who is now seeking to avoid the protection that the defendant would enjoy under his showing of privilege.

§ 6—19 Traditional Defamation Law—Conflicts With the Interests of the Press

Dissatisfaction With Traditional Law. The predicament of the press and other mass media was not a happy one under the Traditional law of defamation. The established rules betrayed little compassion for the unintended errors chargeable to the news media. Such errors are many, and they are of various kinds: News sources may prove false; a culprit may be erroneously confused in identity with some innocent party; an apparently innocuous fact may turn out to be defamatory in the light of facts unknown to its publisher; a typographical error may turn what purports to be an innocent statement into something ludicrous; observations intended as harmless may be regarded as offensive in the eyes of some sensitive persons. Following the Traditional law, courts were obliged to treat all such errors indiscriminately and to entertain no more tolerance for an innocent mistake than for a reckless disparagement.

[*177*]

Even prior to 1964, when the Supreme Court moved into action under the Free Speech Amendment, there was considerable dissatisfaction with the common law's Draconian attitude toward defamation, and efforts by both courts and legislatures to soften its rigors were not infrequent. We have already noted several: There emerged in some quarters a notion of Libel per Quod (§ 6–9, supra), according to which, material that fell short of being defamatory on its face could not support a defamation claim in the absence of affirmative proof of special damages (which requirement was usually fatal to the plaintiff's case). Again, we may recall that in a sizeable minority of the state courts there was an inclination to recognize a qualified group privilege which would justify the making of factual misstatements in good faith on matters of concern to the political community (§ 6–16). In one jurisdiction a newspaper could escape responsibility for the inclusion in its pages of seemingly true or innocuous statements furnished to it by one of the national news gathering agencies. Similarly, it appeared for a time that defamation by radio would be characterized as slander, rather than libel, thus forcing the victim to establish actual damage in most instances. Of even more direct assistance to the press was a sizeable array of statutes (about 20) which were intended to preclude any award of general damages whenever a publisher who had unintentionally defamed the plaintiff offered to publish an appropriate retraction (as defined by the statute in question). Still other measures, would relieve a radio or television broadcaster of liability where the station had merely made its facilities available to others and is itself free of negligence in so doing. Finally, the constitutions in some states were interpreted as affording a measure of protection to the press beyond what was recognized at common law.

New York Times Co. v. Sullivan to Rosenbloom v. Metromedia. Such fortuitous assists to the media as those suggested above should now be viewed in their proper perspective as but small streams which have since been overtaken by a flood of reform under the Constitutional aegis of freedom of speech and press. Prior to 1964 the Supreme Court had cautiously refrained from any effort to contain the law of libel within the confines of the constitutional guarantee of free speech. In that year came the decision in New York Times v. Sullivan (U.S.1964). This case worked a dramatic change in the relationship between the First Amendment and the common law of libel. The *New York Times* case, supplemented by a series of crucial decisions during the following decade, brought into being a radically different version of the law of defamation than had existed theretofore—a version that tended to recognize the interest of the publisher as para-

mount. The defamatory matter that gave rise
to the *Times* case was a paid advertisement in the
New York Times signed by a number of prominent individuals criticizing the behavior of the
Montgomery, Alabama police in dealing with an
incident of racial unrest. The libel suit was instituted by Sullivan, the Police Commissioner of
the City, who contended that the derogatory reference to the police behavior amounted indirectly
to a defamation of him personally. The trial
judge, whose action was affirmed by the supreme
court of the state, instructed the jury in strict ac-
cordance with the Traditional no-fault point of
view as it obtained in Alabama at that time. The
result was a plaintiff verdict of half a million dollars, which was allowed to stand in the courts.
This was reversed by the United States Supreme
Court.

The Court based its reversal on the ground that
the Constitutional guarantee of free speech under
the First Amendment prohibits a *public official*
from recovering damages for a defamatory falsehood relating to his *official* conduct unless he
proves that the statement was made with factual
malice—that is with knowledge that it was false
or in reckless disregard of whether it was false
or not. This constitutional protection was extended both to the press and to the private individuals who instigated the publication. Despite
the fact that the Times concededly did not in-

vestigate the truth of the material submitted to it, it still was regarded as not guilty of that actual knowledge of falsity or callous indifference necessary to liability.

It is noteworthy at this first stage of the Supreme Court's intervention into the law of libel that, apart from its deliberate and unprecedented interposition of a constitutional safeguard to protect a publisher in a defamation suit, the *Times* decision did not itself clearly foretoken the range of radical innovations which were to follow. The general body of Traditional libel law was to all appearances not seriously disturbed in this first case. The Court appeared satisfied to resort to Constitutional free speech in order to shore up a group privilege which had already been recognized under the libel law of a respectable minority of the States: That is to say, it sought to assure that the members of the *political* community (as well as members of a church congregation or social fraternity) would enjoy a substantial measure of freedom to communicate in good faith concerning the demerits of those who serve it.

But at the same time, the new position of the Court bore a noticeable resemblance to the familiar privilege of Fair Comment on all matters of public interest. In keeping with the analogy to Fair Comment, the new constitutional freedom was made available for the protection of the press and other outsiders which were not themselves

necessarily members of the political community
whose interests were at stake. Similarly, the geographic area of dissemination that could be
reached with impunity was much more extensive
than would usually be allowable under a group
privilege designed only to protect the common interest of a limited social, religious or political
community.

But the analogy to Privileged Fair Comment
tends to give way entirely when we consider the
limited scope of the subject matter that could be
safely discussed under the new freedom. In contrast with the wide range of topics that can properly be labeled "matters of general concern" and
which thus fall within the acceptable broad ambit
of Fair Comment, the constitutional freedom as
conferred under *Times* was expressly limited to a
discussion of the character of public officials and
their behavior in public office. This limitation
of subject matter in *Times* was of particular significance. The only victim of defamation who was
placed under a relative disability was the public
official whose stewardship must be subjected to
the critical scrutiny of those who are his ultimate
employers. If the Supreme Court had rested content with this modest ambit of constitutional protection, its introduction of free speech considerations might have been more readily accommodated within the Traditional law of defamation
than, as we shall see, actually turned out to be the

case. It may also be noted that an extension of constitutional protection to the discussion of the conduct of officials can be viewed as an acknowledgment that speech relevant to self government is of a superior order in the hierarchy of constitutional values. Cf. A. Meiklejohn, Public Speech and the First Amendment (1967) 55 Geo.L.J. 234.

An inclination to move toward a broader rationale for the new constitutional freedom became obvious almost at once. In one of the first decisions after *Times* to deal with the public official concept, Rosenblatt v. Baer (U.S.1966), the Court, although adhering to the position that the freedom was restricted to claims by officials, nevertheless ruled that the term, official, embraced any employee, however insignificant his office. For example, the plaintiff, Rosenblatt, whose libel claim was dismissed, was the supervisor of a public ski area. The language of the opinion served to forewarn that a broader operative area for the freedom was in the offing. The objective to be served, said Brenner, J., was freedom to criticize public servants "lest criticism of government itself be penalized." A year later in Curtis Publishing Company v. Butts (U.S.1967), the Supreme Court wholly abandoned the notion that the public official is the only defamation victim whose right to recovery is limited by the Constitution. Significantly, it added a class of persons designated *"public figures"*, whose rights in a libel suit were made subject to First Amendment restrictions. The qualification for membership in this group was not unequivocally defined. Wally Butts, the first claimant so qualified by the Court, was a well known former football coach who at the time in question was employed by the Georgia Athletic Association, a private corporation. Walker, the complainant in a companion suit [against the Associated Press] was a retired army officer who had attracted attention by reason of his dramatic voluntary participation in a disturbance on the campus of the University of Mississippi, which was in the public eye. Both, according to the opinion, commanded "a substantial amount of public interest at the time of the publications in question"—Butts, by reason of his position, and Walker, through his activity in "thrusting his personality into the 'vortex' of an important public controversy." Little more appears in the opinion to cast light on the new term. But a reader may well gather from the overtones of the opinion that the Court is shifting its focus toward the notion that the objective to be promoted is a broad freedom to discuss any matter of public interest or concern.

Rosenbloom v. Metromedia through Gertz v. Robert Welch. Despite the expansion of *Times* protection in *Butts'* and *Walker's* cases so as to include material defamatory of "public figures", there remained substantial areas which appeared to be outside the reach of the Constitution. The availability of protection for the publisher still depended on the proper characterization of the defamed person, rather than upon any importance the reported event might have in the public eye. It was in a later sequel in the *Times* chain, Rosenbloom v. Metromedia (U.S.1971) four years later, that the growing court sentiment for a virtually unfettered press reached its full tide. In a plurality opinion, joined by only two other members of the Court, Justice Brennan announced:

> "The public's primary interest is in the event; the public focus is on the conduct of the participant and the content, effect and significance of the conduct, not the participant's prior anonymity or notoriety. . . . Freedom of discussion, if it would fulfill its historic function in this nation, must embrace all issues about which information is needed or appropriate to enable the members of society to cope with the exigencies of their period."

The transition is complete. With respect to all matters that could be regarded as of public or general interest, the victim of defamation—whoever he might be—must establish by clear and convincing evidence that the publisher was either aware of the falsity of his statement or that he was consciously indifferent to whether it was true or not. Clearly the policy that dominated the

Rosenbloom plurality opinion was a strongly felt need to avoid the specter of self-censorship by the press. To this need all interest in reputation was subordinated. The freedom accorded the press fell only slightly short of the unqualified privilege to defame enjoyed by judges and legislators. The Court declined to venture in advance how the conception of *public interest* or *concern* might be bounded. It left the reach of that term to future cases. There is little doubt that decisions during the ensuing four years treated *public interest* as virtually synonomous with "newsworthy", although it should be noted that the Supreme Court did not use that expression. *Rosenbloom* was unhelpful on whether others than members of the press enjoy constitutional protection.

There was a conspicuous lack of unanimity of opinion in the disposition of the *Rosenbloom* controversy. The rationale set forth above was acceptable to only three Justices: Brennan, Blackmun and Berger. Black, J., although concurring in the result, adhered to an extreme position which he and Douglas, J. had espoused consistently since the beginning—namely, the First Amendment was intended to leave the press wholly immune from the harassment of any libel claim whatsoever. In all, there were three separate opinions, none of which commanded more than three votes. There were three dissenting Justices —Harlan, Stewart and Marshall—all of whom shared a common view that the rationale of the plurality opinion was unacceptable because it exacted a greater sacrifice of the interest in reputation than was necessary to recognize the press' interest in freedom from fear of censorship. The features of these proposals will be brought into focus in our discussion of the *Gertz* decision, to which we should now turn.

The battle to determine the acceptable point of balance between conflicting values, as it was waged in *Rosenbloom* with the outcome in virtual stalemate, gave rise immediately to intense discussion and debate among lawyers and law writers. The struggle in the Supreme Court was renewed and a fresh resolution attempted three years later in Gertz v. Welch (U.S.1974). Gertz was employed as an attorney by the family of a youth who had been shot and killed by a Chicago policeman, Nuccio, who was ultimately convicted of the murder. Gertz' only interest in the matter was as the representative of the family in a civil proceeding against Nuccio, and solely in this capacity he attended the coroner's inquest. Otherwise his connection with the entire criminal affair was remote. American Opinion, a publication of the Birch Society under the editorship of Welch falsely charged Gertz with active participation in an alleged conspiracy to discredit the police, and it described him as a member of left wing organizations dedicated to violence. The opinion made clear that Gertz was not a public figure. On the other hand, there was little doubt that the article in question concerned his purported involvement in an event of 'public interest or concern'. Furthermore, the plaintiff was unable to prove that the article was published with knowledge of its falsity or in reckless disregard of its truth. It therefore was clear that recovery for libel must be denied unless *Rosenbloom* were to be disregarded or overruled. Again there was a sharp division of opinion, and again, similarly to the *Rosenbloom* alignment, a majority of five was made possible only through the expedient of a reluctant concurrence by one Justice (Blackmun) who conceded that his preference was for an opposed position, but who joined only because he felt that a majority opinion was essential. Each of the four dissenters wrote his own separate opinion. Nevertheless, a majority opinion subscribed by five Justices did manage to make an appearance.

The chief features of the new position can be summarized as follows:

First, the Constitutional requirement of proof of knowledge or conscious indifference as to falsity was again restricted by the Court to claims by public officials or public figures, as in *Times* and *Butts*. The *Rosenbloom* approach, resting on the test of public interest or public concern, was expressly repudiated.

Second, the states were declared free to define for themselves by statute or decision the appropriate standard of liability for statements defamatory of a private individual *so long as they did not impose liability without fault.*

Finally, whenever liability is imposed in favor of a private individual under any standard less exacting than the guilty knowledge test of *Times,* the recovery must be limited to actual injury sustained.   In such cases presumed general damage and punitive damage are not available.

The *Gertz* position marks in general an adoption of the dissenting opinions of Justices Harlan, Stewart and Marshall in *Rosenbloom.* The point of balance between the interest in reputation versus that of free speech has shifted back so as to favor at least a limited protection of the interest of the defamed individual unless he is a public official or public figure. But it should be noted that in one respect the *Gertz* opinion marks a more serious intrusion into Traditional defamation theory than had been the case under the *Rosenbloom* approach. The plurality opinion in *Rosenbloom* would have carved out for constitutional protection those areas of defamation that are matters of public interest or concern, but it would otherwise have left the basic structure of defamation theory unchanged. Under the *Gertz* opinion, however, the traditional ideas of liability without fault and recovery of presumed damages are completely uprooted from the law. This basic restructuring of Traditional libel law by the majority opinion prompted dissents by the Chief Justice and Justice White.

The Views in Rosenbloom and Gertz Compared and Appraised. The following observations by critics merit close attention when the *Rosenbloom* test of public interest or concern is compared with the position of the majority in *Gertz,* which makes the public status of the defamed victim the touchstone.

A critic of *Rosenbloom* can point out that resort to the test of that case would charge the courts with the responsibility of an *ad hoc* determination on the public interest aspect of virtually every item of defamatory material that is litigated. The unpredictability of the outcome of litigation that would follow a resort by the courts to any selective or exclusionary formula of public interest would be certain to bring about self censorship by the public media. It could follow that the desired objective of a free press would be defeated through the very means devised by the court to protect it. This uncertainty could be avoided under the *Rosenbloom* formula, but only at the cost of abandoning virtually all restraint upon the press. For if it were to be announced that all material that is *newsworthy* is automatically a matter of public interest or concern, only a deliberate falsehood by defendant could lead to liability. Under this view the public media might indeed go its way rejoicing, but the reputation of the individual would be virtually stripped of protection.

The *Gertz* decision is similarly vulnerable to criticism: It has been suggested that the technique for resolving the conflict between reputation and free press adopted by the *Gertz* majority is awkward and poorly designed to attain the objective of a fair compromise. If the defamed victim is a private person, the publisher must face the prospect of an adverse judgment whenever the plaintiff can induce the jury to believe that the objectionable matter was published through his "fault". The absence of any better explanation of this term by state court or legislature invites the conclusion that the "fault" requirement will probably be met by a showing that the publisher failed to use reasonable care with respect to the truth or falsity of his statement. Whenever negligence on the part of the publisher becomes the touchstone of liability the issue may frequently fall into the lap of the jury. Under these circumstances it may be that the publisher, aware of the risk of an unfavorable verdict, would hesitate to undertake any publication that might expose him to substantial danger of a suit. The need for caution may be appreciably enhanced where, as here, the jury will be expected to pass judgment upon the accepted professional behavior of publishers—a matter it is ill equipped to understand and evaluate. On the other hand, it can be argued in defence of the negligence test that the obligation to use reasonable care for the protection of the reputation of others is no different from the restraint that is recognized and accepted in other walks of life, and that an alert use of the power to direct a verdict is an adequate antidote to excesses of a jury.

The "Public Figure" Conception in Gertz. The Court in *Gertz* reverted to the *Butts* rule which would require both public officials and public figures to establish knowing or reckless falsity by the publisher as a condition to recovery. This singling out of the public figure for special treatment was justified in the court's opinion by its expressed belief that the private individual is more vulnerable to defamatory harm than the public official or figure. These persons, observed the opinion, enjoy a more realistic opportunity to counteract false statements through rebuttal in the public media than does the private person. In further support of the distinction the Court advanced a notion somewhat akin to assumption of risk: The individual who seeks public office must accept certain necessary consequences of that involvement. The arguments supporting the imposition of a heavier burden with respect to proof of fault upon the official serving in public office appear to have considerable merit. Freedom to discuss the stewardship of public servants may well deserve a special degree of protection. Furthermore, if the public official is to enjoy an unqualified privilege to defame others in the course of performing his duties, perhaps it is not unfair to place him under a handicap when he, in turn, seeks to sue for defamation (cf. § 6–14, supra).

On the other hand, an imposition of the same burden upon public figures who are only private citizens may be more difficult to defend, and the reasoning of the court with respect to them is less convincing. An observation that public figures have ready access to the media for self defence is hardly a dependable generalization. Furthermore, there are serious administrative problems. Unlike the classification of public official, which can be readily bounded, any attempt to isolate public figures and distinguish them from other private persons is certain to prove difficult. When can it be said that a defamation victim has achieved a general notoriety sufficiently broad to justify his being singled out for special treatment? In the *Gertz* case the plaintiff was a very active attorney who was the author of several books and numerous articles. His activities had been discussd many times in the newspapers. He had appeared frequently on television and radio and he had served as an officer in many civic and professional organizations. Nevertheless, the majority opinion refused to classify him as a public figure for those reasons. The opinion observed significantly that the "instances of truly involuntary public figures must be exceedingly rare." (418 U.S. 345).

If this view is accurate, the public figure who is not also a public official must be identified by means of some criteria other than merely by reference to the extensive public recognition accorded him. This suggests a focus upon the remaining distinctive characteristic of the public figure, as a person who has thrust himself voluntarily into the vortex of a public issue (as the court put the matter). It is to be expected that an approach to the public figure following this line of inquiry should begin with an appraisal of the event or happening in which the plaintiff has become involved. As the event in question becomes increasingly fraught with overtones of public interest, all those who were prominent participants in the event would be more properly regarded as public figures. The Court, however, by moving in this direction would return in effect to the rejected *Rosenbloom* criterion, and this by way of an awkward and circuitous route. Such was clearly not its intention. In Gertz' case the occasion in question was an official inquest growing out of a sensational killing. Certainly there is here an event fraught with public interest. The Supreme Court, however, found that Gertz did *not* become a public figure merely because the incident in which he was involved was sensational. It explained significantly that the most frequent instances of public figures are "those who have thrust themselves to the forefront of particular public *controversies* in order to influence the resolution of the *issues* involved." (Ital. added) Gertz was merely among those present at the inquest. Notice that the stress in the quotation above is upon the aggressive character of the plaintiff's participation and the motive that prompted him into action. The court clearly draws a distinction between the mere involvement in an event of public interest and the active interjection of oneself into a public *issue* for the purpose of influencing its resolution. This restrictive feature of the public figure concept was stressed again by the Supreme Court two years later in Time, Inc. v. Firestone (U.S.1976). The issue in that case centered around a derogatory press commentary upon a sensational divorce proceeding to which plaintiff, a prominent society woman of Palm Beach, was a party. The defendant claimed that she was a public figure both because of her social prominence and because of her participation in a "cause celebre". Both arguments were rejected in the opinion of Rehnquist, J. The opinion noted that the defendant

> "seeks to equate 'public controversy' with all controversies of interest to the public. Were we to accept this reasoning, we would rein-

state the doctrine advanced in the plurality opinion in Rosenbloom v. Metromedia."

It reiterated the language quoted above from the *Gertz* opinion.

We may note that under this more restrictive approach the effort exerted by the public figure to sway public reaction and to influence the outcome of something with which the public is concerned serves to cast him in a role not entirely dissimilar to that of the public official. The public figure approach should enable the Court to draw a narrower but more meaningful ambit within which the constitutional freedom would operate than would be the case under the matter-of-public-interest approach.   This, of course, does not wholly dispose of the specter of self-censorship, which will continue to haunt the publisher as long as he is beset by that uncertainty which is characteristic of the interpretive process in its first fumbling stages.   But there will remain fewer occasions when a delicate interpretation will be required.

§ 6—20   The Fault Requirement After *Gertz*

Actions by Public Officials and Public Figures. As indicated heretofore, the public official or public figure must establish "actual" malice on the part of the publisher. This the Supreme Court defines in *New York Times* as knowing or reckless falsity, which means that the defendant entertained conscious doubt concerning the truth of what he published. It is not enough that the statement, though honestly believed to be true, was actuated by some sinister motive, by ill will, or was made with disregard of the rights of the plaintiff.

Actions by Private Persons. The majority opinion in *Gertz* declined to establish any definitive meaning with respect to the element of fault which the private individual is required to establish in a defamation suit. Instead, it left the states free to establish for themselves the appropriate "standard of liability" to which the publisher should be held. Its only prescription was a constitutional minimum that no-fault liability could not be imposed. Even this requirement, however, works a basic alteration of Traditional defamation law, and it is this feature of the majority position that prompted sharp dissenting opinions by Justice White and the Chief Justice.

One of the most troublesome inquiries arising from the part of the *Gertz* opinion that would leave the states free to establish an "appropriate standard of liability" relates to the meaning of this latter term. Several observations in the opinion together with the Court's deliberate use of the term *standard* suggest that it was thinking along the lines of negligence—a failure to conform to the standard of reasonable care with respect to the prospect of making a false statement. Certainly this version has been accepted by Restatement of Torts Second (§ 580B) which then continues by setting forth the familiar factors used to determine the makeup of an unreasonable risk in cases involving physical injuries to person and property.   But many questions are still unanswered.   For example, can the defendant be held if it is shown that he failed to make an affirmative investigation, or must it be made to appear that he failed to investigate in the face of suspicious circumstances that would have prompted an investigation by a reasonable person?   If the defendant is a professional publisher is his liability to be judged by reference to accepted practices in the publishing business?   A realistic attack remains to be worked out on a case-to-case basis.

Although it is to be expected that most States will adopt a negligence standard, they are nevertheless free to define fault as they see fit, so long as they avoid strict liability.   Several options are open to the State courts and legislatures: They may choose to apply the *Times* knowing-or-reckless-falsity test to *all* suits by private individuals, or, as an alternative, to suits by private individuals only when the subject is a matter of public interest.   An adoption of this latter choice would resurrect the *Rosenbloom* test through preference as a matter of State law, and this has been the expressed preference in a few jurisdictions.   It is safe to assume that no State would elect to make the publisher answer where there is only "slight" negligence. At the other extreme, it is highly unlikely that any court or legislature would follow the proposal of Justices Black and Douglas that defamation claims against the public media should be abolished even when the libel is deliberate and known to be false.

Defendant's Behavior With Respect to Falsity. The assumption that the fault issue centers around the defendant's behavior with respect exclusively to the truth or falsity of his statement is one that requires further examination. Fault may have an important bearing on the resolution of several issues other than falsity. One example is that of publication. A focus upon wrongdoing is invited whenever there must be considered the manner in which the defendant released the material or allowed it to become public. Here a showing of negligence at the least has always been required under Traditional defamation law, and no change of position in this respect is likely to be forthcoming. Again, the publication of matter that is innocent on its face but which becomes defamatory in the light of circumstances unknown to the publisher, raises the question of what duty to investigate, if any, rests on the defendant? A similar question arises where the defendant, although appreciating the defamatory character of his statement, was unaware of facts which, if known, would cause him to realize that the statement referred to the plaintiff. In both the above

situations the Traditional position has been that
of liability without fault. But even when the defamed victim is a private person the conclusion
appears inescapable that fault of some kind must
be shown under the *Gertz* rule. Again, the negligence approach offers a sensible solution: Would
a reasonable man situated as the defendant fore-
see an unreasonable liklihood that the material
might turn out to be defamatory, or that it would
be understood as referring to the plaintiff?

**Qualified Privilege and the Constitutional Fault
Requirement.** In considering the Fault requirement it is well to bear in mind that *Times* and
the line of cases that followed it were concerned
almost entirely with the problem of the public
media. Although the Supreme Court did not expressly recognize that the press as an institution
is entitled to enjoy any special protection under
the Constitution, yet the single thrust behind the
opinions was clearly a concern to minimize a
risk that the public media would resort to self-
censorship when faced with the prospect of frequent and costly law suits. The central point
of attention was the mistake of fact—the inadvertant falsehood: When was the error prompted
by such blameworthiness that the publisher
should be penalized? Fault was identified with
Falsity. Unfortunately, this emphasis upon the
press and its needs served to detract Court attention from areas of private controversy that in-

volved other important aspects of the phenomenon of fault. The reference here is to those defamation suits whose outcome depended on some qualified privilege. We observed earlier that Traditional defamation law remains indifferent toward any lack of blameworthiness on the part of the defendant until the trial reaches that stage where he establishes that the occasion on which he spoke was qualifiedly privileged. By raising the privilege issue the defendant thrusts into the foreground the specific beneficial purpose his communication was designed to serve: He was seeking to protect his own interest or that of some other private individual (§ 6–16). When this showing has been made, the plaintiff will find himself obliged to counter with the claim that the privilege was abused by the defendant.   From this point on, the outcome will depend upon the character of the defendant's behavior, and the fault element emerges sharply into the foreground (§ 6–18). The abuse issue is characteristically framed in terms of "malice." But this cryptic phrase has merely meant that the claimed conditional privilege ceases to afford protection for the defendant because the statement was published in such way as to serve some purpose other than that for which the privilege was created. If the statement is a deliberate falsehood, it can serve no purpose other than to injure. Hence, the fact that the defendant was aware of the falsity of his statement *always* serves to defeat any quali-

fied privilege, and in most jurisdictions the result
is the same when it is shown that there were
absent any reasonable ground for his belief in its
truth (§ 6–18).

It does not follow, however, that a showing by
plaintiff of defendant's knowledge of falsity or
lack of reasonable ground to believe in the truth
of the statement are the only means recognized
under Traditional law for defeating a qualified
privilege. "Malice" embraces a far wider range
of abusive behavior. A privilege can be abused,
for example, whenever the defendant has inflicted
more harm than would appear reasonably necessary to attain the desired objective. Hence publication that is excessive amounts to abuse, and
the same is true whenever the defendant resorts
to language more abusive or more extensive than
is reasonably required in order to convey the necessary information, or where the statement is
made to the wrong person. In short, the defendant
may frequently be found to have abused his qualified privilege despite his reasonable belief in the
truth of his statement (§ 6–18).

In the light of the foregoing we can appreciate
the complexity of the picture presented by the
emergence of Constitutional protection such as is
afforded by *Gertz*. If the *Gertz* opinion should
be interpreted as a requirement that the plaintiff
who is a private person is obliged to establish defendant's negligence with respect to truth or fal-

sity as a part of his prima facie showing, this would render the status of the qualified privilege precarious to say the least. For under this view, whenever the plaintiff does succeed initially in establishing a lack of reasonable care by defendant in ascertaining the truth, he will have demonstrated by the same token that any issue of qualified privilege which may be raised thereafter would be utterly unavailing. If, on the other hand, the private individual is unable to establish even a lack of due care with respect to truth or falsity, he will find his attempt at a prima facie claim dismissed even before an issue of privilege or abuse thereof has been reached. It would appear to follow that the qualified privilege would have no meaningful role to play once there has been accepted the view that *Gertz* requires proof of negligence with respect to truth or falsity in the suit by a private individual. The Restatement of Torts Second accepts this unexpressed postulate. See Restatement, Second Torts, Special Note introducing § 593 et seq. It concedes that future decisions may lead to the conclusion that qualified privileges and their abuse have no further role to play in defamation law. But the Restatement retreats from any announcement that such is the present state of the law. Instead it concludes that the private individual, having once succeeded in establishing negligence as to truth or falsity, can defeat a claim of qualified privilege by going further and demonstrating that the defendant was a conscious liar or was indifferent to the falsity of his statement. In brief, according to the Restatement, the private individual who seeks to defeat the defendant's qualified privilege can do so if he can make the same showing with respect to truth or falsity that is required of the public official or public figure. R. § 600. On the other hand, at least one recent state court decision has recognized that a qualified privilege can be abused either by a reckless disregard of truth *or* by other circumstances which would support a conclusion of "ill tempered manner or ill will". General Motors v. Pisker (Md.1975). Although no decision supporting the Restatement's conclusion has been found up to this point, the concession it makes is difficult to refute when it is considered that proof of at least negligence with respect to truth or falsity is essential to recovery in cases where no qualified privilege whatever is asserted. Certainly the existence of a qualified privilege should not operate to the *disadvantage* of the defendant.

Is Constitutional Protection Restricted to Public Media? There is another important angle to this entire unsettled matter. It has been contended that the line of cases from *Times* to *Firestone* are intended to afford constitutional protection only to the public media. If this is correct, a statement made by one individual to another and which concerns only a private individual is a matter that remains outside the protection of the Constitution and within the full control of the States. Hence no proof of negligence as to falsity is required and the traditional system of qualified privileges and their abuse continues to prevail until voluntarily altered by state law. This position has considerable merit and it has met with approval recently in several decisions. Calero v. Del Chemical Corp. (Wis.1975); Harley Davidson v. Markley (Ore.1977); Rowe v. Metz (Colo. 1978). However, it has been rejected by the Restatement (§ 580B comment *h*), and by at least one state court. Jacron Sales Co. v. Sindorf (Md. 1975). The arguments of those opposed, briefly, center around the apparent unfairness of affording less Constitutional protection to the individual defendant than to the mass media whose wider circulation is likely to result in more serious harm and whose assets, or at least access to insurance, leave them in a superior position with reference to the absorption and distribution of the costs of defamation. In answer to this criticism it has been pointed out that the language of the First Amendment affords explicit recognition of a distinct freedom of the press. A reading of the *Gertz* opinion reveals clearly that the Court's concern was to avoid media self-censorship, not the chilling of protected speech generally. In pointing this out, one writer observed: "That preference arises not because (the media) are less culpable or less likely to cause injury, but because the media serve and personify the unique First Amendment interest in a flow of communication and debate that is 'uninhibited, robust and wide-open' " Robertson, Defamation and the First Amendment, 54 Tex.L.Rev. 199, 218 (1976). If this view comes to prevail generally, courts will be faced with the task of determining what constitutes the public media.

Two Special Qualified Privileges Affected by *Gertz.* Two qualified privileges noted heretofore (§ 6–17) are unique in that neither their existence nor their operation is affected by the defendant's ignorance or his awareness of falsity. These are the privilege of fair comment and the privilege to report official proceedings.

Fair Comment. The Traditional privilege to comment on matters of public interest was available only whenever the material stated was solely the opinion of the publisher, or, if the comment was made with respect to revealed facts, such facts were either true or were independently privileged. Such characteristics as truth or falsity (or knowledge thereof by the defendant) can have very little meaning with reference to sheer opinion. Of course one may express an opinion which he does not honestly entertain. But this could hardly be a matter of serious concern in a suit for defamation, and even if it were important, the lack of honest belief in ones own opinion could hardly be established with any satisfaction. The opinion need not even be a temperate one that a reasonable man would entertain. However, so long as expressions of opinion in the form of comment were recognized only as giving rise to a qualified privilege which was restricted to matters of public interest, Fair Comment was regarded as an affirmative defense that must be placed in issue by the defendant. But here the Court's opinion in *Gertz* has worked a basic structural change. It announced a position long advocated by several commentators: Naked opinion is not actionable as a defamation. Suit can be maintained only for statements of fact, and these must be established as such by the plaintiff. As a result it is quite immaterial whether the matter in question is, or is not, a subject of public interest. In short, the Traditional privilege of fair comment has lost its meaning and has disappeared.

Reportorial Privilege. The qualified privilege to report public proceedings, like the privilege of fair comment, does not lend itself readily to discussion in terms of truth or falsity. This privilege, as we have seen (§ 6–17) is grounded upon the law's interest in public access to official reports and records. The undertaking to make such material available to the public is encouraged through the recognition of an immunity, so long

as the report is an accurate one or, if condensed
or fragmentary, is a fair representation of what
appeared on the public record. The reporter is
not accountable for the truth or falsity of the
public matter he reports. Hence, knowledge of
falsity of what is contained in the record or innocence with respect thereto is wholly immaterial.
Fault *does* have a role to play, however, if the
report is either untrue or unfair. Inaccuracy in
transcribing the record or in condensing it or in
selecting fragments for publication are not infrequent. They can be the result of an intention
to convey an erroneous impression of the record,
of negligence resulting from undue haste or lack
of understanding, or finally, the errors may be
virtually unavoidable. In Time Inc. v. Firestone
(U.S.1976) the Supreme Court held that the litigant who is a private person can recover for harmful inaccurate reporting without the necessity of
establishing knowledge of, or indifference toward
the inaccuracy of the report. It is sufficient that
"fault" as established by state law is discoverable.
The opinion did not elaborate further, and the
nature of an acceptable standard in any detail is
yet to be evolved. Failure in some way to conform to acceptable professional standards will
probably serve as the determinant of liability.

Very recently the suggestion has been made by
the Court of Appeal for the Second Circuit that
the reportorial privilege is available for protection

of an accurate report of a serious charge against a public figure when the charge was made by a "responsible prominent organization," even though the reporter had been alerted to its falsity. Edwards v. Nat. Audubon Soc., Inc. (2d Cir. 1977). The implications such a proposition might bear for the already-precarious state of defamation law are disturbing. The matter is well discussed in 2 Utah L.Rev. 347 (1978).

Proof of Fault under the Constitutional Requirements. The *Times* requirement that the public official or public figure establish the defendant's knowledge or conscious indifference as to falsity is one that the plaintiff can meet only by proof of "convincing clarity". The determination here is one on which constitutional rights stand or fall. Hence it will be carefully scrutinized on appeal, and a jury verdict based on evidence insufficient to meet the exacting requirement will be set aside without hesitation. It might be contended by analogy that proof of negligence with respect to truth or falsity in a suit by a private individual would be subject to similar treatment since the fault requirement is again one imposed by the Constitution. Certainly there is little reason to doubt that the fault issue will be subject to constitutional review throughout the course of appeal. It does not follow, however, that negligence or such other fault as may be recognized must be proved to the same virtual certainty that is required with respect to knowledge whenever the suit is by a public official or public figure.

§ 6—21   Defamation Damages After *Gertz*

Damage at Common Law. One of the most notable elements of the *Gertz* decision is its treatment of damages. Under the rule layed down, the victim of defamation must establish that he sustained "actual injury". The full implications of this reform become apparent only when the complexities of the treatment of damages for libel and slander at common law are understood and kept in mind. The three Traditional elements, briefly, were as follows:

(1) Special Damage. This was restricted to specific economic or pecuniary losses. Special damage, when established by satisfactory proof, can always be recovered in either libel or slander. This is still true after the *Gertz* decision. It is not to be confused with "actual injury", as defined by *Gertz*. The latter includes special damages sustained, but it is not limited to pecuniary losses, as we shall see. Special damage is the only damage recoverable in suits for slander at common law, unless the defamatory words were slanderous *per se* (§ 6–3).

(2) General Damage. This is a variety of compensatory (as distinguished from punitive) damage. Unlike Special damage, General damage is not restricted to economic loss, and when avail-

able, it is compensation for the general harm
caused to the plaintiff's reputation, to which may
be added emotional distress and resulting bodily
harm. The distinguishing characteristic of General damage is that it represents compensation
for harms which are normally deemed to flow
from defamation and which therefore need not be
established by specific proof. Traditionally General damage was allowable at common law for the
publication of *any* written defamation (libel) as
well as for the utterance of any oral defamation
which was either slanderous *per se* (§ 6–3) or
where Special damage had been independently
established. It served as the mainstay for a substantial recovery in most libel claims, where specific losses of any kind were difficult or impossible
to establish through affirmative evidence. Hence
the abolition of General damage could work a
serious disservice to most defamation claimants.

(3) Punitive Damage. Damages beyond those
necessary to compensate the victim could be
awarded in a defamation proceeding at common
law solely to punish the offender for his outrageous conduct. Such Punitive damages are to be distinguished from the broad General damage, which
is regarded as wholly compensatory (although
the two may frequently be difficult to distinguish
in practice). There must be an actionable defamation supporting an award for General or Special damage before an award of Punitive damage

can be made. But compensatory damage in a trifl-
ing amount and substantial Punitive damage are
not necessarily inconsistent. It is a fair surmise
that the enormity of Punitive damage awards
against the press was an important factor im-
pelling the Supreme Court to impose First Amendment restrictions in *Sullivan* and the cases that
followed it.

**Constitutional Limitations on Recoverable Dam-
ages—"Actual Injury".** In the *Gertz* decision the
Supreme Court held that the presumption of General damage could not be tolerated under the First
Amendment. With one possible exception to be
noted hereafter, there must be proof of "actual
injury". Although this term has not yet been
specifically defined, it appears that the elements of
harm which may constitute "actual injury" are
basically the same as in General damage. No
out-of-pocket loss need be shown (although such
losses are also obviously recoverable as "actual injury"). Included are "personal humiliation, and
mental anguish and suffering". The important
restrictive requirement is that such damage must
be affirmatively established, and the inference
that harm to the reputation flows from defamatory words without need for proof no longer obtains under the Constitution. But the evidence
need not "assign any actual dollar value" to the
harm sustained. There is still need for considerable clarification. How, for instance, are "person-

al humiliation and mental anguish" to be established except as they may be expected to follow the very defamatory words that were used? Of course the plaintiff's own testimony of the severity of his suffering and the word of his family and friends concerning the visible symptoms of his concern may be available. But how does one establish that he is held in less esteem in the community? It might be ventured that the requirement of affirmative proof is imposed principally as an assist to the court as a means for directing a verdict or otherwise maintaining a controlling hand over the jury in the face of overly generous impulses.

The *Gertz* opinion leaves open several important damage questions: For example, does the requirement that damages must be proved obtain even when it is shown that there was knowing or reckless falsity on the part of the defendant? Does the difference between this attitude and mere negligent misstatement justify a difference in the treatment of presumed damage? The Restatement has felt obliged to impose a Caveat on this matter (R. § 621). A similar question arises with respect to punitive damages. The *Gertz* opinion makes clear the fact that punitive damages cannot be imposed where the only fault established is the defendant's negligence with respect to falsity. Whether or not knowing or reckless falsity is a sufficient fault to justify additional damage by way of punishment remains open. One possible solution would be to allow General damage without affirmative proof whenever knowing or reckless falsity is shown, but at the same time to refuse an allowance of punitive damage unless actual malice, such as ill will, appears from the evidence. The problem is still unsolved.

The *Gertz* Opinion and the Libel-Slander Distinction. Nothing in the *Gertz* opinion suggests that the distinction between libel and slander has been affected in any way. General nonpecuniary damage is still recoverable in libel provided that proof is made of the harm sustained. It is hardly to be expected that damages for nonpecuniary loss can now be recovered in an action for slander whenever these can be established by proof even though there is no showing that the words were slanderous *per se* or that Special damage was sustained. Nothing in the line of decisions on the Free Speech amendment would suggest that any former impediment to recover in defamation has since been obviated.

§ 6—22   Proof of Falsity—Recent Developments

Although falsity has always been referred to as an essential element of the law of defamation, we have seen that it was not necessary at common law that the plaintiff establish by proof that the statement was false (§ 6–14). Once the utterance was regarded as defamatory, its falsity was

[*214*]

presumed. If the statement was true, this must be set up as an affirmative defense. There is no express observation in *Gertz* to the effect that the traditional presumption of falsity no longer obtains. However, the requirement that the public official or public figure must establish the defendant's knowledge of falsity or his indifference thereto necessarily implies that falsity in fact must be shown by these claimants. The same conclusion appears inescapable with reference to suit by a private person who is now obliged to show negligence with respect to the falsity of the statement. However, we cannot overlook the fact that no express requirement on proof of falsity appears in *Gertz*. The obvious administrative advantage of assigning the burden of proof to the defendant who is in a superior position to proceed with the evidence could arguably induce the Court to leave the burden of establishing truth as it was at common law except in those situations where fault and falsity are inseparable.

PART IV

THE TRADE RELATIONSHIP

CHAPTER 7

PHYSICAL AND APPROPRIATIONAL HARMS

§ 7—1 Dimensions of the Problem

The Nature of the Trade Relation. The interest in acquiring and maintaining satisfactory trade relations is basic in even the most rudimentary society whose material needs must be satisfied through barter, lending, selling, buying, hiring and the like; and law has been pressed from the beginning with demands for the protection of the processes and benefits of trading. Most people live by their enterprise, and the protection afforded by law to even their physical person and property reflects government concern for their trade relations. To illustrate: When a wrongdoer destroys or injures the goods of another he impairs the other's advantage in the market place. Hence damages to property represent the loss of this market value. Similarly, the reparation afforded by law for the wrongful destruction of an enterprise, such as a factory, includes restoring the profits that otherwise would have accrued from sales of the establishment's product. The same is true when a person sustains a bodily injury that deprives him of anticipated wages—the trade value of his labor. In all such situations protection of the trade relation is afforded through the assessment of damages as one element of loss for tortious conduct that invades other interests with which we are familiar. But the bare interest in access to trade itself has been the beneficiary of some measure of direct legal attention from the beginning, and with the increase in complexity of modern trade and the devising of infinitely more subtle means to injure it there has evolved a considerable body of law dedicated exclusively to the protection of the trade relation alone.

Difficulties of Compact Treatment. The undertaking to compress the law's struggle with the trade relation within the confines of a "nutshell" is difficult. This must be attributed in large part to the fact that the problem of trade competition has assumed such dimensions that the judicial process of the common law, imbued with nineteenth century individualism, has proved to be unable to cope unassisted with the complexities of the market place. Elaborate doctrinal innovations have been devised by the courts in an effort to work out some acceptable abstract standard for competitive behavior against which the defend-

[*217*]

ant's conduct might be measured. There is frequent talk in the opinions of "unfair competition", "unlawful act", "malice", "disinterested malevolence", "free ride" and "prima facie tort", most of which terms have proved to be of only limited help. Instead of explaining, they themselves have required explanation. One notable byproduct of the incapacity of common law doctrine to meet the need has been a proliferation of statutes dealing with all aspects of competition. Trademarks, copyrights, patents, pricing and advertising practices, combinations in restraint of trade, and monopolies—all these and many more aspects of competitive behavior have fallen under the aegis of special legislation which has been extended far beyond the possibilities of naked common law. The administration of many of these complicated measures has demanded a watchful eye, a strict reporting system and an expertise beyond that which could be supplied by the courts alone. As a result, much of the regulation of competition has passed into the hands of specialized commissions created for the purpose. Hence it can be readily seen that the subject flies apart and does not lend itself well to a single compact treatment. Much common law thread still interlaces the fabric, but the statutory overlay makes cohesive treatment difficult.

With these considerations in mind it becomes obvious that sharp limitations must be imposed on the proportions of the treatment we can afford here. Professor Kionka has pointed out that the purpose of the Nutshell series is primarily to afford an overview—the "big picture" as he calls it. Torts in a Nutshell—Injuries to Persons and Property, *VII* (1977). In a volume of this kind we can only undertake to gain a perspective of trade regulation as an aspect of the broader domain of tort: How does treatment of the trade relation compare with the treatment accorded other relations we have seen? What networks of tort theory with which we have already become familiar have a significant role to play in the setting of competition? What doctrinal accretions have developed to assist in the solution? What novel concepts have emerged, and to what extent have they succeeded? Was the break down of the common law complete, or did it survive as a material adjunct to the later statutory innovations? Perhaps the outer limits of our present venture come into view as we approach the boundary between statute and common law. We cannot profitably go much further in these pages. The coverage afforded here is approximately only that of most first year torts casebooks. The full range of competitive practices as they are regulated under our modern statutory framework will be the subject of a forthcoming Nutshell by Professor Charles McManus, and the highly specialized problems of copyright and the protection of intellectual property will require still a further Nutshell, which is now on the drawing board.

The Structure of the Tort. All those characteristics of the relational interest with which we have already become familiar reappear in the setting of the trade relationship. We find the same rudimentary three-party structure: The plaintiff, who enjoys the prospect of a profitable trade advantage with another (or others) finds his expectancy frustrated through the tortious conduct of the defendant. The latter is usually a competitor of the plaintiff, who hopes to turn the plaintiff's prospect to his own advantage. The expectancy interfered with may take the form of a single existing contract whose breach is brought about through the defendant's machinations, or it may be a more generalized and remote expectancy of an indefinite number of deals with potential customers. The possible gradations in terms of the immediacy of the anticipated benefit are considerable. Similarly, the means adopted by the defendant to interfere with the relationship may vary greatly and may lead to the infliction of any of the three kinds of harm we have already seen— physical, appropriational or defamatory (§ 1–2).

§ 7—2 Physical Harms to the Trade Relation

Actionable harms to the trade relation which are the result of physical injuries inflicted upon the person or property of the tradesman are commonplace. So long as there can be discovered some independent actionable wrong toward the plaintiff he is entitled to recover damages representing a loss of profits or other economic expectancy which he suffered thereby. This holds true even though no injury to his trade was anticipated by the defendant. However, where invasion of the trade relation is the only injurious conduct that can be discovered, the situation is more complex even though the defendant's behavior was unlawful and may have amounted to an actionable tort of a familiar kind committed upon the person or property of some third party.

Interferences With The Customer's Person. A tradesman whose best customer was assaulted and killed by defendant would have little chance to recover the benefits he otherwise would have enjoyed from trade transactions with the deceased. If, however, the assailant were aware of an impending transaction with the plaintiff, and furthermore the assault on the prospective customer was made primarily for the purpose of frustrating the deal, the tradesman may have a right of recovery for his loss. Physical misbehavior engaged in with the object of working an injury on the trade relationship itself has long been regarded as an actionable tort, R. § 766B. The molesting of third parties in order to injure the plaintiff's business or to turn it to the defendant's own advantage may take the form of an actionable assault or imprisonment with respect to the injured customer or other third person, or it may amount only to an annoyance, harassment or abuse which alone would be beneath the law's notice. In either event it may amount to an actionable wrong when the plaintiff's trade is deliberately injured thereby.

Interference With Access To Customers. Similarly, liability may follow when the defendant erects a structure on his own land for the purpose of impairing the public's view of a tradesman's sign from a travelled public street, or where he deliberately misdirects the plaintiff's potential customers to his own place of business or he barricades an access route to his competitor's establishment in order to cut him off from trade. Although the decisions are not harmonious, there is also authority to the effect that picketing a competitor's place of business may be actionable. Such obstructive conduct overreaches the stage of mere persuasion or resort to reason. People confronted with an appeal by picketing (frequently carried out through large numbers) often feel embarrassed or intimidated as they approach the plaintiff's establishment and are not free to proceed as their purchasing instinct dictates. Even though the object of picketing may be to force conformity with some commendable trade practice favored by a majority, coercion through picketing is arguably a doubtful means of accomplishing the purpose (§ 7–11, infra).

Interference With Property. A recovery in trespass or case for appropriating, damaging or otherwise molesting personal property in the possession of the plaintiff will likely include an award of damages representing loss of the sale value of the property or the trade use to which it might have been put. But even where the required "property" interest of plaintiff is lacking, deliberate intermeddling with chattels in such way as to impair a trade relation may be actionable. For example, to secretly loosen the nails in the shoes of horses shod by plaintiff and thus discredit his skill as a blacksmith may make the defendant liable for any loss of custom occasioned thereby. Similarly, recovery has been allowed where the defendant, a tire manufacturer, furtively substituted his own tires in place of those manufactured by the plaintiff, his competitor, on a vehicle exhibited at a trade fair.

Entering on land may similarly entail liability even when the injured plaintiff lacks any property interest. The solicitation of taxi passengers on a station platform open to the public may give rise to a cause of action in favor of a competitor who enjoys an exclusive license from the railway, where the defendant knows of the arrangement. At times a delicate problem with respect to the protection of a trade interest may be disguised as what appears to be a simple issue of damages for trespass on land. As an illustration, suppose

that plaintiff is owner of a tract of land whose
market value has been greatly enhanced by reason of a speculation concerning the possible presence of petroleum in the general vicinity. The defendant, an oil prospector, now conducts an exploration upon his own adjacent land. The result,
unhappily, is a negative finding which, when it
becomes known, serves to deflate the value of all
neighboring property, including plaintiff's.   At
this juncture we may pause to note that plaintiff's
speculative trade value of his land is not entitled
to protection against any truthful revelation
brought about by reason of defendant's honest efforts in his own behalf. But suppose that during
the conduct of his tests the defendant trespassed
on the plaintiff's land and established one or more
testing points there. Suppose further that the information thus gained through the unlawful entry
made possible or more certain a conclusion that
there were no minerals. The difficult problem
posed by these facts might be stated thus: Is
plaintiff's access to a speculative market for his
land entitled to protection against defendant's
truthful exposure of the unsoundness of the speculation if it should turn out that the information
upon which the exposure rested was gained or
verified by defendant through unlawful trespas-
sory conduct? The conflicts of policy involved
here will only be obscured if the question is in-
genuously posed merely as an inquiry as to wheth-

er the damages were "proximately" caused by the trespass. But, however the problem may be framed, the courts have not been uniform in their conclusions. The entry by defendant may be deliberate and furtive; it may be a good faith entry made under a negligent mistake as to the title; or it may be an entirely unavoidable trespass. Furthermore, the information gained through the trespass may have been absolutely essential to the conclusion reached, or its role in the complicated testing procedure may have been trivial or merely confirmatory. Should these matters make a difference as to the outcome? Malone, Ruminations on a New Tort, 4 La.L.Rev. 309 (1942).

Nuisance as Trade Injury. The maintenance of a public nuisance, such as an obstruction of a highway or interference with the beneficial use of a public place is not actionable on behalf of a private individual unless such individual can show that he sustained a special harm different in kind from that suffered by the public generally. An appreciable injury to one's trade is commonly regarded as supplying the necessary element of special loss. Commercial fisheries may recover for the wrongful pollution of a public body of water, although one not engaged in fishing for a livelihood may have no redress when denied his sporting pleasure by reason of pollution. Recoveries by tradesmen for interferences with the public way are not infrequent. A taxi driver who was unable to fulfill a contract to carry passengers due to the defendant's obstruction of the public way was entitled to recover the resultant loss of business, although other members of the public may be obliged to suffer considerable inconvenience without remedy.

A difficult situation arises when a tradesman finds that access to his place of business is obstructed by queues or other large gatherings of people in the public street who are attracted there by some business activity conducted by his neighbor. If the latter's conduct is highly extraordinary and calculated to invite unnecessary congestion or to incite noise or misbehavior, injunctive relief against the nuisance thus created may be available, and damages are not infrequent. If, however, the defendant has done nothing to attract crowds other than to conduct his business with such success that the public is regularly present in the adjacent street in large numbers, the neighboring tradesman may be obliged to tolerate the inconvenience. The availability of some practical means of adjustment that will allow each tradesman to enjoy a maximum benefit from the public way while working only a minimum interference with the other's needs often determines the outcome. The needs of a sensitive trade operation may exceed what can be afforded by way of legal protection. Such was the situation presented when the operator of an outdoor drive-in motion picture establishment complained of interference with his business by his neighbor who operated a dog track next door and employed brilliant klieg lights for illumination. See generally R. § 766B.

Negligence. Harm to a trade relation that results from negligence alone is not actionable unless it is accompanied by some injury to the person or property of the plaintiff. The operator of a truck whose negligent driving knocks down a power line may be liable to the power company not for only the cost of replacing the pole but as well for the loss of revenue sustained due to its inability to deliver power to its customers. Its trade loss flowed from an actionable injury to its property and which had the effect of denying it the value of its use. The same customers, however, who sustained losses in their trade because their source of power was cut off would be denied recovery for the same negligent misbehavior. The only rational explanation of this denial is a fear that the extensive range of damage to which the defendant could be exposed would be too costly to be borne by a wrongdoer who is chargeable with negligence only. The plaintiff's chance of recovery is not assisted by the fact that the injured trade interest was an existing contract benefit rather than a bare trade expectancy. As Justice Holmes observed, "The law does not spread its protection so far." R. § 766C.

If, however, the harm suffered is to the person or property of the plaintiff, the fact that the harm resulted from a deprivation of a benefit or protection supplied by some third person under contract, does not prevent a recovery against the defendant whose negligence impaired the physical capacity of the third party to supply the benefit or protection as promised. Thus, if my factory were in flames and the supply of water from a utility were denied me when the defendant negligently caused a water main to be severed, recovery may be forthcoming if causation and other elements of liability can be established.

§ 7—3 Misrepresentation and the Trade Relation—Introduction

In our consideration of the various harms to which relational interests may be subjected we have already observed several situations within the family relationship in which a defendant's resort to falsehood and misstatement has served to deprive a family member of some gift or other expectancy he otherwise would have enjoyed (§ 4–6). Similarly we have encountered other situations in which a calculated deception has lured some credulous person into a highly undesirable marriage (§ 4–5). But when we turned thereafter to the harms that may be inflicted on the social relationship we discovered that injurious falsehoods in this area have gone unnoticed by law except where they have taken the form of defamations injurious to the plaintiff's reputation.

Deceitful practices are obviously intolerable in the world of commerce and trade, for here the success of any venture rests largely on the dependability of promises and representations made by others. The law's effort to protect against deception has resulted in the development of an elaborate body of doctrines and formulas which make up the law of fraud and deceit. These received their formative development as an outgrowth of the struggle of the courts to fix the boundaries of legally acceptable behavior which must obtain between the parties themselves at the bargaining table. This should be borne in mind when later we attempt to fit these same rules into the three-party setting of a relational injury. So long as the parties themselves serve as the sole actors in the transactional drama, law recognizes that they should be left free to fix the bargaining climate within which they elect to deal with each other; and it is only with due deference to this climate that their rights should be judged. In some areas of commercial dealing custom has permitted a relatively free range of representations, puffing of wares, and the like. When this is the setting, each party has been expected to form his own unfettered judgment and to look upon the representations of his adversary with a skeptical eye. But in other types of transactions an entirely different

range of expectations may prevail. The subject
matter of the deal may be a specialty which requires considerable expertise if the judgment ex-
ercized by the parties is to be intelligent. Here
an uninitiated party may feel entirely justified in
letting down his guard and may entrust himself to
the acknowledged superior judgment of his adversary. When this is the case much more in the way
of honesty and accuracy is to be expected of the
latter. Between these extremes there exist marked differences with respect to the extent of the confidence or the distrust that may obtain between
the parties to the varied types of transactions
with which law must deal. In order to meet these
diverse needs of the commercial world with respect to honesty courts have evolved a body of
tractable doctrines which lend themselves readily
to the juridical maneuvering which is essential in
any effort to cope with the multiple needs of commerce.

Fraud and Deceit. The law of fraud and deceit
can be considered in outline as embracing four
components. First to be considered is the required mental state of the defendant. Fraud is characterized as an intentional tort. Prosser has pointed out that the intent which underlies misrepresentation is a more complex matter than the relatively simple intention discoverable in the case of
assault and battery. The intent to deceive, which
has been given the name *scienter*, has at least

two aspects which must be treated separately. The first deals with the awareness of the defendant that he is making a statement which is false; and the other deals with his desire to influence the particular person who claims to be deceived. Second, assuming that the requisite *scienter* is present, there arises the question as to whether the plaintiff did in fact rely on the misstatement to his detriment. Third, did the victim who acted upon the misstatement forfeit his right of recovery through his own behavior? Finally, was a loss incurred, and if so, what did it amount to?

Erroneous Information Supplied By Third Parties. The issues mentioned above supply only the bare framework, which has been fleshed out with an elaborate arsenal of doctrines and rules. We must confine our present consideration of these within the limits of their effective use in a relational interest setting. This setting, we know, is an arrangement wherein the defendant is an outsider whose misleading conduct has served to affect adversely a trade relationship existing or in prospect between the plaintiff who claims to have been deceived and another person or persons. It is this deceptive practice by the defendant, a stranger to the negotiations, rather than the behavior of the other party to the transaction, that merits our present attention. We shall be dealing primarily with the alleged misconduct of professionals. Typical is the scene in which one or both the negotiating parties requires specialized information which must be supplied by some third person or agency. The needed information may be statistics concerning the ability or creditworthiness of the other party. This will likely be supplied by one who is a professional accountant or credit agency. Or the needed information may relate to the state of the market within which the proposed deal falls. Hence the services of a trustworthy broker or consultant may be required. Again, there may be a need for specialized information concerning the legal prospects of the deal; or professional skill may be required in the execution of some proposed transaction. All these call into play the talent and skill of the lawyer, tax expert or title abstractor. If the subject matter is highly technical there will be required the services of engineers or other specialists, and so on. Even if there is no pressing demand for the personal services of some third person, there may be a need to resort to specialized literature which, if it is inaccurate, can bring one or both parties to grief. Under what circumstances should the counselor, author or publisher be held to account for a transactional loss incurred as a result of misreliance by one of the parties on information supplied by some technical consultant or which appeared in a book or periodical?

It is clear that professional consultants and writers would be driven out of business quickly if they were made answerable in damages for every erroneous statement of theirs upon which someone chose to rely and who sustained a loss by so doing. Such limitations on liability as courts have felt obliged to impose fall into one of two orders: The first relates to the ethical behavior of the supplier of information. What can properly be demanded of him in terms of honesty, skill or attentiveness? Are his mistakes to be ignored by law so long as they are not deliberate nor made with reckless disregard of their falsity? Or, to the contrary, is the person who chooses to traffic in information for the guidance of others to be held for his carelessness just as physicians, storekeepers and truck drivers are held for theirs? We shall examine this hereafter. Second, assuming that the supplier's behavior is such that he should be held liable, who is entitled to recover? Consider the variety of the persons who may choose to rely upon a given misstatement. The range of such confiders may include the trusting client who paid for the information and upon whose request it was prepared, and may extend finally to the eavesdropper who learns and acts upon that which was never intended for his ear. Between these extremes the variations are profuse. These two aspects of the problem—the character of the defendant's behavior and the fixing of the class of persons whose reliance is protected by law—are not independent of each other. The farther the informant's conduct departs from a standard of meticulous care and complete trustworthiness and moves toward callous deceit the broader and more inclusive becomes the range of persons who may be entitled to hold him responsible at law for their misreliance on his statements.

Who is Entitled to Recover?—Negligent Misrepresentations. The landmark case, Ultramares Corporation v. Touche (N.Y.1931) serves to illustrate the contours of the problem under discussion, and the opinion of Cardozo, J., addresses the principal factors that must be borne in mind in seeking a solution: Defendant, Touche Niven & Company, a firm of public accountants, was employed by Stern, a rubber importer, to prepare an annual balance sheet in thirty-two certified copies, which the accountant knew would be shown to various creditors, stockholders and the like of the employer, according to its needs. The defendant's certificate was to the effect, first, that the firm had examined the accounts and that the balance sheet was in accord therewith, and second, that the sheet presented a true and correct picture of the resources of the business of the company. In fact there was no accurate correspondence between balance sheet and accounts. The general ledger had not been posted for nine months, and while this task was under way at the hands of the defendant several fictitious entries were surreptitiously made by Stern's employee. Furthermore there were numerous other suspicious circumstances. As a result the balance sheet showed the capital and surplus as intact when in reality both had been wiped out. On the faith of the certificate, plaintiff, a factor who had had no previous dealings of any consequence with Stern, made to the latter a series of sizable loans, which were unpaid when Stern passed into bankruptcy. The present suit was instituted, initially, on a theory of negligence. The New York Court of Appeal concluded that although the evidence supported a finding that the audit was negligently made, nevertheless recovery could not be sustained on that basis because the plaintiff was not a member of the class of persons to whom the defendant owed a duty of reasonable care. The opinion conceded that reliance upon the defendant's report by some future lender of funds, such as plaintiff, was readily foreseeable, and if the harm sustained as a consequence had been an injury inflicted upon the plaintiff's person or property, recovery against the careless defendant would have been forthcoming under familiar negligence principles. But where, as under the facts shown, the harm was a transactional loss sustained by the trusting plaintiff and affecting solely a trade expectancy, something more than negligence must be established if recovery is to be allowed. Here again, as in the preceding section, we find that the trade relation is denied protection against negligent misconduct of third persons.

The practical considerations which prompt a denial of recovery are well explained in the opinion of Cardozo, J.:

> If liability for negligence exists, a thoughtless slip or blunder, the failure to detect a theft or forgery beneath the covers of deceptive entries, may expose accountants to a liability in an indeterminate amount for an indeterminate time and to an indeterminate class. The hazards of a business conducted on these terms are so extreme as to enkindle doubt whether a flaw may not exist in the implication of a duty that exposes to these consequences.

The difficult problem is where the line of exclusion in negligence cases should be drawn if it is to fall short of those persons whom reasonable foresight would suggest as likely to rely on the defendant's misstatement. It has been only within the past twenty years that the English courts have recognized any cause of action whatever in favor of third parties for negligent misrepresentation. Who is to recover? Certainly the person who requested the information and paid for it is entitled to assume that reasonable care would be exercised in supplying it. In this country, even though the recipient is not the one who solicited the service and paid for it he may still be protected against negligence if the service was rendered with the understanding that the information was supplied for his use in a transaction known to the supplier. Whether the information was supplied directly to such person or was furnished to the supplier's employer, who, to the knowledge of the defendant, procured it for the purpose of forwarding it to the plaintiff is immaterial. Nor is it fatal to the plaintiff's claim that he was not designated by name as the intended user or that he was merely an unidentified member of a relatively small class of persons who, to the defendant's knowledge, would use the information for a specific purpose for which the defendant supplied it, as distinguished from the much larger and more disparate class whom the defendant could have contemplated might at some time have access to the information and rely upon it in some indeterminate transaction. It is not enough, as the Restatement observes [R. § 552(2) Comment *h*] "that the maker knows of the ever-present possibility of action in reliance upon it, on the part of anyone to whom it may be repeated." Yet it must be conceded that the two classes of victims cannot readily be distinguished from each other. Consider the *Ultramares* situation just discussed: If Stern had advised defendant that he wanted a balance sheet in the standard form in order to attempt to negotiate a loan with Ultramares, a recovery based upon negligence alone would apparently have been forthcoming. The same might well be true if the defendant was advised that

Stern needed the balance sheet in an effort to secure the loan of a substantial sum of money from
whomever he could interest, and the defendant
had prepared it for that express purpose. The
salient point of distinction appears to lie in the
wide variety of appropriate purposes to which the
balance sheet could be devoted under the facts
presented in *Ultramares* without the employer's
having specified any particular transaction for
which it would be made (even though many uses
were foreseeable). A more explicit delineation of
the purpose in prospect would possibly afford the
defendant some indication of the amount of money
that expectably would be hazarded in reliance on
his report, together with a beforehand view of
the exactness of the need he must meet. This, in
turn, might well be determinative as to the extent
of detailed attention that would be required of
him and the price that he must exact for his services.

The instances in which there has been a denial
of liability for some not unforeseeable transactional loss where the negligent defendant had no
special reason to expect that the plaintiff would
rely on his statement are legion and varied: A
letter of credit addressed to one person but read
by another; erroneous information conveyed by
a stock ticker service that prompted plaintiff to
invest; a negligently prepared abstract of title
relied upon by a purchaser in a later transaction

affecting the land; an error by a surveyor, or by a telegraph company in the transmission of a message causing a transactional loss to someone other than the sender or receiver.

Who is Entitled to Recover?—Deceit and Negligence Compared. It must be noted further that where only negligence can be established the plaintiff must be able to show that the transaction through which he sustained loss was the same or substantially the same transaction for which the information was supplied. It is at this point that negligent misrepresentation must be distinguished from intentional misrepresentation, or deceit, as it is called. The ambit of recovery for the latter tort is broader. Liability for deceit extends to "any of the class of persons which the defendant intends or should expect to act in reliance on it, and to losses suffered by them in any of the general type of transactions in which he intends or should expect their conduct to be influenced" (R. § 552, Comment *i*). Perhaps the difference in the reach of the two torts is only a reflection of the closer specification of conformity between statement and reliance required in negligent misrepresentation as compared with deceit. Yet, even if it is a difference in degree rather than kind, it cannot be ignored. Returning again to *Ultramares* as an illustration, we find that the New York Court of Appeal, after denying recovery on a basis of negligence for the misreliance by the

lender, Ultramares, then continued by remanding
the controversy to the trial court with an announcement that the facts would justify a finding
of deceit on the part of defendant. He had falsely
stated in the certificate that the balance sheet
was in accord with the accounts of Stern's company, when, in fact, there was no such accord.
By reason of this misrepresentation a recovery
could be allowed the lender, Ultramares, because
he was a person engaged in a type of transaction
in which the defendant contemplated there would
be an inducement to act on his (defendant's) representation.   The fact that the specific loan by
Ultramares was not the immediate transaction in
prospect when the certificate was made does not
preclude liability when based upon a deceit.   It is
to be noted, however, by way of caution that even
a finding of deceit does not serve to justify a recovery by everyone whose reliance on the defendant's misstatement was reasonably foreseeable.
The plaintiff must be a person who chose to rely
in the course of one of the types of transactions
which defendant intended or had reason to expect
his conduct to be an influence.   R. § 531.

Intent to Deceive.   Once it has been noted that
a deceit can result in liability toward a wider
range of claimants than could be recognized under negligence doctrine, it becomes pertinent to
inquire, how does deceit differ from negligence?
They are distinguished chiefly with reference to

the mental ingredient involved: Deceit is an intentional tort, requiring *scienter*. This does not mean that the defendant acted from any unworthy motive, but simply that he was conscious that he was making a misstatement. This presents no problem where the defendant had no honest belief in the truth of his statement (although he may not have been positively aware of its falsity) or where he was recklessly indifferent as to its truthfulness. R. § 526(a)(b). But from this point on the shadings become more difficult. Where the misstatement is as to a positive fact which is entirely susceptible of knowledge, and the defendant states that the fact exists, when in fact it does not, can we conclude that he has stated a matter as of his own knowledge when in fact it was not of his own knowledge, and hence he has told a knowing lie? See R. § 526(c). If intentional deception can be thus defined, the determinative inquiries are only two: First, is the matter stated susceptible of accurate knowledge? And, second, was the defendant reasonably to be understood as affirming the matter as of his own knowledge (as distinguished from a venturing of the matter as something defendant hoped or believed was true)? Once it is conceded that the requirement of intention or *scienter* with reference to knowable facts can be satisfied in this way there remains little, if any, distinction between intentional falsehood and negligent misrepresentation in this area. This suggests that the exact character of the information conveyed by the defendant will be an important factor in determining whether *scienter* has been proved. For example, the blunt certification of the accountant in *Ultramares* that there was a conformity between the balance sheet and Stern's accounts was one susceptible of exact knowledge, and its unqualified affirmation by defendant when in fact it was untrue was sufficient to justify a finding of deceit and a consequent recognition of a wider range of persons whose misreliance could be protected. By contrast, the second statement in the certificate relied on in *Ultramares*, to the effect that the balance sheet presented a true and correct picture of the business of Stern's company is one that should be understood as expressing only the professional conclusion of the accountant arrived at after a consideration of pertinent data according to acceptable practices. This must be treated as a negligently made misstatement and the ambit of liability must be restricted accordingly.

Statements Required by Statute. Frequently statutes require that certain specific information be certified by designated public officers, such as recording clerks or public inspectors. When such is the case the question as to which misinformed persons or classes of persons may recover is answered by determining the class of persons and the type of transactions whose protection was contemplated by the statute, rather than by reference to the intention of the person supplying the information. Of particular interest here are the provisions of the Federal Securities Act of 1933, which imposes civil liability upon a wide range of persons (including accountants, engineers and appraisers) engaged in the preparation of registration statements required prior to the issuance of securities. The liability is absolute, except as the issuer "can sustain the burden of proof that he did not know, and in the exercise of reasonable care could not have known of (the) untruth   . ." (15 U.S.C. Sec. 77k). However the right to proceed under this Act against those who participated in the issuance is limited to those who were initial purchasers from the issuer. Another regulatory statute affecting securities (Securities Exchange Act of 1934 § 10b and regulations thereunder) does afford protection to later purchasers who were not in privity. This measure, however, has been interpreted to cover only intentional misconduct. Ernst & Ernst v. Hochfelder (U.S.1976).

Note of Caution. Only a moment's reflection is required to realize that our treatment has been confined to only a fragment of the law of misrepresentation. We have restricted our attention to those relational interest situations where misleading information was furnished by a third party to persons who contemplated entering into some transactional arrangement with each other. Misrepresentation, as it appears in the relational interest framework shares all the characteristics present in situations where the misrepresentation obtains between the contracting parties themselves. All the usual requirements for recovery must be shown. These include the requirement that the plaintiff must have relied on the misstatement and that this reliance played a substantial part in prompting him to enter into the transaction. He must establish further that the loss of which he complained flowed from his misreliance and that he did not conduct himself in such manner as to disqualify him from recovering. See generally R. §§ 525–552C.

§ 7—4   Confusion of Source

Misrepresentation Through Passing Off Goods as Those of Another. A common means of injuring the trade relation through misrepresentation is the not unfamiliar practice of Passing Off. Here the producer or dealer falsely induces a potential customer or customers to believe that the goods or services he offers are those of his competitor. By resort to this device he manages to take a free ride on the good will or trade expectancy of the latter. In such situations the direct victim of the deceit is of course the customer who is induced by the misrepresentation to accept goods other than those he expected, and for this deception he may be entitled to maintain his own action in deceit for rescission or damages. However, due to the triviality of the amount customarily involved this is done only occasionally. The principal loser is more likely to be the competitor whose goods or services were simulated. He is harmed in several respects: First, he loses a sale to the defendant each time the latter's deceit lures away one of his potential customers. His good will is thus appropriated by the defendant. Second, if the goods or services happen to be inferior to those the purchaser expected to receive from the plaintiff, the reputation of the latter will suffer, and the benefit of future patronage may be denied him. Finally, apart from loss of sales or harm from defamation, the value of the tradesman's distinctive symbol may be cheapened through overfamiliarity, and offences against good taste may be chargeable to the defendant's indiscriminate use— all of which can prove to be highly detrimental to the plaintiff's standing in the trade.

Decline of Reliance on Traditional Tort Law. Protection against simulation of trade symbols is of long standing. From its origin in the practices and regulations of the trade guilds it found its way into the common law during the 17th Century. Protection was afforded through a network of rules and doctrines known as "passing off." In view of the fact that the plaintiff's chief aim in instituting suit has been to bring his competitor's practice to a halt, the body of passing off law received its development largely through courts of

chancery. Statutes regulating trade marks were
regarded at first chiefly as supplements to the
common law. As such they served to enlarge the
remedies available and they made for uniformity.
However, the need for protection became increasingly acute as possible geographical areas for
competition expanded and advertising and other
marketing devices became increasingly sophisti-
cated. The result has been a decline in the influence of common law precepts and an increasing
reliance on legislation, until today virtually every
problem in the field of passing off centers around
an interpretation of the federal trade mark statute
(known as the Lanham Act), the Federal Trade
Commission Act and other regulatory measures.
As this has occurred, familiar common law doctrines have become mere importees within a legislative setting and hence must be interpreted and
developed with due regard to the statutory framework in which they are found. For this reason
the subject of passing off demands a more
elaborate discussion than is possible here, and even
a compact treatment must be entrusted to a forthcoming volume of this series devoted to Trade
Practices. In passing, however, we may indicate
a few of the highlights and may touch on some of
the policies that underlie the law.

The Highlights of Passing Off. Passing off is a
misrepresentation to the buying public that it is
securing the goods or services of the plaintiff

when in fact they are those of the defendant. This is usually achieved by means of copying the plaintiff's name or other trade designation, by imitating the shape or packaging of his goods or simulating the distinctive appearance of his place of business or even the vehicles used by him in supplying services. In making the appropriation the defendant is usually aware of the likelihood of deception, and frequently this is the sole purpose behind his conduct.

Trademark. The devices most frequently abused and misappropriated through passing off are the trademark and the trade name. The trademark is a designation that enjoys many attributes of property. It belongs to the tradesman, and it is protected as something owned by him. It assumes its role as trademark as soon as it is adopted and used to identify goods from a particular source, even though that source may be anonymous. Thereafter, the use of any confusingly similar mark by a competitor constitutes an infringement even though the plaintiff's mark has not become known and no confusion in fact can be established. Since the protection of the trademark symbol serves arbitrarily to exclude from general use the word or combination of words in question there arises the unhappy prospect that other tradesmen will thereby be denied the use of a trademarked word necessary for the effective description and marketing of their own wares.

This danger of a monopoly on the vocabulary by prior use is minimized at law by requirements limiting the words or designations whose employment as a trademark is allowable. Frequently a purely fanciful mark or logo is used. Excluded are common or generic names for the goods. Neither can the trademark consist in a designation of the geographical origin of the goods or the personal name of the maker. Nor can it serve to describe the goods or their qualities or their function. Much of the law of trademarks has centered around the question as to whether a given term can be properly regarded as a trademark. It should also be noted that competitors are free to use any trademark term so long as they do not employ it as a means of designating the origin of their own wares.

Trade Name. It does not follow from the preceding observation that terms which are descriptive of the origin or the qualities of the product are open game for imitators. Although such items cannot be accorded the same arbitrary protection as technical trademarks, they may, nevertheless, enjoy a limited protection as trade names. Unlike the trademark, which is entitled to protection immediately upon its adoption and use, the designation of a term as a trade name must be earned through actual user over a considerable period of time. The descriptive term must acquire a "secondary meaning." That is to say, through its constant use by the plaintiff in association with the marketing of his goods or services the word or term no longer serves solely to describe some characteristic or quality of the goods or service, but has now come to be commonly understood by the public as indicating also their origin in some single source.   After repeatedly seeing the term Buttercrust as a label on bread, for example, the buying public no longer regards it merely as a description of some characteristic or quality of the bread.   It comes likewise to think of the expression as an indication that the loaf came from the same source as other loaves which it had purchased with satisfaction in the past.   This remains true even though the source is anonymous and the buyer does not know who is the maker.   It is enough that a purchaser's inclination to select this loaf has been incited by his desire to return to the same familiar source as before.   A buying habit that benefits the plaintiff is shown to have been established and this will be accorded at least a limited protection.

It must be noted that by acquiring a secondary meaning a descriptive term does not cease to be descriptive, and there remains the same need as before to accord competitors the continued use of the word in question to describe their goods or to indicate where and by whom they were made. For this reason the principal objective of the administration of the law of trade names is to recon-

cile the need of the trade name holder that he
be as free as possible from deceptive imitation, on
the one hand, and the need of other tradesmen for
as free a range of language as possible in acquaint-
ing customers with the qualities of their products,
on the other. To this end the qualified injunction
of a court of equity is an invaluable instrument.
The qualifying feature of the decree may relate to
the geographic limits within which relief may
prove effective; or provision may be made for specific uses of the name which are forbidden or are
expressly permitted. The alleged infringer may
be required to include in his label or advertising
an explanation distinguishing his product from
that of the complainant or by clarifying certain
features which might otherwise be confusing.
Again, a change in the style of lettering or its position on the label or package may afford some
protection to the plaintiff and still allow some opportunity for the competitor to get his message
across to the public.

It is noteworthy that a term which was originally appropriate for use as a trademark on some
unique or patented article may with the passage
of time lose its once arbitrary character and become a generic name designating the kind of product to which it refers. At this point the symbol
which once served as a trademark must be demot-
ed to trade name status and as such can command
only a qualified protection. (i. e. Aspirin, coined

originally as a term indicating the maker, Bayer Company, has now become the common name for a specific pain reliever. What customer would ask for it by the technical name, acetyl salicylic acid)?

Although the trademark need no longer be attached to the goods or package, yet it can be used only as a symbol which appears at least on displays physically associated with the goods themselves. The trade name, on the other hand, can be employed in an unlimited variety of ways to indicate the source of either goods or services or to identify a business establishment or accessories.

The trademark's validity does not depend upon its appearance in any official register. Federal registration under the Lanham Act, however, confers a number of important procedural advantages, such as assured access to the federal courts. It affords prima facie evidence of the validity of the registration and of the registrant's exclusive right to the use of the mark. Another prominent advantage of registration is that it serves as notice of the registrant's claim of ownership in geographical areas outside his own neighboring territory. A proceeding can be brought by a competitor for the cancellation of an unqualified trademark.

Imitation of Shape or Color of Article or Container. The use of a trademark or trade name

may not afford sufficient protection against passing off in certain markets where instant recognition or recognition at a distance is essential if the
product is to be effectively distinguished from ·
that of competitors. Illustrative of such markets
are the newsstand where mints or gum are displayed for instant purchase and the taxi stand on
a crowded thoroughfare where the chosen cab
must be selected from a distance. As a result, confusion of purchasers as to the source of a product
may be brought about solely by imitating the
shape or color of the product itself or the package in which it is marketed. Such protection as
can be afforded against the simulation of product
appearance follows the same general line of attack
as with trade names. The adoption of a distinctive shape in a product or package does not confer an immediate right to protection. An association of the shape or appearance of the product
with a single, although perhaps anonymous source
is essential. This must be established by repeated use, as with trade names. Although the
decisions are not harmonious, it appears to be
enough that the customer did recognize the feature in question and regard it as an indication of
the article's source, even though this awareness
may have played no part in motivating his choice
of the article. But unless the feature did serve in
fact to indicate the source it cannot be protected
under any form of passing off doctrine. The pro-

[*252*]

ducer's ingenuity in devising a novel design, shape or color must find whatever protection is available under the carefully circumscribed law of patent or copyright (which protects only a limited variety of designs for a limited period). Otherwise a perpetual monopoly would be conferred upon the first established user. The means adopted under traditional passing off law for assuring competitors a free range in the exercise of their own skill in production and merchandising has been the requirement that in order to enjoy protection, the shape, color or design in question must qualify as being *nonfunctional*. That is to say, the feature in question must serve no object other than to point to the origin of the article. If the design, shape or color affects the purpose, action or performance of the object in question or if it is a feature which makes possible a more facile or economical production or marketing of it, the feature is regarded as functional. Hence it is open for free competitive use. The fact that the copied feature enhances the aesthetic appearance of the goods and makes them more attractive does not cause it to be regarded automatically as functional. But where the goods are marketed with an eye alerted primarily to the buyer's artistic taste, any feature which serves to enhance their appeal in this respect may well be regarded as functional and excluded from protection.

The same requirement with respect to function can be approached from the defendant's point of view by regarding functionality in terms of a privilege enjoyed by him. He is free to incorporate any feature into his competing product that enhances its function or its adaptability to the trade or which assists him materially in his effort to produce it and market it efficiently and economically, even though the result is an exact copy of his competitor's product.

But even if the feature copied by the defendant cannot be regarded as entirely nonfunctional, it may still be accorded a qualified protection in proper instances. The defendant may be required to take such steps as are reasonable to inform purchasers that the goods he offers are not those of the plaintiff. This may be done through the adoption of an appropriate legend, distinctive mark or arrangement of features which tend to distinguish the source without depriving the defendant of a functional benefit. In fine, the court may endeavor to devise some means through a qualified injunction to individualize the situation with the hope of reconciling the needs of both parties.

The Shredded Wheat Case. Many of the foregoing observations on passing off can be well illustrated by the fact situation and the opinion of the Supreme Court in Kellogg Co. v. National Biscuit Co. (U.S.1938), the well known Shredded Wheat case. Shredded Wheat was a name devised and used by the predecessor of plaintiff, National Biscuit Company, since 1893 for its patented food product, which is still known only by that name. The pillow shape and the size of the shredded wheat biscuit was the same then as it is today. So long as the patent remained valid, both the name, shredded wheat, and the shape and size of the biscuit continued to be associated in the public mind with the sole maker, plaintiff's predecessor, as well as with the generic product itself. But when the patent expired defendant Kellogg, a competitor, produced the same food item in the same shape and size and under the same name, Shredded Wheat. National sought to enjoin both the use of the name and the continued employment of the same size and shape of the biscuit. Relief was denied in both respects. As to the name, shredded wheat, it had become the generic name to denote the unique food product itself. Since all competitors had become free to market the product they were of necessity free to tell the public what it was that they offered, even if this resulted in confusion with the plaintiff's product. The same freedom for competitors must be recognized with reference to the shape and size of the biscuit. This had become functional. The familiar pillow was the appropriate shape and size for marketing the commodity, and it was thus that the public had come to recognize it. It remains functional despite the fact that some other shape might be devised and ultimately accepted by the purchaser.

Federal Preemption of Passing Off. Within recent years there have appeared indications that the States are powerless to prevent deceptive copying of the shape or size of a product so long as the characteristic copied is outside the protection of the federal patent laws. In Sears Roebuck Company v. Stiffel Company (U.S.1964) the Supreme Court ruled that even a total absence of functionality of the copied feature is irrelevant because whenever the object is in the public domain due to the absence of federal patent protection it is open for free imitation irrespective of the deception that may result. What appears to be an underlying notion of federal supremacy may portend drastic changes with respect to other aspects of unfair competition, as we shall see hereafter (§ 7–13).

§ 7—5   Competition in Violation of Statute

Those actionable harms to the trade relation which we have previously considered (physical harms and deceptive practices) have all involved misconduct of a kind that can be readily recognized as tortious under traditional common law principles. But there are other injurious competitive practices in trade which are unlawful because they either are not authorized or they are in violation of some statutory prohibition. If such unlawful conduct serves to bring about an injury to a competitor who himself is in compliance with the law, can the latter maintain a claim for damages or injunctive relief? The answer here depends on the purpose underlying the statutory provision in question. We must ask whether protection of the defendant's competitors was at least one prominent objective for which the statute was intended?

At times the competitor's interest appears obviously to be uppermost in the mind of the legislature, as where he has been granted an exclusive franchise to carry on some operation such as a public utility or a transportation enterprise, which the defendant now proposes to conduct without authority. Relief in such cases is nearly always sought by way of injunction, and the customary property interest required for equitable intervention is readily found in the exclusive right to the monopoly conferred on him by legislature. Not infrequently the claim is regarded as one to abate a public nuisance. Even if the franchise is not exclusive, it is treated nevertheless as though it were whenever the competitor has acted without legal sanction in failing to qualify himself.

A license, unlike a franchise, is usually granted primarily for protection of the public against incompetence, dishonesty, financial instability or for reasons of public welfare, health or safety. There is nevertheless a further public interest (although perhaps less pressing) in protecting those who by training and ability have equipped themselves for

the practice of the calling in question and who
have a material stake in the profession. It is they
who are most likely to be alert and prompt in an
effort to bring the unlicensed operation to a halt.
Because of divergent views concerning the extent
to which various licensing statutes may contemplate protecting those who practice the profession
in question, the decisions are not in accord as to
whether the individual professionals, or an organization of professionals, can successfully seek an
injunction against unlicensed practice. Bar As-
sociations and even individual attorneys are frequently, but not always, regarded as proper parties to proceed against those who engage in an
unauthorized practice of law. The issue is most
frequently raised in suits instituted to enjoin the
preparation of tax returns, title certificates or
patent applications. The fact that the attorney
is regarded as an officer of the court is frequently
assigned as a special justification for his right to
proceed. Other professional persons have not
fared as well, but the right to relief is not infrequently recognized. Efforts on the part of op-
tometrists, physicians, dentists and chiropodists
have met with varying success. If the activity in
question is regarded as the conduct of a business
rather than the practice of a respected profession,
relief will usually be denied. A denial will also
be forthcoming if the licensing provision is for
police purposes, such as a required showing of
good character for the operation of a saloon, or

if the provision is merely a revenue raising measure.

Even though the statute merely regulates the manner in which a business is to be conducted or imposes other duties on the operator under criminal sanction, it may still appear that the legislature had prominently in mind the protection of other traders whom the defendant has placed at a disadvantage by engaging in practices which they could meet only by becoming violators themselves. The results here, however, have been uneven, and on the whole they have not been favorable to competitors. Injunctions against the use of lottery schemes to attract trade have frequently been granted. The question most prominent in these cases has centered around whether the device was in fact a lottery as defined by the statute. Resort to premiums and prize practices, although perhaps unhandsome, is seldom outlawed, and hence does not serve to ground relief to the competitor who has abstained. Efforts by one competitor for injunctive relief against another who persists in operating his business in violation of a Sunday closing law have usually been denied. Preservation of the public interest in peace and quiet has been dominant in these measures, although it can be argued that allowing tradesmen a day of rest is an equally plausible reason for such closing laws.

We can appreciate the reluctance with which courts view the prospect of injunctive action on behalf of a competitor solely on the basis of a violation of some penal measure regulating the operation of business. Such statutes are wide in variety wtih respect to the dominant purpose which they serve. Prohibitions against telephone or house-to-house canvassing; regulations concerning the methods or the appropriate places for advertising; regulations of weights and measures or requirements concerning the quality of foods or drugs or the installation of sanitary facilities all these, and others, are potential sources of a loss of business by law-abiding competitors. It is certainly arguable that the latter who have gone to considerable trouble or expense to comply, or who have foregone advantages seized by the violator, should not be denied injunctive relief. Perhaps it can be answered that as a practical matter those regulations which most profoundly affect the competitive balance are likely to fall today within the administrative control of some specialized agency which would be armed with suitable enforcement machinery and hopefully would be responsive to the complaints of injured competitors.

§ 7—6   Unfair Competition—A Tort?

In our approach to the trade relationship we were obliged to observe that competition, as it developed in the nineteenth and twentieth centuries came to assume such complexity that the judicial process of the common law was unable to cope satisfactorily with anything more than the crudest excesses of the marketplace. So long as the courts faced only those abusive trade practices that fell within the reach of some already familiar conception such as physical harms, nuisance, deceit or defamation, they could make their way on a case-to-case basis with fair success. But as competitive misbehavior became increasingly subtle and the marketplace tended to assume a decorum all its own, the demand that a means be devised to protect the offended tradesman from his competitor was one that challenged conventional legal theory almost beyond its breaking point.

The challenge faced by courts may be framed this way: Do courts, and, we may add, *should* courts attempt to frame a code of prohibited business behavior that can be dependably regarded as unfair competition? Such a task would be disheartening. Practices that are tolerated or even encouraged in one segment of trade may be regarded as scandalous in another. What was forbidden yesterday may be commonplace today. Even at a given moment in a single area the reactions of individual traders are likely to differ widely. Furthermore, an assemblage of assorted grievances into a list of specifically forbidden practices is not the common law's way of doing things. The more acceptable approach is to unfold a body of broad principles under which disputes between competitors would be resolved. Unfortunately our inquiry here must be limited. There is no opportunity to concern ourselves with definitions of unfair competition as these have emerged under special legislation or pursuant to action of some administrative body such as the Federal Trade Commission.

We should start by recognizing that the very act of making an offer in competition affords all the basic ingredients of an intentional tort. There is present the intent, the act and the resulting harm to the competitor. By offering goods for sale the tradesman deliberately attempts to attract to himself patronage that would otherwise be enjoyed by some competitor. He thus knows that harm to his fellow tradesman will follow, and he is willing that it should do so. If it is admitted that such an intentional infliction of harm is a tort, then each tradesman must be regarded as a chronic tortfeasor. But we also know that his cannot be so, and, indeed the Court of Common Pleas so held more than five hundred years ago. The Schoolmaster Case (C.P. 1410).

Competition as Justification. Even though the sheer act of engaging in competition is not actionable, there remains the inquiry as to whether certain harsh tactics of persuasion in the market place can be regarded as tortious. In England this question was first faced by the Court of Appeal in the celebrated "Great Mogul" case, Mogul Steamship Co. Ltd. v. McGregor (1889). Both the plaintiff and the several defendants were engaged in the international tea trade in China. The defendants formed themselves into a conference with the objective of driving the plaintiff out of the market. To this end they offered substantial commissions or rebates to shippers who would deal with them exclusively, and they established freight rates at a level that would not repay the shipowner, expecting to recoup their losses through higher rates after the plaintiff's competition had been disposed of. In denying relief the court dismissed the plaintiff's claim that a duty obtained at common law which prohibited traffic below a fair freight. It observed that beyond the obligation of a trader to refrain from fraud, molestation, intimidation and the like he is free to set the terms upon which he will trade or refuse to trade. Thus the claim that unfair competition was a tort was disposed of. It was immaterial, observed the opinion that prices were set below a level necessary to insure a present profit if greater profits in the future may be encouraged by so doing.

Bowen, J. then made the pronouncement that has been stressed in some quarters as the "prima facie tort" theory:

> " . . . intentionally to do that which is calculated in the ordinary course of events

to damage . . . another in that person's
property or trade is actionable.   .   .   .
The acts of defendants which are complained
of here were intentional, and were also calculated, no doubt, to do the plaintiff damage in their trade. But in order to see whether they were wrongful we have still to discuss the question whether they were done
without any just cause or excuse. Such just
cause or excuse the defendants on their side
assert to be found in their own positive right
(subject to certain limitations) to carry on
their own trade freely in the mode and manner that best suits their own advantage.
. . . "

In the occasional situation where the competition is entirely feigned and one person allures
away the patrons of another out of sheer disinterested malevolence, intending to cease business as soon as the enemy is ruined and disposed
of, recovery should be forthcoming. Such a situation, however, is indeed a rarity. Usually the
motive is mixed, and so long as the defendant
intends to further his own economic situation as
well as to satisfy his ill disposition toward his
competitor a court will not intervene to determine
which motive was the stronger.

Refusal to Deal. Each business enterprise must
be free to choose with whom it will deal and to
fix the terms upon which it is willing to do busi-

ness. Except in the area of public utilities, which enjoy a monopoly and are consequently obliged to serve all comers at rates approved by law, the freedom to refuse to deal includes the freedom to fix the price at which the enterprise will sell or serve. Even though the figure is unreasonable in the eyes of others and even though the choice of patrons is determined by caprice or prejudice, the interest in preserving freedom of action for the tradesman was of greater importance in the eyes of the common law than the attainment of some other meritorious social or economic objective. Exclusive dealing arrangements are not generally obnoxious at common law. The task of prohibiting discriminatory practices deemed offensive to the economic or social order is one that must be undertaken by the legislature. As a result, much regulation depends upon measures such as the Clayton Act (15 U.S.C. § 12 et seq.), prohibiting efforts to enforce certain exclusive dealing arrangements and tying restrictions; the Robinson-Patman Act (15 U.S.C. § 13 et seq.) forbidding unjustifiable discriminations between purchasers; various statutes prohibiting sales at below cost and Fair Trade statutes prohibiting vertical price fixing. Similarly, hiring and selling practices may be subject to measures outlawing racial discrimination between customers or employees.

Conditional Refusal to Deal—Competition as a Justification. The freedom to impose conditions upon one's willingness to deal includes freedom to refuse to deal with a person who, in turn, deals with one's competitor: A and B are competitors for the trade of C. A is free to refuse to deal with C unless the latter is willing to surrender his right to deal with B in any type of transaction in which A and B are competitors. This freedom obtains irrespective of the level of competition between A and B. They may both be wholesalers competing for the business of a retailer. Or, A may be a manufacturer who sells to independent retailers such as C, and A may refuse to deal with C unless C refrains from dealing with B, a wholesaler who competes with A by selling the goods of another manufacturer. Furthermore, so long as A and B are competitors it is arguable that A may refuse to deal with C in a type of transaction that is foreign to the area of competition between A and B so long as A's purpose is to gain a competitive advantage over B in the area in which they do compete. Thus A, who is an insurance salesman, may refuse to sell his house to C unless C agrees that he will buy all his insurance from A instead of from B, who is A's competitor. There is reason, however, to regard the propriety of this latter situation with a skeptical eye: So long as A's refusal to deal is made with reference to goods or services in which A and B are competitors we can support A's right to refuse as being consonant with sound economic principles. C is a

free agent. Presumably he will accept A's proposition only if it is to his advantage to do so. It
follows that if B's goods or services are cheaper
or sufficiently superior in quality to offset whatever advantage C would gain from dealing exclusively with A, C will refuse to accede to the
condition. Thus the superior goods or the cheaper price will likely determine the choice; and
this is as it should be. The same is not so clear,
however, when A's refusal is conditioned on a
matter foreign to the competition between A and
B. In the illustration of the insurance proposal,
for example, C may greatly prefer B's insurance
to A's, but his overwhelming urge to buy A's
house compels him to ignore the relative advantages of B's insurance offer. On the other hand,
this is perhaps not a matter of great concern pol-
icywise. The allurement of an accessory benefit
offered by one competitor is fairly commonplace
and need not be frowned upon. The Restatement
adopts the position that A is free to refuse to deal
with C only in transactions *related* (sic) to the
business in which A and B are competitors. R.
§ 708(1)(b), comment (e). This is by no means
clear from the decisions. The Restatement position would be strengthened if it could also be made
to appear that A enjoyed some marked bargaining
advantage over C, as if A were C's employer who
threatened to dismiss him if he should deal with
B, or if he were C's landlord who threatened to

oust him.   Even here, however, several cases recognize A's freedom of action and deny recovery to
B, the competitor.   Deon v. Kirby Lbr. Co. (La.
1926) (employer); Celli & Del Papa v. Galveston
Brewing Co. (Tex.1921) (landlord).

§ 7—7   The Prima Facie Tort Theory

Unprivileged Inducement.   Up to this point we
have seen that the existence of competition between plaintiff and defendant serves to shield the
latter from any tort liability arising from his inducement of a refusal to deal with the plaintiff.
Are we now to assume that, conversely, whenever
it appears that the inducement was *not* undertaken for the purpose of furthering the defendant's competitive position the inducement may
lead to liability?   Let us begin our exploration by
reexamining the rationale of the *Great Mogul* decision, from which we quoted earlier.   (§ 7–6)
We are left by the opinion of Bowen, J. with the
clear impression that conduct that induces a refusal to deal does amount at law to an actionable
injury unless there is "just cause or excuse."
Hence there appears to emerge a new intentional
tort with distressingly indefinite boundaries with
respect both to the types of conduct that may give
rise to liability and to the policy limitations that
may be expressed in the notion "just cause or excuse."   The structure of the proposed tort is interesting: It follows the pattern of familiar inten-

[*268*]

tional injuries to person and property wherein the plaintiff establishes that his body or belongings were injured intentionally. By making this showing he has entitled himself to recovery, nothing more appearing. He has made out a prima facie case. We see, then, that an inviting analogy does obtain between this trespass procedure and the inducement of a refusal to deal. But here we should pause. Intentional physical harms such as assaults, batteries, trespasses and the like are subject to a sharply limited group of privileges with which we are all familiar, such as self defense, protection or recaption of property, and necessity. These privileges the defendant must plead and undertake to support by proof. Thus the trial proceeds through two successive stages and the burden of proof shifts accordingly. In the traditional area of intentional trespass, considerations of policy have been pre-fixed. New privileges will not be readily recognized, and there is little room for innovation. Although the procurement of a refusal to deal is likewise classified as an intentional tort, it does not follow that the prima facie approach offers a satisfactory technique for administering disputes in the trade area. The difficulty will appear as we look again at the history of inducement.

Malicious Inducement. In contrast with trespass, the tort of inducing a refusal to deal through conventional persuasive tactics has been the product of comparatively recent efforts to throw a measure of protection around business expectancies in a highly competitive world. The tort had its origin as an outgrowth of the cause of action for inducing a breach of a subsisting contract (discussed hereafter, § 7–9). This latter cause of action came into recognition only in the second half of the past century. During most of its history the new tort was referred to as a procuring of breach of contract through *malice*. It soon became obvious that "malice" did not signify ill will or other wicked state of mind. "Malicious" inducement came to be regarded as virtually synonymous with inducement without a privilege. Quinn v. Leathem (H.L.1901). But the term was retained, and it was required that the plaintiff show affirmatively that the procurement was "malicious". This, obviously, led to confusion as to whether the existence of a privilege was a matter to be raised and established by the defendant in order to defeat the plaintiff's prima facie case, or whether, on the other hand, the absence of privilege was a matter to be established by the plaintiff in his effort to show that the inducement was "malicious". This confusion concerning the establishment of privilege, served to impair seriously the usefulness of both the "prima facie" theory and the theory of "malicious procurement" as means of attacking the inducement problem.

It can be further urged against the prima facie approach with an attendant list of privileges that such an approach fails to encourage a sufficiently broad focus upon the wide variety of policy considerations which the court must face. By following the prima facie approach the court may be tempted to confine its attention to the motive that prompted the defendant to act as he did. And indeed the motive *is* often the proper controlling consideration. But, as we shall note hereafter, policy considerations other than the defendant's purpose or motive may prove to be of paramount importance. A court's attention may be centered upon the means that were employed to prompt the refusal, or upon the relationship that obtained between the defendant and the person whom he incited, or upon the nature of the expectancy that was frustrated by the defendant's conduct. In order to bring these multiple considerations into a useful perspective there is required something more than a catalogue of privileges which a defendant can establish and thus escape liability. Much legal scholarship has been devoted to the evolution of a formula that would at least suggest the variety of factors which have a role to play in determining when and under what circumstances an inducement of a refusal to deal or to breach a contract should be treated as actionable. To this end we should turn now to the analytical structure proposed recently by the Restatement, Second, Torts in §§ 766–774. Hopefully, we may find here a model which is both thoughtful and usable.

§ 7—8   Protection   of   Trade   Expectancies Through the Factor Approach

The American Law Institute in the first Restatement of Torts in 1938 evolved a technique which has been employed with considerable success in an effort to make a determination of the circumstances under which the procurement of a breach of contract or the incitement of a refusal to deal may be properly regarded as actionable. It undertook to list those factors which have been demonstrated by experience to play a decisive role. If these factors, when viewed in the aggregate appear to recommend that the defendant be exonerated from liability, the court treats the defendant's conduct as "privileged". Thus the term, privilege, was employed as a word of art that served to express in a single adjective the court's response to an entire complex of factors. The process is similar to the balancing operation with which we have become familiar in negligence where a determination must be made as to what conduct involves an "unreasonable" risk of injury. Cf. R. § 291. The soundness and practicality of the factor approach has been demonstrated by judicial experience. The only difficulty encountered with respect to the original Restatement approach was the choice of the term, Privilege. The establishment of a scheme of privileges is remindful of the Prima Facie Tort pattern of the *Great Mogul* decision and its awkward allocation of the burden of proof, already discussed in § 7-7, supra. In order to retain the advantages to be gained by balancing the factors involved and yet avoid the limitations of the prima facie attack, the Reporter of the Restatement of Torts Second, has focused upon whether the defendant's conduct is "proper", rather than whether it is "privileged". The essential factors, however, remain the same and the respective weight to be accorded each of them has not been disturbed.

Section 766 of Restatement, Second provides as follows:

> One who intentionally and *improperly* interferes with the performance of a contract (except a contract to marry) between another and a third person by inducing or otherwise causing the third person not to perform the contract, is subject to liability to the other for the pecuniary loss resulting to the other from the failure of the third person to perform the contract.   (Italics added.)

Interference with a mere expectancy of making a future contract is treated by the Restatement Second in a separate section (§ 766B), but the language remains the same, and, as before, liability is imposed for intentional and *improper* interference. The all-important Section 767, which lists and comments upon the separate factors which must be considered in determining whether the interference is *improper* draws no distinction between the two interferences separately listed in §§ 766 and 766B. For most purposes the two invasions can be subjected to the same analysis, although the weight to be accorded the various factors involved will not necessarily be the same. As we shall see, it is only when the defendant seeks to justify his interference by showing that he was seeking to further his position as a competitor with the plaintiff that it becomes a matter of vital importance that the interest he interfered with was that of a subsisting contract rather than the mere expectation of a future deal. This, however, is no infrequent occurrence. The procurement of a breach of contract was the first tort to emerge as a distinctive cause of action, and as such it developed a character all its own. Only within recent years has its identity merged with the procurement of a refusal to deal into the single broad tort we know today. For this reason it is advisable to gain a brief understanding of the history and distinctive characteristics of procuring a breach of contract before turning to the various factors which influence the court's determination as to whether a given interference should be regarded as "improper" and hence actionable.

§ 7—9   Inducement of a Breach of Contract

Inciting a servant to leave employment under his master has been recognized as a tort since the adoption of the Ordinance of Laborers following the Great Plague in the Fourteenth Century. This however, remained a unique situation for five hundred years. Most servants were indentured and their role was somewhat analogous to that of a member of the family (Cf. § 4–3, supra). Hence the separate treatment of their contracts is not unexpected. It was not until the decision in Lumley v. Gye in 1853 that any steps were taken to condemn the procurement of a breach of any other type of contract. That case involved an agreement by Johanna Wagner, a prominent singer, to serve as a performing artist at the plaintiff's theater from whence she was lured by means of a more attractive offer by the defendant, Gye, the manager of a competing theater. The allowance of a recovery against Gye might have gone unnoticed if the court had been content to regard Mrs. Wagner's engagement as a mere contract of hire actionable by analogy to the Ordinance of Laborers. However, it rejected that approach, and the decision in Lumley v. Gye has come down in history as the first announcement of a general principle that the intentional and "malicious" procurement of a breach of contract is an actionable wrong. The principle lay virtually dormant for about thirty years and during that interval it was invoked only occasionally for inducing a breach of a contract for service. It finally gained its footing in 1893 when it was affirmed and enlarged by the Queen's Bench in Temperton v. Russell (Q.B.1893) so as to protect contracts beyond those of service. In the same case the doctrine was extended in principle to protect relations that were merely prospective as well as binding contracts.

Intention. It was observed earlier that an injury to a trade relation through negligence alone is not actionable, even if the injury is the result of physical misconduct (§ 7–2, supra). This obtains a fortiori where the only misbehavior is that of inducing a breach of contract through persuasion. At the very least it must be shown that the defendant realized to a substantial certainty that his conduct would bring about a breach. It is not enough that he *should* have appreciated the likelihood of an injury to a contract relation. Nor does it matter that a reasonable investigation would have revealed that such a result would follow. An awareness that a breach will be induced is enough to satisfy the requirement of intent even though the defendant was motivated primarily by a desire to achieve some other object. It does not follow, however, that the absence of a motivation to affect adversely the plaintiff's contract is entirely immaterial. When we come to consider the policy factors which must be balanced in ultimately determining whether the defendant's conduct was "improper" the fact that the defendant's behavior was serving some purpose other than to impair the contract in question is a matter that may weigh appreciably in his favor. The problem here is particularly acute whenever the defendant, instead of inciting the other party to breach, intentionally does an act which has the effect of disabling that party from performing a contract with the plaintiff. If, at the time he acted, the defendant was aware that his conduct would have the effect of depriving the plaintiff of a performance he otherwise would have received, his interference must be regarded as intentional. The question as to whether or not the defendant should be held liable for the plaintiff's loss as a matter of policy must depend upon other considerations. These could include the objective the defendant hoped to serve by his conduct, the circumstances under which he acted, and the exact nature of his behavior. Even if the behavior was independently tortious it may still be necessary to consider the policy that made it wrongful. For example, a murderer would not be subject to liability to a third person who suffered a contract loss because the murder victim's death prevented his performance. This would remain true even though the culprit were aware of the contract's existence.

Malice. As we have seen, the cause of action is still commonly referred to as the "malicious" or "wrongful" procurement of a breach of contract, and decisions are common in which courts have denied liability by noting that the procurement was not malicious or wrongful. This, however, has proved to be misleading. Once it has been determined that the defendant had a proper purpose in view, the fact that he also entertained ill will toward the plaintiff does not serve to create liability. Ultimately the answer is reached by a resort to those factors whose balance determines whether the interference was proper or improper.

Contracts Protected. The clearest instance of a contract right that is entitled to full protection against an effort by a competitor to procure its breach is an agreement that is untainted by illegality and whose performance can be enforced at law. Certainly an agreement to effectuate an immoral purpose or to create a prohibited monopoly or carry out an unlawful determination not to compete will not be protected. Accordingly a court may refuse to condemn a retailer's conduct in inducing a breach of a fair trade agreement between a manufacturer and a distributor where such agreement is opposed to state or federal policy. Argus Cameras v. Hall (Mich.1955). We have already noted that a cause of action will not lie for inducing a breach of a contract to marry. (§ 4–5 supra). In view of the seriousness and permanency of the marriage relation it is probably advisable to leave the field free for a change of mind up until the time the marriage vows have been exchanged.

Voidable Contracts. The fact that a contract is unenforceable because of infancy or a lack of mutuality or because it was not in writing as required by the Statute of Frauds does not deprive it of protection against third party interference. The requirement of a written memorandum for certain agreements was not enacted in order to sanction interference by third persons with contracts already in existence. The refusal to enforce oral agreements relating to certain subjects rests instead on a felt need that there should be due deliberation by the parties preliminary to their unequivocal commitment.

Contract at Will. When it appears that a party to a contract enjoys an option to terminate the agreement at his pleasure it can be argued that a third person who induces him to exercise such option does not thereby procure a breach of contract. Supporting this position is the argument that the breaching of a contract is itself a wrong; and hence the inducement of a breach can be regarded as tortious because it amounts to the procurement of a wrongful act. Under this view, the inducement of one party to a contract merely to exercise an option (a privilege accorded him under the contract) would not be wrongful with respect to the other party, who, it can be said, must anticipate that the option might be exercised.

Refusal to regard an inducement to terminate an "at will" contract as an actionable tort in a suit against a competitor could serve a policy advantage when viewed with respect to contracts of employment (many of which are at-will). Mobility of labor is encouraged if a prospective employer is enabled with impunity to offer a better opportunity to the worker who serves another under an at-will contract, or if one worker who seeks employment urges his own services upon the plaintiff's employer. But other policy considerations could lead to an opposite conclusion: Many stable employment relations rest on an at-will basis, yet they are maintained intact over long periods of time if they are not interfered with. An employer who has gone to considerable trouble and expense to train an employee for specialized work may suffer a serious loss if a competitor is free to reap the employer's harvest for his own benefit by luring away the worker just as his performance was beginning to justify the investment in time and labor. As may be expected, the decisions are not in accord as to whether the competitor is free to interfere. The conflict of policies that is brought into focus when there is an interference with an at-will contract betrays the need for more elbow room in an effort to arrive at a mature conclusion. The fact that the contract with which the defendant interfered was terminable at will does not mean that it is left wholly without protection.　Such an agreement represents a picture where there persists a strong expectancy that an economic benefit will be forthcoming, even though it cannot be enforced at law against the party whose performance is optional.　The existence of so immediate an expectancy is entitled to sympathetic consideration when the effort is made to determine whether the interference was "improper".

Means of Interference.　It has already been seen that a use of force or coercion or a resort to misrepresentation or other conduct which is independently tortious is clearly actionable when it brings about an interference with either a contract or a trade expectancy. But, even in the absence of such recognized predatory wrongs, persuasion exerted upon a contracting party to induce a breach or a refusal to deal with him unless he is willing to avoid his contract obligation is actionable when engaged in by a competitor if it interferes with rights under a subsisting contract.　The same is not true, however, where the defendant's purpose is merely to induce a refusal to deal with one who is the actor's competitor (§ 7-6, supra).　Persuasion by a competitor short of actual fraud is tolerated by law up until the negotiations have been concluded by a contract.

The question remains as to what behavior amounts to an inducement of a breach of contract?　There must be something by way of positive conduct. Merely to decline an offer is not actionable, even when the person declining is aware that his failure to accept will cause the offeror to default in the performance of some contract. On the other hand, an expressed threat to reject an offer unless the offeror indicates his willingness to breach a contract is quite another matter, for it serves as a positive inducement. The clearest instance of an inducement to breach is a direct request accompanied by a proffer of some benefit if the request is complied with. But what effect should be given the sheer act of making an offer to sell goods to one whom the offeror realizes cannot accept unless he breaches a previous contract to purchase the same goods from the offeror's competitor? In such situation the offeror must be viewed as deliberately choosing to present a temptation in the face of a virtually certain prospect that acceptance of his offer will cause a breach. The inducement must therefore be regarded as intentional. The fact that the primary motive is to conduct business in the regular manner does not alter the intention. But at the same time, an imposition of liability for procuring a breach of contract under such circumstances would have the unfortunate result of seriously hampering a normal practice of soliciting business. A tradesman should not feel obliged to avoid customers who appear to be committed to other tradesmen. If, under the same circumstances the prospective purchaser should express his reluctance to breach an existing contract and thereafter the offeror should persist in urging him, an entirely different picture might be presented. Here again, as with our discussion of the at-will contract, it appears that the wiser course is to maintain a flexible approach and to regard the circumstances attendant on the negotiations as factors which should exert their influence when the trier seeks to determine whether the procurement was "improper."

Impeding the Performance of a Contract, or Impairing its Value. Although the tort with which we are concerned is commonly referred to as that of inducing or procuring a breach of contract, it is not necessary that there be persuasion of any kind; nor is it essential even that the contract be breached, so long as its value to the plaintiff is impaired or its performance is made more burdensome by reason of the defendant's conduct. Such conduct may consist in a physical act, or refusal to act. It may be the creation of a condition wherein performance of the contract cannot be carried out fully or advantageously. The conduct may be directed toward either the plaintiff or the other contracting party. Or it may be the destruction of the subject matter of the contract or its alteration so that performance is impeded. The defendant may call an unlawful strike or boycott, refuse a work permit, breach his own contract to supply material or labor, or refuse to carry out an undertaking which, if completed, would have entitled the plaintiff to a commission. A contract right intended to be conferred upon the plaintiff to the exclusion of others may be seriously impaired in character when the defendant acquires a similar right or interjects himself at some place intended under the contract for the plaintiff's sole occupancy. It does not follow, of course, that all such behavior is actionable even if it is intentionally carried on and serves to frustrate the plaintiff's contract benefit. It must be shown upon a balance of the factors to be "improper."

Cause. The issue of cause is one of fact and is resolved by proof. Little difficulty is encountered if it appears probable that the breach of contract would not have occurred apart from the defendant's inducement, or that the performance would not have been prevented or made more onerous if the defendant had not intervened. His behavior, however, need not be the sole inducing cause. Furthermore, where the alleged cause of the harm was the influence exerted by the defendant on the mind of the person who failed to carry through, it is sufficient that its persuasive effect amounted to a substantial operating factor in prompting the conclusion to breach. And this would be true even though there were other powerful inducements present at the same time which were exerting a persuasive effect. If a balance of the factors establishes that the inducement was "improper" there remains no meaningful problem of proximate cause. The wrongful breach by the defaulting party can hardly be regarded as a superseding cause of the loss when it is borne in mind that the procurement of the breach was the very object of the defendant's effort.

Damages. The fact that the victim of a breach of contract is entitled to damages against the defaulting party does not serve to defeat the tort action against a third person. However, amounts paid by the defaulter, including satisfaction of a judgment for breach, should serve to reduce the amount recoverable in tort. Nor can the insolvency of the party who defaulted under the contract be asserted by way of defense in the tort claim. Performance, not damages for breach, was the object for which the plaintiff bargained and this has been denied him by the defendant's intervention. This is particularly clear with reference to contracts for service. The remedy more commonly sought is that of injunction, with the hope that if the defendant's power to entice away the contracting party is denied him, the latter will be satisfied to continue performance for the plaintiff.

The measure of damages for which the procurer may be held is not necessarily the amount recoverable against the defaulting party to the contract. An intentional tort has been committed and the damages should represent all loss proximately caused, even though it was not foreseeable. The reparation can properly include emotional disturbance and injury to reputation, even though the defendant was not chargeable with defamation. In extreme cases punitive damage may be allowed.

There arises an interesting question as to whether the contracting party who breaches his contract pursuant to the inducement of a third person becomes a tort feasor as well as a defaulter on his contract. If such is the case he may subject himself to liability for more extensive damages than would be chargeable against him if he had breached the contract on his own motion. The decisions are not in accord on this matter. Cooper, Civil Conspiracy & Interference With Contract Relations, 8 Loyola (L.A.) L.Rev. 302 (1975).

§ 7—10 "Improper" Interference With Trade Expectancies

In its effort to deal with injuries to trade expectancies the common law has neither managed to devise any broad formula of acceptable behavior similar to the standard of reasonable care to which the defendant's conduct could be referred, nor has it been able to catalog many groups of specific circumstances whose presence could serve dependably as justification for the defendant's behavior in appropriate instances. Specious generalities, such as malicious wrong, prima facie tort and unfair competition which have been ventured in an effort to provide an underlying theory of some kind have served little purpose other than to lend a deceptive appearance of order to conclusions otherwise arrived at.   The tort, we know, is a newcomer in which the courts have groped their way cautiously toward acceptable conclusions while relying on such analogies as they could muster.   But a body of usable law has managed to emerge as certain common factors have appeared and reappeared singly or in combination so that the effect of their presence is to make possible a fairly orderly procedure for discovery.

In the formulation of Division IX of the Restatement of Torts Second in 1977 the Reporter, Professor John Wade, listed seven factors which, operating in harness or in opposition to each other, appear to exercise the determinative influence in fixing liability for inducing breach of contract or for other interferences with trade expectancies. These are set forth in § 767 as guides to aid in determining whether the defendant's conduct should be regarded as "improper."   Liability is imposed (R. § 766) only upon one who "intentionally and *improperly*" interferes.   The factors set forth in § 767 and which thus exert a profound influence in the disposition of most controversies are as

follows: (a) the nature of the actor's conduct;
(b) the actor's motive;   (c) the interests of the
other with which the actor's conduct interferes;
(d) the interests sought to be advanced by the
actor;   (e) the social interests in protecting the
freedom of action of the actor and the contractual
interest of the other;   (f) the proximity or remoteness of the actor's conduct to the interference;   and (g) the relations between the parties.

The choice of those factors which appropriately
control the dispute at hand and the determination
of the balance to be made between them are tasks
which must be undertaken by the court in each
controversy, and the outcome is tailored to fit the
occasion.   This on the one hand makes for flexibility of judgment; but on the other hand it tends
to frustrate the search for an outcome which can
be predicted in advance with any certainty.   However, as Comment b to R. § 767 points out, "factual patterns develop and judicial decisions regarding them also develop patterns for holdings that
begin to evolve crystallized   .   .   .   rules defining conduct that is not improper." Hence we may
profitably begin with a limited group of situations
which have occurred and reoccurred to a point
where the outcome is fairly predictable: In the
first place, we can observe that whenever there
is encountered a situation in which courts have
persistently refused to characterize the defendant's conduct as improper even in the face of a

claim for procuring the breach of a subsisting contract we can be certain that the same conduct will not be regarded as improper when the only complaint is that it interfered with a prospective contract or with patronage.

Interference for the Assistance of Another. There are many situations in which one person is charged with responsibility for the physical, economic, social or religious welfare of another. This holds true for parents, physicians, attorneys, religious counsellors and frequently for teachers and employees (particularly those who are officers or directors). A person so entrusted is free to persuade the individual in his charge to refuse to deal with anyone where such dealing is honestly believed to be contrary to the welfare of the person whose protection is at stake and which falls within the scope of the actor's responsibility. He can even go so far as to procure the breach of a subsisting contract. His interference may be vigorous, and he may withhold benefits which are within his control and without which the transaction in question would be impossible. He may not resort, of course, to predatory means, such as violence or fraud (unless force is independently privileged, as with parent and child). But otherwise a wide range of interfering conduct is tolerated as being proper. R. § 770. An occasion must exist which would appear to call for interference. Although there is little authority here, it is submitted that a reasonable appearance that intervention is needed or appropriate should be sufficient. If information which turns out to be false is supplied by an agent or hired consultant to support his advocacy of a breach of contract or to incite a refusal to deal, the falsity of the facts furnished does not serve arbitrarily to render the advice improper with respect to any claim by the party who suffered by reason of the incitement. The person, however, to whom the information is afforded and who is induced to breach in reliance thereon may recover his contractual loss from the adviser who failed to use reasonable care with respect to its truth or falsity (§ 7-3, supra). Furthermore, even the other party, against whom the breach has occurred, might recover against one who deliberately furnishes information which he knows to be false. Under these circumstances it could be contended that the untruthful defendant was not honestly seeking to serve the interest of the party whom he purported to protect.

Although the defendant is under no legal or moral obligation toward the person with whom he communicates, he is generally free to make available to others useful information even though he is aware to a substantial certainty that it will have the effect of influencing the hearer or reader to decline to deal with another or to breach an existing contract.

The Restatement has adopted the position that under such circumstances information that is volunteered without any prior request must be true (R. § 772(a)) before its dissemination can be regarded without question as conduct that is proper as that term is used in the Restatement. This, however, may be debatable. It is difficult to avoid the same considerations that prompted the Supreme Court, acting pursuant to the First Amendment, to require a showing of at least negligence with respect to truth or falsity as a prerequisite to a successful claim for defamation (§ 6–20, supra). Arguably, the same should be true where the claim is for inducing a refusal to deal, or even a breach of contract.

So long as a defendant confines his conduct to the furnishing of information he will not be regarded as acting improperly even though the facts he assembles are selected with an eye toward inducing a breach of contract or are arranged in such order as would serve to encourage a breach. Beyond this, however, he must not go. He cannot actively and expressly sponsor such a course for a stranger to whom he owes no duty without running the risk that his conduct will be found improper.

In order to actively counsel a breach of contract by someone to whom he owes no protective duty he must await the making of a request. But once this is done he need not withhold any advice

that was asked for. The only remaining requirement is that he act in good faith and that he avoid
exceeding the boundaries of the request. R. § 772.

A court needs freedom to exercise a wide range
of judgment in facing situations of the kind suggested above: An intimate friend acting out of
genuine concern for the welfare of another may
proceed on his own motion and urge a course of
action in derogation of the plaintiff's contract
rights, where a similar urging by a stranger would
not be tolerated at law. The urgency of the felt
need to protect the other's welfare, the social
value of the object sought to be attained, the unavailability of any other source of advice—all
these factors, which are listed in R. § 767 are entitled to consideration by the court. A few ran-
dom illustrations may be helpful: A dissatisfied
owner of an automobile may properly suggest to
an acquaintance that the latter would be well advised to avoid entering a contract to purchase a
car of the same make. On the other hand it
would be improper for him to place a notice in a
newspaper or erect a sign in a public place urging
that no one purchase such a vehicle. It is also
doubtful that even a close friend could be urged
to withdraw from an existing contract of purchase. And an even closer situation would be
presented if the friend had been previously granted an option to acquire such a car and was thereafter urged to avoid the purchase. By way of con-

trast, a physician might properly insert a notice in the public press warning that the restaurants in a given area are contaminated and proceed thereupon to advise the world at large to avoid such places.   In such a situation the interest sought to be protected is more urgent and hence greater latitude should be afforded.   But even here other complications may arise: The physician's warning against contamination may turn out to be unfounded.   Should this serve to make his conduct improper?   Again, even though he were mistaken, should he nevertheless escape liability for inducing a refusal to deal if he exercised reasonable care in his effort to determine the truth?   Is the fault requirement here the same as in a suit for defamation?   Much of this entire area of liability is virtually unexplored.   Legal theory can do no more than afford a catalog of those matters which should be considered.

Protection of Property.   A defendant who is charged with inducing a refusal to deal or with interfering with future patronage can escape liability by showing that he was engaged in competition with the plaintiff and that his conduct was in furtherance of his competitive standing.   Hence the conduct is not improper.   R. § 768(1).   (See § 7–6).   On the other hand, competition does not afford any protection for the procurement of a breach of a subsisting contract.   R. § 768(2). Apart from competition, the protection of other present interests in property may be asserted in good faith to justify the procurement of a breach of contract if the defendant's conduct was not otherwise improper. One who has reason to believe that he is the owner of property can threaten to enforce his rights through legal proceedings in an effort to induce a breach of a contract to purchase the same property from an adverse claimant. Similarly the owner of a tract of land can properly threaten the prosecution of an abatement proceeding in order to forestall a threat that a neighboring tract will be sold to someone who proposes to maintain a nuisance thereon. The same is true for one who holds a prior contract right. His effort to frustrate the performance of a later contract between other persons with respect to the same subject matter will not be regarded as an improper interference. But the actor's own property right must be in apparent peril of loss or debasement. The mere prospect of financial loss if the contract is carried out is not enough. The fact that there is a threatened sale of my neighbor's property to an undesirable purchaser would not entitle me to procure a breach of the contract to sell, even though the sale, if carried out, would serve to depreciate the value of my own land. Under the same circumstances, however, it is not unlikely that I could properly urge my neighbor not to accept a proposed contract offer to sell his land. This would be true even though I was not in competition with the proposed purchaser.

A threat to institute civil or criminal proceedings against anyone who deals with the plaintiff is a powerful coercive weapon. One who claims to have patent rights can seriously injure the business of a manufacturer or tradesman by broadcasting threats of proceedings for patent violation against anyone who purchases or deals in the questioned item. On the other hand, the right to resort to the courts would be seriously impaired if litigation must be initiated without preliminary announcement. The use of coercive threats of litigation is proper only when it appears that the litigant has an honest belief in the merits of his claim and that he intends to persist in litigation until a final determination of the merits.

Stockholders and creditors of a corporation have a definite financial interest in the welfare of the corporate body and frequently they may seek to influence its action with reference to prospective contracts or they may persuade the corporation's governing body to breach contracts which they regard as detrimental to their interests. Similarly, the citizens and taxpayers of a political community may seek to influence the conduct of a governing body with reference to business negotiations. Where the only interest of the person interfering is the protection of his own economic welfare as a stockholder or creditor and if his status has not served to place him under any obligation to protect the corporation, he is free to interfere only with such negotiations as are still prospective. His procurement of a breach of a subsisting contract may be regarded as improper. Where the interference is by a citizen of a public body, his intervention may be for the protection of some important public policy other than his own private welfare, and for that reason may be regarded as proper.

§ 7—11 Concerted Interferences with Trade Relations

Although inducing a refusal to deal with a tradesman is not regarded as an improper interference when engaged in by one who is a competitor (§ 7–6), there remains the question as to whether several persons may similarly act in concert to interfere with the trade relations of a competitor without becoming subject to liability. An affirmative answer here was announced by Bowen, L. J. in the *Great Mogul Steamship* case, already discussed in § 7–6. If each of several persons acting singly may lawfully engage in an act, he observed, the same conduct does not become unlawful because they act in concert. This position continued to prevail in England until the Restrictive Trade Practices Act of 1957.

However, the American common law decisions of the same period tend to recognize that a concerted refusal to deal may amount to improper conduct where it is calculated to injure or destroy the business of the person so affected.   In Jackson v. Stanfield (Ind.1894) a group of retailers of lumber, endeavoring to drive from the market all lumber wholesalers who sold directly to consumers, agreed that they would not purchase from any lumber producer who did business with the objectionable wholesalers, and they spread this information abroad throughout the trade. Their conduct was regarded by the Supreme Court of Indiana as improper, and it awarded both damages and an injunction.   This appears sound. There is a far greater potentiality for harm where the members of a group act in concert than where one individual acts alone.   Also, in view of the fact that concerted action occurs only infrequently and is generally outside the ordinary course of conducting business there is a less noticeable frustration of personal liberty in imposing some degree of restraint upon behavior in combination than in an attempt to regulate individual conduct. If the object to be attained is opposed by the dictates of sound policy, this can be more readily ascertained where several parties have determined to pursue a common course of action.

It by no means follows that a group of individuals may not with complete propriety agree to trade only with those whose behavior meets some standard agreed upon by the group.   If the purpose to be served is a proper one, such as an imposition of uniform requirements for good credit or sound sales practices, concerted action may prove to have a salutory effect on the quality of operations within the trade affected.   There is no reason why fair arrangements for mutual protection should not be tolerated.   On the other hand, tactics that are basically oppressive become more oppressive when they are carried out by a sizeable segment of traders.   They can quickly have an adverse effect on freedom of trade and can frustrate innovations by ostracizing those whose practices meet with the displeasure of the group.   Under such conditions they become improper and require strict regulation.

As a result of the growing complexity of the subject of concerted action, the influence of the common law regarding monopolies and combinations in restraint of trade has continuously declined since the Sherman Antitrust Act of 1890, 15 U.S.C.A. § 1 et seq.   Under this act combinations in restraint of trade are dealt with as a distinct subject.   Hence the work of the courts has been largely that of interpreting the federal statute and the state statutes modeled after it.   The controlling determinant of the illegality of combinations is the test of *unreasonable* restraint of trade.   Some types of combinations are condemned in advance as unreasonable "per se".   At this point the subject passes beyond the purview of any limited treatment possible here.

Concerted Action in Employment Disputes.
Concerted refusals to deal may have as their objective the promotion of the economic welfare of a group even though the participants are not competitors of the individuals whose trade they are seeking to disrupt. This is descriptive of the strike or boycott which is designed to secure an enhanced wage or to remedy some other aspect of the employment relation to which the actors object. The concerted action may be a simple refusal to deal unless the desired objective is met. Here we have the strike. Or their operation may include physical demonstrations with a dramatically persuasive impact which borders on coercion—the picket line, whose purpose is to dissuade those who might otherwise agree to accept employment with the person picketed, or to urge the public to refrain from dealing with the recalcitrant employer and thus bring him into line. Virtually all forms of the labor boycott are regulated exclusively by statutes (usually federal), such as the Norris-LaGuardia Act (which assures the right to strike) and the Taft-Hartley Act (whose purpose is to insure collective bargaining). The purposes of a group of laborers may be furthered by mass appeals to the consuming public, as exemplified by the appeal on the part of the National Farm Workers Association in 1968 for a nationwide boycott of table grapes to assist in the labor struggle of migrant farm workers.

Again, the objective of economic gain may be furthered in combination with an effort to insure some civil right, as evidenced by the wave of racial boycotts by non-employees directed against merchants whose employment practices allegedly discriminate against minorities. These have been treated as analogous to labor disputes and hence protected by the Norris-LaGuardia Act against injunctive relief. New Negro Alliance v. Sanitary Grocery Company (U.S.1938). An important new area for the exercise of the boycott is that of consumer protection. See Comment (1971) 42 Miss.L.J. 226.

The social or economic purpose to be served by a concerted procurement of a refusal to deal is important as one factor to be weighed in the balance along with the means adopted. If nothing more than peaceful persuasion is exerted by the group in order to induce others to avoid the objectionable individual or object or institution, a court is not likely to condemn the conduct as improper solely by reason of the triviality or personalized character of the object being served. A pastoral letter read widely in all Catholic churches in Wisconsin complaining of the plaintiff's newspaper as being injurious to the faith of the church, and even going so far as to proscribe the possession of the journal by the faithful was not regarded as improper interference with plaintiff's business. Kuryer Publishing Company v. Messmer (Wis.1916). (But cf. § 5–2, supra).

On the other hand, the object to be served through mass action may be one that is itself discriminatory, as in Hughes v. Superior Court (U.S. 1950) where a race boycott was instigated against a store in order to oblige the employment of blacks proportionate to the number of black customers served by the establishment. This was held to be improper. The fact that a dispute has a racial overtone does not qualify it, without more, as an effort to attain a protected civil rights objective. A neighborhood of black persons, for example, may be denied the privilege of picketing a store whose owner, a white person, was popularly believed to have assaulted a black employee.

A resort to violence or threats of violence is clearly an improper interference, and the same is true when there is an interference with the right to use the public streets. However, the fact that violent behavior is revealed does not without more justify the imposition of a broad unqualified injunction against picketing as a racial boycott tactic. Sandifer & Smith, the Tort Suit for Damages, the New Threat to Civil Rights Organizations, (1975) 41 Brooklyn L.Rev. 542. See generally, Coons, Non Commercial Purpose as a Sherman Act Defense (1962) 56 Nw.U.L.Rev. 305; A.L.I. Restatement of Torts (1938) § 765.

§ 7—12 The Appropriation of Trade Intangibles

Some of the most highly prized assets of a tradesman consist in intangibles. Almost beyond

measure is the commercial value of abstract ideas,
saleable information, methods for operation or
achievement, schemes of arrangement, formulas
for creating things, the ordering of items into
meaningful and useful categories, the contrivance
of attractive merchandising devices, and the like.
These are things that are subtle in their nature
and almost endless in their variety. They all
have a commercial value that can be destroyed
through appropriation by a competitor, and the
task of protecting them poses a challenge which
law has not yet been able to meet successfully
through the evolution of any single formula. To
the extent that physical possession or control of
the material embodiment of an intangible can
serve in practice to forestall its capture or spolia-
tion, law has been able to afford some measure of
protection through such familiar possessory actions as trespass, trover or replevin. Also intangibles can sometimes serve as consideration or
subject matter for an enforceable agreement, and
be secured in that way. But beyond this the going has been very rough. An almost irrecon-
cilable conflict of values stands in the way of a
comprehensive solution of any kind. The dimensions of the problem of protecting the intangible
are well illustrated in the notable decision of Mr.
Justice Pitney in International News Service v.
Associated Press (U.S.1918). The situation that
prompted this dispute arose during the tense

period leading up to the First World War. The British, who completely controlled American access to cabled news from the western war front, shut off all communication to the United Press whose owner, William Randolph Hearst, had insisted on maintaining an outspoken anti-British editorial policy. When Hearst's frantic appeal to his arch rival, the Associated Press, for a share of their news facilities met with a cool reception, Hearst undertook in desperation to save at least that portion of his news empire which lay on the west coast through resort to three tactics which were somewhat less than handsome. First, he bribed employees of eastern newspapers published by Associated Press members; second, he induced members of the press to violate its bylaws —all in order to secure news for INS before its publication so that it could be transmitted by phone or telegraph to the latter's westcoast papers where the three hour time differential made commercially effective publication possible for INS. Both these tactics were clearly actionable interferences with contract rights of the Associated Press, and were subject to injunctive relief. Cf. § 7–10 supra.

It was the third method adopted by INS for securing news that raised serious questions: Agents of INS openly copied news from issues of the plaintiff's papers which were available for

public purchase or they took the news from bulle-
tin boards in public places.

Does such conduct resemble any common law
tort considered up to this point? Little can be
gained by labeling the appropriation as "unfair
competition" without some explanation as to what
makes it such. Is there present some kind of actionable deception? We have become familiar
with the offense of passing off. But that epithet
is hardly applicable here. Hearst had practiced
no deception whereby the newspaper-buying public was induced to purchase news which it would
have rejected if it had known the true source.
Public misreliance, the essence of passing off, is
wholly missing. In a dissenting opinion Mr.
Justice Holmes refers to "passing off in reverse".
He suggests that the west coast reading public
was induced to believe that the news purchased
from the defendant was the product of its own effort, whereas it was news gathered by the plaintiff.
But this hardly amounts to the inducement of any
false belief which in turn would prompt the making of a purchase. Furthermore, as Mr. Justice
Holmes concedes, such harm as might result from
deception could be readily remedied by a printed
notice in International Press papers making full
acknowledgment of the source. There were no
lies, no furtive conduct, no pretense. What else
may be available? Was there perchance an invasion of property?

Literary Property and Copyright. Fairly generous legal protection has been made available for intellectual literary and artistic products. For more than a century common law has recognized a "property" right in unpublished manuscripts which exists separate and apart from the paper or other material on which it is written or impressed. Beginning in 1802 the federal copyright scheme was gradually unfolded, and by 1909 copyright was available for books, periodicals, maps, prints and reproductions of works of art. Both the state common law property scheme and the federal copyright have coexisted side by side at least prior to the latest amendment of the copyright act, effective in 1978. Until that date the line of cleavage beween the common law and the statutory schemes had been that of "publication". An intellectual or artistic creation could be revealed or communicated through oral or visual delivery or performance or by means of exhibition without becoming "published" and hence suffering the loss of its former common law protection. But the creator who attempted to profit by authorizing tangible reproductions of his creation must publish with notice (as required by the copyright act) and upon so doing he would enjoy protection exclusively by way of federal copyright. Copyright protection is arbitrarily limited to a period of years, while common law protection was perpetual. Much thought and labor has been devoted by legislators, courts and writers in an effort to lay out a proper ambit of overall protection for literary property of all kinds and to establish an acceptable boundary between literary property and copyright, culminating in the Copyright Act of 1976. This elaborate body of law is obviously beyond any treatment possible here.

However, what is important to note in connection with the INS controversy is that neither common law literary property nor copyright could afford any assistance to Associated Press in the odd dilemma in which it found itself. The only creations which are recognized and protected by either common law or copyright are the literary, dramatic or artistic ingredients which are added from the creator's own personality. The raw material on which his intellect has operated is beyond the pale of any protection available here. It is the expression only which is protected, not the idea behind the expression. The mere record of isolated happenings—the raw news element— is information that is available for narration by all who gain knowledge of it directly or through others. Furthermore, if common law literary property protection were invoked by the Associated Press, this must be denied because it had reduced the news items to written form and displayed them for the public to see—they were published and passed beyond common law protection.

Misappropriation of Intangibles—a New Tort Theory? With access to both the doctrines of deception and of literary property denied the Associated Press, the Supreme Court nevertheless allowed injunctive relief against the copying of news from public bulletins and from copies of newspapers offered for public sale. It did so through resort to a novel notion of unjust enrichment in the world of trade. The concept of unfair competition was restated by Pitney so as to include the misappropriation of intangibles as well as passing off and deception. It is obvious that what the court sought to protect are the processes involved in the production of news. These the court hoped to guard against competitive misbehavior by means of which the end product of the plaintiff's labor and expense would be captured just at the moment of its fruition. The latter's effort has been diverted so as to enrich the defendant who is thus enabled to turn the product back in competition against its originator. As a result the incentive to produce is destroyed, and with it eventually disappear both the producer and his imitator. The Court's expression of censure of the conduct of INS has been termed the "free ride" doctrine, and it has been captured in the seemingly virtuous phrase, one should not be allowed to reap where he has not sown. The injustice is dramatically apparent in the INS setting. Many hours of labor, elaborate facilities and much capital have been invested to produce a few published facts which for the short period of their novelty become a source of profit. Anyone who is enabled to broadcast the same facts without any expenditure of effort can destroy their creator.

However, admitting that an invocation of the "free ride" doctrine seems appropriate under the special facts of the INS controversy, does the doctrine represent indeed a sound and workable generality when one attempts to apply it in the broad world of competition? Despite the moralistic tone of the INS doctrine, one might well question whether copying or imitating are indeed practices that deserve to be condemned under all, or even most, circumstances. In opposition to the notion that the fruits of every man's efforts should be secured to him alone for his own use or disposal, is a proposition which also has much to commend it: It is a reminder of the fact that progress depends upon the full utilization, development and expansion by us all of the intellectual products of others, and that no single individual should be allowed to usurp for his exclusive use and profit an idea or other intangible solely on the asserted ground that he thought of it first or that he developed it or concretized it before any other would-be user. The need to protect creativity, on the one hand, but to assure a maximum utilization of intellectual resources, on the other, are needs that require thoughtful compromise.

The objections that can be voiced against any wholesale prohibition of appropriation are many. There is available an abundance of moralistic theology to support either side of the controversy. The one who appropriates can be condemned as a pirate or a free rider; but, similarly, the one who resists any use of his creation unless he is remunerated therefor can readily be dubbed a monopolist. A certain amount of permissible free riding is inescapable in a competitive society. From a practical standpoint, to administer any generalized prohibition against all appropriation would be impossible. How great, for instance, must be the expenditure of originality, resources, or labor before the claimed creator can properly insist upon a right to exclusive use and exploitation? Seldom does an idea spring like Minerva full blown from the head of Zeus. How great must be the harm suffered by reason of the copying? Under some circumstances the creator's competitive standing may be threatened with extinction. Or again he may be denied a secondary market, as in the case of the fight promoter who wants the full profits from broadcasting or television. Finally the reproduction of the originator's product may merely expose him to some measure of competition, which he can sustain without tragic loss. Even beyond this, we must look at the behavior that is claimed to amount to free riding: It may amount to a total usurpation of the plaintiff's creativity. But on the other hand, what the plaintiff created may serve simply as the germinal seed which some later user develops, modifies or improves, or readapts. If now a second usurper appears who uses the ultimate product, must he, in turn, reimburse both the originator and the equally ingenious author of the improvement? The impossibility of administering any general formula here is obvious. The doctrine of the INS case has been accorded an uneven reception. As authority it has become less impressive by reason of the fact that it was decided as a matter of general Federal law prior to Erie v. Tomkins (U.S.1938). Its appeal to a sense of fair play became somewhat lessened several decades later when the Associated Press was convicted of a Sherman Act violation by limiting its membership. Assoc. Press v. U. S. (U.S.1945). Finally, as will be seen hereafter (§ 7–13, infra), the doctrine, as it applies to uncopyrightable news, may have been largely displaced by reason of Federal preemption under the copyright law. Sears Roebuck & Co. v. Stiffel Co. (U.S.1964).

The influence of the INS doctrine on later decisions has depended largely on the subject matter rather than on any appeal that a general free ride principle may possess. Relief is frequently granted in news cases involving facts very similar to those of INS itself. These have included the appropriation of news from newspapers for use in radio broadcast (Assoc. Press v. KVOS, Inc. (9th Cir. 1935) and the unauthorized broadcasting of a sporting event (even where the game was reported by defendant without trespass or breach of confidence). The mechanical copying by record of an exclusive broadcast by the Metropolitan Opera Association was protected by the New York courts in Metropolitan Opera Assoc. v. Wagner-Nichols Corp. (N.Y.1951). On the other hand the commercial use on a juke box of plaintiff's orchestral performance was denied protection, despite a restrictive notice on the record. RCA Manufacturing Co. v. Whiteman (2d Cir. 1940). Although occasional instances are found where relief is granted against free riding in situations outside the news and broadcast area, the clear tendency is to deny recovery in cases where there is no deception nor inducement of breach of an exclusive contract nor other unlawful behavior. A court has refused to enjoin the copying of dress designs observed in public or purchased in open market and which were unprotected by design patent. Cheney Bros. v. Doris Silk Corp. (2d Cir. 1929). Where, however, the copying was effected by means of trespass or breach of confidence relief has been granted by way of the INS doctrine. Dior v. Milton (N.Y.1956). Similarly, ingenious business methods and trade devices which must be exposed and publicly used are usually open for copying and emulation by competitors, and the unique personality or characteristics of an actor or other performer can be imitated without risk of injunction so long as there is no confusion in the public mind resulting in a belief that the plaintiff is an actual participant in the spectacle. Columbia Broadcasting System v. De Costa (1st Cir. 1967).

The factors that may affect the outcome in the appropriation cases are many. Among them is the extent of the harm sustained. One writer finds decisive the question as to whether the appropriation has served to deprive the originator of a primary market. The bare fact that he is exposed to unwanted competition when his device is turned against him is not enough. Rahl, the Right to "Appropriate" Trade Values 23 Ohio St. Univ.L.Rev. 56 (1962). Also must be considered the use to which the appropriator has put the material. If he has taken it bodily and without improvement or change, his conduct is more likely to be condemned than if he has mingled it with other material and through accretion and ingenuity has produced something of independent value to society. Again the task of administration may be too specialized for judicial talent, as where subtleties of style and artistic value must be passed upon.

Protection of Ideas. The demand for the protection of abstract ideas offers a challenge which legal ingenuity has never successfully met. To the extent that a novel idea can be embodied in a machine or other concrete device it can be processed and protected under federal patent law for a limited period. The same is true when the idea consists in a novel allocation of words, figures or sounds which can be reduced to concrete form in a writing or on a record or tape. Here copyright protection is available, and the scope of copyright has been substantially enlarged through the Copyright Act of 1976 (17 USC §§ 101 et seq.). It must be borne in mind, however, that copyright protection extends only to the expression or expressions used:

> "In no case does copyright protection for an original work of authorship extend to any idea, procedure, process, system, method of operation, concept, principle, or discovery, regardless of the form in which it is described, illustrated, explained or embodied in such work."

17 U.S.C. § 102(b)

The raw idea, like news, is free for the taking once it has been made public. Naturally this is a source of consternation to creators, who are not in a position to derive any profit from their ideas except as they may be able to place them into action in public or to merchandise them to others for remuneration.

Ideas as Merchantable Commodities. An idea can serve as the subject matter of an express contract if the requirements of consideration and definiteness of promise are met. This, however, affords but cool comfort for the disappointed creator who seeks to market his idea in advance. Obviously, rare is the person who would be willing to commit himself to become the purchaser of an idea whose quality, novelty and usableness must remain wholly unknown until it is revealed by his adversary in the course of the negotiations. Nor would it normally be sensible to promise in advance that one is willing to pay for the proferred idea if he should elect to use it. Whatever is revealed to him in return may be utterly commonplace, or it may have occurred to him before and was rejected. If the re-presentation happens to revive the hearer's interest, should he be obliged to pay for the mere reminder? Many ingenius suggestions for the marketing of ideas have been advanced, but these have seldom met with success.

A disclosure of a worthwhile idea under an expectation of remuneration has occasionally been accorded protection. New York and California have manifested considerable liberality in this direction. Attempts at protection have been predicated on either of three theories: First, literary property, where it is found that a publication in confidence has taken place; second, the discovery of an express or implied-in-fact contract; and finally an obligation implied in law to pay for the disclosure as part of a service performed by the creator for the user of the idea. This latter theory for recovery is particularly inviting whenever the person making the disclosure has also undertaken to assist in placing it in operation. Relief is more readily available where the very matter disclosed is itself an intellectual product, such as a title, a slogan, a plot or a program format, than would be the case where the idea is a method of accomplishing some objective which method would remain the same irrespective of the form in which it is expressed when it is revealed. See the treatment in Havighirst, The Right to Compensation for an Idea (1954) 49 Nw.U.L.Rev. 295.

Trade Secrets. We have seen that apart from such protection as may be afforded by the free ride doctrine intangible material that is unpatented and uncopyrighted and which is open to public view can be freely imitated by competitors so long as there is no passing-off, deception or other improper means of acquisition or use. But the converse also holds true: The creator of an idea may attempt to conceal it from his competitors and may have the means or be so situated in private that he has a fair chance to do so. The object of his safekeeping may be a formula, a pattern or a process affecting the goods he expects to merchandise. Or it may relate to operations involved in the course of conducting the business itself, such as a credit system or some device for identifying and reaching buyers, such as a compilation of trade data or a list of customers.

If the attempt to conceal is frustrated by a breach of contract or abuse of confidence or through resort to predatory means, such as trespass or electronic surveillance or bribery, relief by way of injunction and damages may be made available. This is commonly referred to as trade secret protection. Although the right to exclude others from the creation is often discussed by the courts as property, the remedy finds its true basis as a corrective of the improper means adopted by the defendant. In keeping with the property approach is the fact that a remedy is available even against a third person to whom the secret was revealed by the original appropriator, and who uses it with knowledge that it was improperly acquired. Strictly speaking, a trade secret, as explained by the Restatement of Torts (1938) § 757, Comment *b*, "is a process or device for continuous use in the operation of the business", and this is certainly a common characteristic. But a single item of information may also be protected when it is exposed through breach of a fiduciary obligation.

The "secrecy" required for protection must certainly be more than a bare hope that the information will not be discovered by others. Although the information need not be utterly unique in order to meet the secrecy requirement, yet matters commonly known or readily discoverable through public observation or analysis are not protectable as trade secrets. Absence of general knowledge, the exertion of substantial efforts by the plaintiff to preserve the secrecy with expectable promise of success, together with a substantial value possessed by the information are all matters to be taken into consideration in determining whether a protectible trade secret exists.

The trade secret is protected only against procurement through improper conduct. The impropriety depends on the means employed and not on the purpose that prompted the acquisition. Any tradesman is free to expend both effort and money to analyze a competitor's substance or device which is on the open market or is available in public places. The means which is most obviously improper is a resort to trespass or the use of violence or fraud. The availability of scientific means of surveillance makes surreptitious observation a constant threat; but the secret character of the information is not lost by reason of the fact that its discovery can be managed without technical trespass. E. I. DuPont de Nemours &

Co. v. Christopher (5th Cir. 1970) (passage over plant by airplane with camera enabled defendant to discover chemical manufacturing process).

The most numerous and the most difficult instances of breach of contract or abuse of confidence are those involving the skilled employee who, upon severance of the relationship, seeks to turn to his profit confidential information gained during the course of his former employment. The conflict of interests here is sharp. The knowledgable or highly skilled employee should be entitled to utilize the experience he gained through prior employment. But on the other side of the equation, the employer should not be denied the exclusive benefit of information gathered through expense and effort behind closed doors in the operation of his establishment. The real problem here, like so many others we have observed, can be attacked only through an undertaking to balance these competing interests.

In the cases of normal employment where there is no trespass or deception the employee should be free to carry with him into the labor market all the knowledge he has acquired in past employment, except as he may have promised expressly or by implication that he would retain in confidence what he had learned. Hence it is important to focus on the terms of the contract of hire and ascertain whether the employee had a fair opportunity to decide whether it would be to his advantage to surrender his normal freedoms in exchange for better pay or other allurement. If the employer desires to expose the employee to sources of knowledge which he intends to protect against being revealed once the employment has been severed, he should be obliged to make this clear at the beginning. Even if the employee did understand and consent, the understanding may impose such an undue burden on him that it should be regarded as voidable as against public policy. A refusal by the court to countenance the restriction may be more expectable where the hiring agreement is in stock form and should be treated as a contract of adhesion. In seeking to attain a balance between the conflicting interests it may appear that the secret information was highly valuable to the business affected and that it was attained at great effort or expense, or, on the other hand, the facts for which protection is sought may be only a minor part of the general know-how of operating the business. Such difference in the value of the information may tilt the scales one way or the other. On the employee's side of the equation it may appear that possession of the knowledge in question forms only a minor part of his marketable qualifications for employment. Or, on the other hand, expertise in using and developing the information may be the most attractive of his assets when he seeks employment elsewhere.

Customer Lists. A similar problem exists with respect to information gained by the employee in the general course of his employment concerning the names and locations of customers and their trade preferences and buying habits. It is normally to be expected that the sales agent who has served as a public relations representative will be free to take with him such knowledge as he has gained in the course of his duties concerning the range of available customers. Many such customers may have been acquired for the employer through the efforts or personality of the employee, and it seems fair that he should be allowed to seek them out later for his own purposes. Furthermore, such information can hardly qualify as secret so long as it can be learned from public observation by any interested person. For these reasons the employee upon leaving his employment is usually free to renew his old acquaintances and to solicit their business for himself or for a new employer. However, recovery of damages or injunctive relief may be awarded where the employee goes to the pains of preparing a customer list when the information is too elaborate for his own memory. Again, as we observed in connection with trade secrets, the employee is free to elect in advance to contract away his normal freedom to solicit business from his employer's customers. Such an agreement will be effective unless it imposes an undue hardship on the employee. See Restatement, Second, Agency (1958) § 396(b).

§ 7—13   Federal Preemption and the Protection of Intangibles

Until recently common law doctrine intended for the protection of intangible trade values, such as passing off, free ride, common law literary property and trade secrets, managed to survive along side the federal statutory protection scheme embraced within the copyright and patent statutes. Federal supremacy controlled, of course, whenever a direct conflict was unavoidable. But in general, acceptable boundaries were established. In the field of copyright the controlling law depended upon whether "publication" had taken place. Similarly, federal patent law prevailed only when there was found the requisite novelty required under the statute and the idea was embodied in some concrete form or device, and when the discovery had been properly and timely made public through an entry in the federal patent registry. The protection afforded by both patent and copyright extended for only limited periods as specified in the statutes. Outside these boundaries there remained intangible values which were generally regarded as amenable to such protection as the states chose to extend.

A sudden change of position with reference to the federal-state relationship became evident in

1964 with the decision in Sears, Roebuck & Co. v. Stiffel Co. (U.S.1964). Relief had been sought against passing off by defendant through an imitation of mechanical design. The appearance of Stiffel's pole lamp was not such as to qualify it for a design patent. Thereafter certain features of the Stiffel lamp's appearance were copied by Sears, Roebuck & Co. The copied characteristics were non-functional and the deceptive similarity of appearance between the two competing lamps might have entitled Stiffel to a qualified injunction under state passing off doctrines. (Cf. § 7–4, supra). The Supreme Court, however, speaking through Black, J., stated that "an unpatentable article, like an article on which the patent has expired, is in the public domain and may be made and sold by whoever chooses to do so.   .   .   . To allow a state by use of its law of unfair competition to prevent the copying of an article which represents too slight an advance to be patented would be to permit the state to block off from the public something which federal law has said belongs to the public."

This version of the conflict when accepted at its face value would appear to affirm federal preemption of most of the entire field of protection of intangibles, and would render inconsequential much of what has been previously observed in these pages.

Debate over the meaning of the *Stiffel* decision raged among judges and writers immediately, and the new preemption doctrine was both applauded and criticized. It should be observed that the *Stiffel* decision did leave room for some state action against source confusion, such as federal tolerance of a state requirement that there be appropriate packaging or labelling. The relief afforded, however, could not include an injunction against product simulation. Furthermore, in a concurring opinion by Harlan, J., in Compco Corp. v. Day-Brite Lighting Co. (U.S.1964) a companion case to *Stiffel*, it was suggested that state law might still be properly applied whenever there was affirmative evidence of palming off beyond the mere fact that a copy was made. These suggestions indicate that there still remained some as yet undefined area of operation for state doctrine even in the face of patent or copyright law.

While professional reaction to the *Stiffel* opinion was still in ferment the Supreme Court tackled the problem again in Goldstein v. California (U.S. 1973). At issue was the validity of a California statute which made criminal the transferance of any performance fixed on a tape or record onto other records or tapes for commercial purposes without the express permission of the owners of the master recording. The contention was made that since federal copyright law did not protect sound recordings, an uncopyrightable recording

[*323*]

could no more be protected by state unfair competition law than an unpatentable design could be protected by a state prohibition against passing off. This contention was rejected. The opinion of Burger, C. J., appeared to outflank the preemption announcement in *Stiffel* by launching into a fresh attack on the problem of state-federal conflict. The opinion observed that no simple formula can capture the complexities of conflicts that may develop between state and federal action. Reference must be made in each controversy to the fields to which congressional action may apply. The California statute was upheld in a 5–4 decision. Almost immediately thereafter the contention was made in Kewanee Oil Co. v. Bicron Corp. (U.S.1974) that a chemical process for which no patent application was made could not be protected under state trade secret law. The Court disagreed and ruled that a state may exercise regulatory power over intellectual property relating to invention "so long as its action does not conflict with the operation of the laws in this area passed by congress." The Court determined that there was no such conflict. The purpose of the patent laws, it observed, was to encourage discovery by making available a limited statutory protection for the discoverer after he had elected to make his invention public. The purpose was not to *require* publication of the discovery at the risk of a loss of protection under state law if he attempted to maintain secrecy. The shift from *Stiffel* to *Kewanee* was a shift away from an arbitrary rule of preemption of all State efforts to regulate intellectual property, and toward an individualized determination of the attendant policy considerations in each instance. Obviously the problem in its entirety must be solved on a case to case basis. But the fact remains that common law efforts to protect intellectual property which was threatened with almost complete extinction in *Stiffel* continue to have a suitable although as yet not fully defined role.

Legislative Preemption of Copyright. One aspect of the federal-state conflict is beyond question: Congress is free to preempt any area appropriate to patent and copyright which it may choose. The only remaining inquiry is when and to what extent has it done so? With respect to copyright, the congress in 1975 moved expressly to take over virtually the entire field. The technical fact of "publication" which theretofore had marked the boundary between the area protected by common law literary property and the domain of federal copyright, was abolished. Under the terms of the new copyright statute protection attaches whenever the "work of authorship" has been "fixed" in tangible form. The notebook secretly concealed in a drawer serves nevertheless to "fix" the author's expressions contained in it. They have thus become subject to copyright pro-

[*325*]

tection. Since "publication" no longer serves as a dividing line between the two regimes there remains no area to be designated as common law literary property. Section 301 of the Copyright Statute makes this explicit. In view of the fact, however, that news, raw ideas and the like are not afforded copyright protection under § 102(b) it appears that they may still be accorded some protection under such free ride doctrines as state law may recognize. (Cf. § 7-12, supra). The same is true of any intellectual creations that have not been "fixed" in tangible form. 17 U.S.C.A. § 301 (b)(1). An excellent treatment of the subject of peremption will be found in Goldstein, Kewanee Oil Co. v. Bicron Corp.: Notes on a Closing Circle, 1974 Supreme Court Review 81.

CHAPTER 8

DEFAMATORY HARMS

§ 8—1 The Trade Relation and the Law of Defamation

Although the law of defamation serves primarily the purpose of safeguarding the social relationship, it also affords a measure of protection for trade expectancies. Spoken words which are regarded as slanderous because they tend to injure the plaintiff in his trade or calling are regarded under Traditional defamation law as actionable per se without need of proving that any actual damage was sustained (§ 6–3, supra). The words, however, must reflect adversely upon the plaintiff's personal character or his behavior. It is not enough that they are critical of his merchandise. The same is true of written defamation. Words that impute to the plaintiff some characteristic which would render him unfit to carry on his trade or perform the duties of his vocation would be regarded as libelous even though they do not otherwise hold him up to contempt or ridicule. For this reason a corporation can maintain a suit for a libel even though it can have no reputation in the social sense of the word. Language which casts an aspersion on its credit, honesty or efficiency is actionable without more.

§ 8—2   The Emergence of Actionable Falsehood

Even language which cannot qualify as slanderous or libelous per se may still give rise to a cause of action if it brings about a specific monetary loss. Such recoverable losses are not limited to injuries to the trade relation. Liability extends for any pecuniary loss resulting from untruthful statements concerning the plaintiff. Included are the loss of a marriage (which may have economic value), the expense of curing an illness brought on by the offensive language or the cost of instituting a lawsuit. This apparent willingness to confer a cause of action for monetary losses occasioned by language which is false although not defamatory had become evident as early as the sixteenth century when courts began to recognize a cause of action for slander of title to land. By the middle of the nineteenth century there were indications that a distinct tort had emerged. It has since been called Injurious Falsehood. The tort resembles defamation in that the false statement usually refers to the plaintiff, his behavior, or at least to his property. In injurious falsehood, however, it must be shown that there was misreliance intentionally induced by the defendant's untruthful statement. The effect of this misreliance is to deprive the plaintiff of some specific financial gain which otherwise would have accrued to him. The loss may be of a single transaction or it may be represented by an established decline of general patronage. But there is no presumed loss, as was frequently true with respect to libel per se under Traditional defamation law. Even the constitutional requirement of proof of "actual injury" (§ 6–21, supra) in all defamation claims does not serve to obviate the distinction between defamation and injurious falsehood with respect to damages. The only damage recognized under injurious falsehood is a specifically established monetary loss, while "actual injury" as defined by the Supreme Court may be wholly nonpecuniary in nature.

There are other differences between the two torts. The mental element required in injurious falsehood stands in sharp contrast with the treatment of intention under the Traditional law of defamation. The defendant in a defamation suit was formerly not relieved of liability because he was ignorant of the falsity of his statement or he did not intend to harm the plaintiff's reputation (§ 6–10, supra). In a claim for injurious falsehood, on the other hand, it must appear that the defendant was aware of the falsity of his statement (or was consciously indifferent thereto), or that he acted with ill will toward the plaintiff. Recent constitutional reform has tended to blunt the distinction. A showing of conscious indifference toward the falsity of the statement, or at least negligence with reference thereto, is now required of the plaintiff in every suit for defamation.

Hence the two types of claims are almost indistinguishable in this respect. Whether the defendant who was excusably ignorant of the falsity of his statement can nevertheless be held in a suit for injurious falsehood if his action was prompted by ill will or a desire to injure has not yet been made clear. See R. § 623A and Caveats thereto. Another former distinction between injurious falsehood and defamation has probably disappeared. According to the Traditional view of defamation, the victim who succeeded in establishing that the statement was defamatory enjoyed the benefit of a presumption that it was false, while the claimant in injurious falsehood has always been required to show that the statement that injured him was a false one. This distinction is probably not supportable today. Compare § 6–11 and § 6–22, supra.

Misreliance and Causation. With respect to slander of title, the requirement previously noted that the defendant must have acted with the intention of inducing misreliance should be accepted with qualification: It is sufficient for liability that the defendant was aware of facts which would prompt him to realize the likelihood that some third person or persons would be induced by his statement to refrain from purchasing the property in question. Of course it must also appear that the decision of some prospective purchaser was in fact altered by his awareness of the statement.

The falsehood need not have been the sole cause of the decision not to buy, but where there were present other persuasive inducements it must be made to appear that the defendant's statement served as a substantial factor in prompting the decision.   Injurious falsehood concerning a tradesman's merchandise may cause a serious overall loss in patronage.   A loss of this kind can be satisfactorily established through persuasive circumstantial evidence of a falling off of trade which cannot otherwise be accounted for.   In such cases the usual required showing of loss of specific transactions may be dispensed with.

The Disparaging Statement.   In order to qualify as an injurious falsehood a statement need not have any hostile or derogatory overtones.   A person who falsely asserts his own ownership of a tract of land has thereby slandered the title of the true owner.   It is not even necessary that any words be circulated.   The filing of a lien known to be invalid can be sufficient.

Disparagement of the quality of the plaintiff's merchandise is somewhat improperly referred to as "trade libel", although the injurious statement need not be written, and, as we have seen, it is an injurious falsehood, not a defamation.   The disparaging statement generally points out or refers to some specific deficiency in marketed goods, such as a reference to beer as "adulterated" or to eggs as "rotten" or to gasoline as being deficient in

octane content. It may refer to any trade asset.
A derogatory reference to a hotel, restaurant or
taxi service can serve as an injurious falsehood.

In the past a derogatory opinion could qualify
as an injurious falsehood. This was true although
it may be difficult to demonstrate when a mere
opinion was not honestly entertained and also
whether reliance on it prompted the loss of a
transaction. In view of the fact that statements of
opinion are probably no longer actionable as defamations, it remains to be seen whether sheer derogatory opinion can now qualify as an injurious
falsehood.

It may be difficult to distinguish on the one
hand adverse statements concerning only the
goods in question from statements reflecting on
the honesty or competency of the tradesman himself. If they are of the latter kind, they can be
regarded as libel or slander. As we have seen,
this distinction is probably not as important today as it was under Traditional defamation. Nevertheless, the range of damages recoverable under
a defamation theory may be substantially greater.
A statement defamatory of the competency or
honesty of a tradesman may entitle him to recover
as damage to his reputation such pecuniary losses
in his general business operations as the defamation would expectably tend to cause. On the other
hand, some specific loss demonstrably caused by
the disparaging statement marks the outside

boundary for recovery for injurious falsehood. R. § 573, Comment *g*. Furthermore, nonpecuniary damage is recoverable for a defamation, but not for an injurious falsehood.

Usually a statement confined to a disparagement of a tradesman's goods does not qualify as a defamatory statement concerning his competence or honesty. It may be otherwise, however if he were charged with regularly engaging in the sale of contaminated food, or that he short weighted his customers, maintained his goods under unsanitary conditions, that he ran a "rotten hotel" or sold imitation merchandise which he represented as genuine.

Privilege. In general, the privileges available to the defendant in a suit for injurious falsehood are the same as in defamation (§§ 6–13, 6–16, supra), and in the same way they are subject to abuse (§ 6–17). It follows that the same confusion concerning the present status of qualified privilege in defamation which we have heretofore noted as an outgrowth of the constitutional reform in Gertz v. Robt. Welch '(§ 6–20, supra) must be faced whenever there is a claim for injurious falsehood. See the discussion in R. § 650A.

In two instances the qualified privilege to disparage title or quality is broader than the corresponding privilege for defamation. With respect to slander of title, one who has a bona fide

belief as to the *possible* validity of his own claim
to the property interest in question is privileged
to assert that claim though he may not entertain a
belief in its certain or even probable validity. R.
§ 647.   Somewhat similar is the privilege of a
competitor to compare his own goods favorably
with those offered by the plaintiff. So long as he
refrains from derogatory or disparaging comment
on the qualities of his competitor's wares he may
praise the merits of his own goods by comparison
even though he does not entertain an honest belief in their superiority. R. § 649.

The Outer Limits of Injurious Falsehood. There
are clear indications that the broad concept of
injurious falsehood may support a more extensive
incursion into the regulation of deceitful trade
practices than has been heretofore suggested.
False statements which are knowingly made but
which are in no way disparaging of the plaintiff's
business may nevertheless give rise to a cause of
action whenever it can be demonstrated satisfactorily that the plaintiff suffered a monetary loss
by reason thereof. It has been held actionable,
for instance, to state falsely that the plaintiff is
no longer engaged in business or that he does not
carry in stock goods required by the person to
whom the statement was made. Similarly, in one
instance liability was imposed on an employer
who falsely reported to revenue authorities that
he had paid an employee a salary greater in

amount than was thereafter reported by the latter in his own income tax return, and thereby caused the plaintiff to be faced with embarrassing litigation. Gale v. Ryan (N.Y.A.D.1941).

In another group of situations recovery has been allowed for statements which made no mention whatsoever of the plaintiff or his business. In one instance, the defendant prepared and distributed an exclusive commercial listing of persons engaged in the plaintiff's calling, and deliberately neglected to mention the latter. Similarly, a song publisher recovered damages for the intentional exclusion of his song from a widely published listing of the most popular tunes of the week. The publisher, American Tobacco Company, was not even a competitor of the plaintiff. Advance Music Corp. v. American Tobacco Co. (N.Y.1946). In this latter case it is interesting to note that the plaintiff's complaint was based on his deprivation of an added financial benefit which otherwise would have been conferred solely by reason of the defendant's own enterprise—the listing of exceptionally popular tunes. By way of contrast it may be noted that an artist who painted the first portrait of President Truman was denied a recovery of damages against Time Magazine which knowingly published an account of another and different artist to whom it attributed that honor. Perhaps the discrepancy in the outcome of the two controversies can be explained in

terms of the superior position of the song publisher in being able to demonstrate with some pre-
cision the monetary harm he sustained. After all,
what is it worth in dollars and cents to be the first
(although not the only) artist for whom the President sat?

False Advertising. Inability to establish in evidence an ascertainable loss, discussed above, accounts also for the general refusal of courts to
recognize a cause of action on behalf of an honest
tradesman when a competitor misrepresents the
quality of the latter's own goods.

From the standpoint of trade ethics a court
should frown upon a lie about the quality of one's
own wares just as severely as it discountenances
a lie concerning their source (cf. the passing-off
situation § 7–4, supra). As one court observed,
"The reason, as we think, why such deceits have
not been regarded as actionable by a competitor,
depends only upon his inability to show any injury for which there is a known remedy." Ely-
Norris Safe Co. v. Mosler Safe Co. (C.A.2d 1925).
Such deceits are actionable, of course, on behalf of
the deceived customer (who seldom has sufficient
incentive to sue). But it is usually impossible for
a competitor to show that any customer would
have purchased from *him,* rather than from some
other truthful seller, if there had been no deceit on
the part of the defendant. In the rare case when
he does overcome this inability to establish dam-

ages, recovery is allowed (*Ely-Norris Safe Co.,* supra).

Again, in false advertising claims, for practical reasons, the common law falls short in affording protection for the trade relation, and as a result the phenomenon of untruthful advertising falls into the domain of administrative relief afforded through legislation.   Since 1938 such relief as can be made available must be sought under the Federal Trade Commission Act (15 U.S.C.A. §§ 1451–61).   The advantages and shortcomings of this measure lie beyond the area that can be explored within the confines of our Nutshell.   An excellent although disillusioning survey of the Federal Trade Commission made under the auspices of the American Bar Association has been published (1969) and deserves careful study.   It should be noted that in recent years there has been a substantial increase in the number and the scope of State statutes regulating acceptable trade practices.

*

INDEX

References are to Pages

INDEX
References are to Pages

[*340*]

[*341*]

ESTATE
Loss as damage element in wrongful death, 40

EXECUTIVE OFFICER
Privilege to defame, 154

FAIR COMMENT
See Defamation

FALSE ADVERTISING
False statement of one's own goods,
   Not actionable by competitor, 336
     Remedy under Federal Trade Commission Act, 337
Injurious falsehood distinguished, 336

FALSEHOODS
Non defamatory falsehoods actionable, 122

FAMILY IMMUNITIES
Effect in death action, 51

FAMILY INTERFERENCE
Appropriational harms, nature and scope, 67

FAMILY RELATIONSHIP
  See also Dead Bodies
Gifts between family members,
   Interferences with, 84–87
     Nature of expectancy, 84
     Negligence of attorney, 87
     Wrongful interference, 84
Protection, history, 12, 55

FAULT
Fault in defamation, traditional view, 137

FEDERAL PATENT STATUTE
May preempt area of product simulation, 256

FEDERAL PREEMPTION
Patent statute, effect on product simulation claim, 256

FEDERAL TRADE COMMISSION ACT
Statutory regulation of deceptive trade practices, 246

FRANCHISE
Operation in violation of, as unfair competition, 258

FRAUD AND DECEIT
Elements of, 230
Harm to trade relation through, 228

FREE RIDE DOCTRINE
See Appropriation of Intangibles

FUNERALS
Funeral directors, see Dead Bodies

GIFTS
Gifts between family members, interferences with, 84–87

GROUP
Defamation of group, 133
Exclusion from group membership, 98–102

GROUP INTEREST
Privilege to defame for protection of, 162

HEART BALM STATUTES
Seduction, alienation of affection and criminal conversation
    outlawed, 80

HOUSEHOLD SERVICES
See Wrongful Death

HUSBAND AND WIFE
Alienation of affections, 72–77
  Causation, 74
  Conduct, 73
  Effect of prior estrangement, 74
  Heart-Balm Statutes, effect of, 80
  Intention, 172
  Privilege, 75
Criminal conversation, 70
  Effect of Heart Balm Statutes, 80
Defamation, privilege, 156
Personal injuries to husband, 57

[*347*]

INDEX
References are to Pages

NUISANCE
Trade injury through, 225

OPINION
Statements of opinion as libel, 121
Statements of opinions as disparagement, 332

PARENT AND CHILD
See also Damages; Dead Bodies; and Personal Injuires
to Family
Abduction of minor child, parents action for, 78
Alienation of child's affection from parent, 80
Alienation of child's affection from spouse by parent, 75
Child as wrongful death beneficiary, 26
Child's action for physical injury to parent, 60
Child's interest in avoiding unwanted status in family, 94
Child's right of action for enticement of parent from home, 79
Father's interest in being present at birth, 90
Immunity to suit, 51
Interest in attaining parenthood, 91
Interest in avoiding parenthood, 92–93
Spouses' interests in conflict, 91
Personal injuries to minor child, 62
Fault of child or parent, 63
Loss of services, 58
Right of action for injury to child, 57
Seduction of daughter, 78
Effect of Heart Balm Statutes, 80
Wrongful death beneficiaries, 26

PASSING OFF
See Confusion of Source

PERSONAL INJURIES TO FAMILY
See also Husband and Wife; Parent and Child
Action for, 55–66

PHYSICAL HARMS
Effect on trade relation, 216
Relationships affected, 7

[*352*]

INDEX
References are to Pages

[*353*]

✝